SMUGGLER'S WIND

One mariner's true account of
smuggling under sail

Design by Kateri Drexler

Papaya Press is a registered trademark.

Lomas, John
Smuggler's Wind: One mariner's adventure of smuggling under sail.
John Lomas. -- 1st ed.
ISBN 0-9779831-0-2
ISBN-13 978-0-9779831-0-0

Papaya Press
4252 County Road 1
Montrose, CO 81401
USA
www.papayabooks.com

This book is dedicated to my children.

Names and places have been changed to protect the guilty.
The innocent herein have kept their real names.

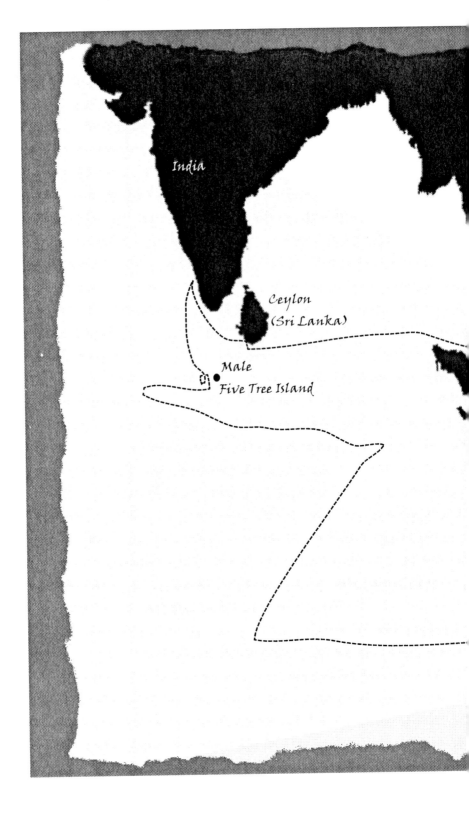

Contents

Being on the land is fine.
But I prefer to be at sea.

Sir Francis Drake
(1540-1596)

ou know the word, synchronicity? I always used to think it just meant coincidence--the meshing or coming together of two or more related events in a coincidental manner, like finding something you desperately need just sitting on the side of the road. One day in Japan, though, something happened that made me think there was a little more to it than that. Perhaps a bit more of the mysticism that Jung seems to apply to the word. I'm not really into all that new-age pseudo science. I like to think I'm a realist. Everything has a rational explanation if you look for it. Even so, what happened that day was very strange and led me into doing something I don't think I would have done otherwise.

I was in Japan building another sailboat, and it was taking longer than I wanted. Building boats is fine, but sailing is even better, and I'd already been on the land for two years, getting on to three. I wanted to get back to the water, back to cruising. Also, the immigration man was beginning to get his trousers in a twist and told me that my visa would probably not be renewed when it ran out in six months time. The problem wasn't time, though. I still had six months and a bit, and most of the big work was finished on the boat. Though there was still quite a bit of finishing to do down below, at only forty-two feet overall, it wasn't like I was building a royal yacht.

The problem, of course, was money, but that shouldn't have been a problem. The last boat I had built in Japan I had sailed to Cyprus and sold it for a good profit that I had planned to invest in my new boat. It was going to be the perfect cruising boat. Everything had been thought out. It was going to be gaff-rigged for downwind sailing; long-keeled for good course-keeping, and broad-beamed for stability, with lots of room below. What it wouldn't be was fast. But, heck, who wants to go fast? The idea of being on the sea is to spend as much time there as possible.

What I should have done immediately after selling my first boat was to come straight back to Japan and start building my new boat. But, I didn't come straight back from Cyprus. I stopped off in Korea on the way. I had thought Korea would be a better place to build a boat, it being cheaper and everything, and, I suppose it is if you're thinking of ferrying around a few million tons of crude oil. When you're on your own, though, trying to get everything together to build a little sail boat, then the problems just don't seem worth it. Things might have been cheaper, but I could never get a price on anything. They were always holding out to see how much they could get out of me. It wasn't like in Japan where the price is the same for everyone. Also, I was with my little seven-year-old daughter, my little blue-eyed Vanesa. Her mum had decided years ago that sailing wasn't her thing. In compensation, though, we had Chantal, a fiery French woman who had stowed away in Sri Lanka when we were cruising around there awhile back and hadn't disembarked yet. These two didn't like being in Korea. They found it cold and bleak. It was the end of winter there, and I suppose it was a bit raw. There was a cold wind blowing straight down from Siberia. What really decided me against building in Korea, though, were the scrap yards. Pathetic places. Not just second-hand junk, had they, but stuff that had been thrown away over and over until not a nut or bolt could you use again. A decent scrap yard is a must for me when building something. Not just for the saving in money, but I like the creative challenge of figuring out how to incorporate a really interesting piece of scrap. So we were going to go to Japan, a much softer land where the scrap yards are like Aladdin's caves.

Just before leaving Korea, however, and quite by chance, we met a salesman with the Hyundai company. You know that name. It must be the largest corporation in Korea. They make all those huge supertankers but are more famous for cars. He was part of an offshoot of the ship building division. They'd just started building pleasure boats but hadn't got a market yet. He said that if we'd be one of their first customers, they'd give us a good deal. So, we took the train to Ulsan on the east coast where the factory was located just to have a look. They must have been desperate to get a client because they treated us like royalty. They put us up in the company hotel and the next day took us on a tour of the sailboat section. There were six or seven boats under construction, from thirty-foot to forty-foot. The one nearest completion was a 32-foot, aft cabin sloop, a beautiful little thing built from the design of a well-known European designer. It had been *Boat of the Year* in Europe the year before. That's what the salesman said, anyway. I don't know about those things. I don't know if he had the rights to build it, either, but they were making a good job. She had all teak decks, and down below, all Burmese teak furniture. The fiberglass hull was flawless, and all the fittings were imported. Sails by Hood, and winches by Hewman. It was a gem. They said it would take a week or so, and they'd put us up, for free, until it was finished. It wasn't the sort of boat I'd like to keep, though. For one thing, it was too small. However, they'd give it to us for half-price if we'd sail it away to show the world what they could do. "Right," we thought. "We'll just take it across to Japan, sell it for a large profit, and get on building a real boat." So that's what we did. Except for the large profit bit.

We entered Japan through the Shimonoseki Straits and sailed through the Inland Sea, stopping at every yacht club and marina we came across. By the time we got to Osaka at the other end of the Inland Sea, a thousand miles and two months later, we were realizing we should have done more market research. It was proving difficult to sell. Everybody loved it. Everybody wanted it. Until, that is, they found out it was made in Korea. Then, they wouldn't touch it with a boat hook. You think England and France have some historical friction, but that's a teenage love fest compared to what these two Asian neighbors have going between them. There is some serious disliking going on. It wasn't until a long time after that I realized I should have told people it was made in Italy. They would have loved that in Japan. I'm a bit slow, but I mostly get there in the end. In this case, I was slower than usual.

We could have taken the boat somewhere else to sell, like New Caledonia or Australia, but Chantal was pregnant at this time and didn't fancy a long sea journey. Our son, Radja, was already born and bawling away before we managed to sell it. When the boat was finally sold, we weren't left with much money to finish outfitting the new boat, but there was an even bigger reason why we were short of money.

We were living in a rough-and-ready fishing town about eighty miles northeast of Tokyo. Not the prettiest place in Japan, by a long way, but it had a wide, slow-running river, lined with unused slipways. Perfect for building. It used to be one of the main centers of the fishing industries on the Pacific Coast. That was when there were lots of fish in the sea, but because of overfishing, the town was declining fast. We had a small wooden house right on the river, which was cold in the winter and hot in the summer, but you could sit in the garden and watch the river going by and dream of the time when you would sail down it, out into the Pacific and down to the tropics. Our son was born there. He was three months old when it burned down.

In a flash, everything went. Clothes, passports, and money, but worst, all my boat things: sextants, charts, binoculars, compasses, and all the tools I had collected for building. At first, it looked a bit dodgy for us. The police thought I had done it for the insurance. When they realized I didn't have any, and they couldn't find any cause--we'd been out at the time and just got back to see it blazing--they, and all the neighbors, pulled around to help. A barber friend found us an apartment over a workshop, which was a stroke of fortune. Upstairs, above the workshop, was a kitchen and two bedrooms, a living room, and a huge empty warehouse. Within a week, this storage place was full to the ceiling with blankets, pots, pans, crockery, knives, forks, spoons, baby clothes, women's clothes, men's clothes. You name it, we had it ten times over. I ended up with five suits and twenty ties. I had never had either before. We were giving clothes away to our friends for years. Vanesa, who was then at elementary school, got clothes and £1,000 from the school who had passed the hat around.

So there we were. Stuck in a bind, it seemed, with funds depleted from natural disasters and human errors. I hadn't been wasting my time while the Korean boat was waiting to be sold, though. I was going to build my next boat in steel, and I had apprenticed myself to an old guy who had a small workshop where he used to weld up steel building frames and things like that. It had taken so long to sell that Korean boat and put some money back in the bank that I had become quite competent in my welding skills. My new boat was now well under way and looking good, but the bank account wasn't growing at the same rate, and I was beginning to pray for a little help.

To put food on the table, I was teaching English at night, which is about all a foreigner can do outside of Tokyo. It was easy work, just a couple of hours in the evening, teaching businessmen and at private cram schools. That's another plus about building in Japan. In England, or wherever, you'd have to work in the daytime to make money and build at night and in your spare time. Here, I could work on the boat all day, knock off about four o'clock, go to the public bath, clean up there, and go off for two hours teaching. That, along with all the good scrap yards, used engines, and discarded fishing boats made it possible to get it all together. Teaching English wasn't going to make me rich, though, and I had still all the sails and things to buy.

You think I've forgotten about the synchronicity bit. Don't worry. I'm getting there. This is the first part now.

My favorite teaching job was going to a doctor's house. He ran the local hospital, which was handy when I sawed off a finger or drilled a hole through my foot. I used to go for dinner every Monday night, and after eating, we would sit around drinking sake and reading *The Japan Times* together. That's an English language newspaper, and he must have been the only person in the town to get it delivered. We would read just a few of the front page articles, with me explaining the more difficult parts, although not, thank God, the grammatical construction of the sentences. I hardly knew the difference between an adjective and an adverb. We never got past the front page, so it was about new when we finished. I got to take the paper home, and because we didn't get one delivered, Tuesday morning was treat day, sitting down on the tatami matting, back against the wall, drinking my morning coffee from a rice bowl, French style.

The article was on page three. Not a big piece. Just a column-wide and a few inches long, but the heading got me: "Italians caught in Gulf of Genoa." Well, I was a sailor. Or thought I was. I loved the world "gulf." Gulf of Mexico, Gulf of Panama. Any gulf will do. There's something bright and brave about the word. In England, all you have are bays and inlets. Not the sort of coastline to stretch the imagination, but a gulf, now that sets you free.

Anyway, what was happening in the Gulf of Genoa? Two Italians sailing there had been caught at sea, carrying some marijuana. It didn't say how they were stopped or what had happened after that. I couldn't imagine how they'd been caught. How did the Coast Guard know? Where did they get the stuff? How did they know where to sell it? "Just give me the chance," I thought. "I'd do it right. Wouldn't get caught. Make some money, make some people happy, and sail off into the sunset." That was going to be my daydream for the day, while I was laying the pinewood decking. I enjoyed doing that job. It was easy to do, made the boat look good, and was the last big work that needed doing.

There was something in the air that morning making me feel good. I was working on the deck in the bright January sunshine, the river sparkling just feet away from the bows of the boat, which sat propped up on the slipway. Half a mile downstream, but hidden by a bend, lay the pull of the Pacific Ocean. Across the river, beyond the discarded fishing boats, stretching into the distance, were miles and miles of paddy fields, green as emeralds in Spring but now a wasteland of winter stubble. Beyond all that, rising blue-grey, was Mount Tsukuba, home of the guardian gods of the Kanto plain. From the summit, you could see Mount Fuji on a day like this, over a hundred miles away, on the other side of Tokyo. Days like these, when the light is so pure, do something to the wiring in my head. I feel alive and optimistic, but they also make me restless. I just want to get up and go, chase the sun around the world. I can't bear to be indoors, and death would be better than having a watch strapped to my wrist. That freedom was so near now. Just another few months, and we could be off, but what to do about the sails and all the other things I had to buy? If only...if only...

At lunchtime, Chantal came over to the boat. Maybe she brought me some lunch. I can't remember. I only remember the letter she was holding. Climbing down from the boat, I took the letter and looked at the stamp. It was from Malaya. I didn't know anyone in Malaya that I could think of, and there was no return address on the back of the envelope. Opening the letter, I had to look at the signature to find out who it was from. Well, that's a surprise! It was from Jack. I hadn't heard from him in years. I thought he was back in his home country of Australia also building a new boat.

I had first met Jack many years before when I sailed into Hong Kong. That was after I built my first boat in Japan, and I was a raw novice. Getting to Hong Kong had been a marvelous feat of disasters avoided. My younger brother had come out from England to give me a hand, but he knew less than I did. Three Japanese friends came along for the ride, and they thought I was Captain Hornblower, but that was because they knew nothing, either. Like most people who had never been at sea, we thought it safer to be near the land. The plan was to sail down the Japanese coast; then a quick dash over to the Chinese coast; and follow China down to Hong Kong, not getting too close, though. In those days, China was a closed country and a terrifying obstacle, especially if you were Japanese.

The sailing part, pulling all those ropes and things, wasn't too daunting to learn. It didn't take long to get the hang of that. The hard part was knowing which way to put the boat. A correspondence course on celestial navigation had given me the grounding. I had spent hours and hours at night studying all the stars. I now knew the earth was a ball and went around the sun, although I still find that hard to believe. We left Japan behind on a sunny November morning, heading west for China. Two days later, I thought I better put into practice what I'd learned, so I took out my brand new sextant and "shot the sun," as they say. Then, after a lot of head scratching, I announced we were a hundred miles off the coast, and it looked like we were pointing in the right direction.

A few hours later in the early afternoon, we noticed a small boat in the water, no bigger than a rowing boat. There was just one man fishing over the side, and I thought "Jesus, he's brave! All this way from land in such a little boat!" When we got nearer, we noticed a line going over the bow into the water. "God, he's anchored!" Then, we saw the water wasn't blue anymore but a dirty brown. On with the echo sounder. "No! It couldn't be!" It was almost shallow enough to stand up in, and there was no land to see in front of us. Maybe it was like Morcame Bay, where at low tide you can walk out to sea for miles with the water getting no higher than your ankles. Whatever. We were definitely not a hundred miles off shore. On with the engine and a quick retreat.

The next morning, now sailing south on what we thought must be parallel to the China coast, we had blue sky and blue sea. But, what were all those trees? "Look! Hundreds of them!" It was a forest in front of us. Nothing was on the chart, though. On a southern heading, there can't be anything in front of us. "These trees are getting nearer!" I thought with alarm. Then, through the binoculars the trees turned out to have boats under them. It was a bit like in Macbeth where the forest turns out to be an army. They were coming straight at us. Huge, really big, Chinese junks, all with tall masts but with the sails furled, under engine. There were about four hundred; we counted them. That is, my brother and I did. The three Japanese hid below. My brother and I quickly dressed as ragged as we could. We didn't want to look like rich kids. This was the cultural revolution time in China when all signs of affluence were death sentences.

On they came until we were surrounded, lost in a vast field of Chinese junks. One right behind. One dead ahead. One near enough to cause a bit of damage when they bumped into us. Looking up to their decks, we had to strain our necks. On the decks, arranged in genealogical order, from very old granddads and grandmums, going down to little babies in arms, there were maybe twenty in a boat, all looking down on us, unsmiling. Very unhappy looking. My brother thought to offer the kids some chocolate, but they made no move to take it. It wouldn't have been possible to get it to them without some nets or the end of a line, anyway. We thought to throw it up, but then they might have thought we were throwing it in anger or something. The guy to our port, the one who had bumped us, began pointing at China. We couldn't escape, and they changed course. We were now forced to follow westward. My brother and I kept rubbing our stomachs like we were hungry and shouting "Hong Kong! Hong Kong!" Why did they seem so keen taking us into port? I'm sure the genuine fishermen onboard didn't really care, but these junks wouldn't have been allowed to roam freely. There must have been some party cadres onboard making sure they didn't make a run for it. We would have been quite a catch for these government watch dogs. They might have been promoted because we would have made five juicy hostages, especially the Japanese guys. They could have sold those three back to Japan for some fancy cars.

Later in the day, around four o'clock, the fleet seemed to be picking up speed. We couldn't keep up, but we were still trapped inside the box of boats. They were spreading out, and they had stopped insisting that we keep up. Why, we never really knew for sure. Slowly, the gaps between the boats opened up until we were able to slip through. None of the boats gave chase to herd us back into line. They probably let us go because they knew a storm of wind was coming, and come it did. But not that day.

The next morning, we were feeling good. We had calm seas, a little breeze, and were going in the right direction. How did we know? Well, there was Taiwan, the island, on our port side, and that bit of land to starboard must be China. "Great." But, then, in the early afternoon, land appeared ahead. "No! Not again!" I thought to myself. "Where are we?" I reckoned that we must be in a big bay on the China coast. I had to turn around quick. The headsails got wrapped around the forestay while the mainsail was flapping and threatening to rip. One of the guys went up the mast and set the jib free. Now, start the engine. Full speed. Six knots. Back out to sea. We cleared the point that we had thought was Taiwan. Now, turn right again, and follow that coast which we can see about ten miles off. No more mistakes. This is the definitely the way to Hong Kong.

About five o'clock that evening, the wind began to pick up. I doubt now it was ever over a Force 9, and maybe it was Force 8, a bit heavy for a small boat but no really big deal for the people who know what they're doing. It was building up the seas, though. By noon the next day, the waves were gigantic, curled up and over like a Yukiyo-e print of Tokyo Bay. We trailed car tires, which we used for fenders, on a long rope to slow down the boat and to try keep the stern into the following seas. Useless. The waves were so steep the tires went up the wave on the inside, then fell straight back down. I had been terrified before.

Now, I was just plain scared, like everyone else. Believe it or not, and most people won't, but when we looked at the depth sounder when the boat was in a trough, it read thirty-six fathoms. On the crest it was forty-six fathoms. One fathom is six feet, which made the waves sixty feet high, and that's why you never sail close to land in shallow water. In the deep ocean the same wind would have given a very pleasant sail going the same way. Anyway, we survived that with just one knock down, which pushed the mast under water and bent the stantions on both sides inward about forty-five degrees.

When the storm died down, we got swept into Hong Kong harbor more by the current and luck than any skill. The first person I saw was Jack on the slip of the Hong Kong Yacht Club. With his full-face red beard, stout build, and his confident sailor's gait, he was everything I wasn't. For some reason, we hit it off, maybe because he knew I had a little bit more money than he did. I told him I was heading for England. "I'll come along with you." He said. "We'll sail in tandem."

We did. He had a new plastic boat he had just bought in Taiwan, not much money left, and he was looking for somewhere to go. We spent months sailing around the Philippines, and he taught me so much. By the time we got to Singapore, the trip, which had started out as a National Geographic-like adventure, had turned me into a sea-loving rover. I wasn't scared anymore. I could use a sextant and find where I was. I could trim sails and talk sea lore with the best. The Japanese guys were now superfluous, and they knew it. They went home. Jack and I went on to have a few more adventures in the Indian Ocean, and then he, too, went home. I hadn't heard from him until I got the letter.

So it was my mate and my mentor who had found me in Japan and was writing all the way from Malaya. I couldn't wait to find out what new sorts of adventures he was up to.

Well, you've obviously guessed what the letter is about so it's no surprise to you, but, it blew me away when I first read it. I was expecting a progress report on the new boat he was building. Or maybe he just wanted to gloat about his life in the tropics.

There was a short postscript after his signature, which I had turned to first, saying to make sure to burn the letter. That was intriguing. I thought immediately, "This has got to have something to do with what I'd just read in the newspaper." I did burn the letter later, just before I left Japan, and being in Japan, we had to make a little ceremony of it. So I can't recall exactly what it said, but it so answered my cry to fate that it was minutes before it all sank in. Just two hours before I had read a short article about some guys trying to smuggle some dope in a boat and me thinking I could do better, and here was a letter from an old sailing buddy offering me just that chance.

Now, that's got to be synchronicity. I don't believe in things like this having any meaning, but no way could I turn the offer down. It was too uncanny. It was like getting a personal message from the Oracle of Delphi. Here was the answer to all my financial woes. How could I refuse to go? Aren't we always taught to grasp the moment? Opportunity knocks once, and all that. Didn't Seneca say "Fate is kind to him who will?" Or to put it another way, as my dad told me, "God helps those who help themselves." I had it on the authority of two good men to jam open the doors of fate, and go for it. I just had to hope fate had got the timing right. If the postman had arrived before I had read the newspaper, then reading the article after the letter, I would have taken the fate of the two hapless Italians as a warning and never would have gone.

Jack had not replied to the letter I sent a couple of years before, so I was surprised to hear that he had finished building his boat and had sailed up to Singapore from Melbourne, literally sailing all the way. It wasn't until Singapore that he had an engine installed. He was now resting up in a small boatyard on the upper reaches of a muddy river near Kelang, on the west coast of Malaya, getting some interior woodwork done. Somehow or another he had got himself a deal to deliver some contraband to New Zealand. He mentioned New Zealand, but I was sure it was going to be Australia. Skirting around the ambiguities, I also figured out that there were no hard drugs involved. I might have drawn the line there. Not that I'm against anyone using them. People can pump what they like into themselves, but that heavy-duty stuff and the pipelines controlling it, run by desperate types, is too heavy a scene for me.

My daughter had gone to England a year before and was going to school there. I had promised her that she could come back to join the boat when it was finished so there would be no awkward face-to-face explaining to do to her. It wouldn't be a lie to say that I was helping Jack to deliver his boat to Australia. As for Chantal, well, everything illegal turns the French on, so there were no words of caution from that side.

I know what you're going to say now. You're going to say, "What about the morality of a scam like that?" And, it's true. It wasn't crates of oranges we were thinking of transporting, but then it wouldn't be crates of guns, either, or other nasty things. Just a bunch of grass. A load of herbs. Poets and philosophers have been using it ever since evolution cranked it out. So, it's a case of one man's poison being another man's inspiration. If you're on the side of the inspirationalists, then there's no moral dilemma to wrestle with. Ah, you mean it's illegal? Come, on! Everything is illegal to someone at some time, but, I don't see the word printed on the leaf when it pops up.

Jack had got himself a ham radio and gave me a call sign to try and contact him. Why he wouldn't use a telephone, I don't know. I would have thought that more secure than broadcasting your message for anybody with a transceiver to pick up. I didn't have a radio and didn't intend to get one for my boat. I like to be alone at sea. That's the reason for being out there in the first place. I had a friend in Japan who knew a guy who was a ham radio freak, though. Jack did not have a license for his radio, however, and was what is called a pirate broadcaster, and serious ham radio operators don't like to talk to them. I came to an arrangement with my new Japanese ham radio friend and started twirling dials and things and eventually managed to get Jack loud and clear. Even though my Japanese friend's English was not so good, many people would be able to hear the broadcast if they happened on the same frequency. So, it was not easy talking in double-speak to get any real information, but I got enough to realize he was serious and he was going to send me a ticket to Malaya. Why did he want me? He already had a young Aussie guy with him whom I had never met, but I gathered this young guy was new to sailing. Jack probably wanted someone who knew something about it and would be into doing something that smacked of piracy.

Jack was the most anarchistic person I'd every met, so I wasn't too amazed at this new career he'd entered into. Did I have a choice not to go with him? I don't know. I don't know if I even believe in the concept of free will. Who knows what those little neurons in the brain get up to. It seems to me they're the one who do what they like. We can't control the pathways they take or tell them which synapses to jump. They just take whatever information they get from out there, buzz about like a cloud of flies around a dying dog, and before you know it, you're walking off to jail or maybe sailing off to the tropics. Obviously, the letter and the newspaper articles were two pieces of information my neurons had put together before they decided I should get on the plane. They would determine the outcome later.

I was a little worried about leaving Chantal alone in Japan, but she still had about five months on her visa left, and the trip was only going to take two or three months. So, I locked away all of my tools, secured my boat, and when the ticket arrived, got Chantal to drive me to the airport to take the plane to Kuala Lumpur, where Jack would be waiting.

Chantal and I had decided a code to let her know where we were going. We would stay in contact on the ham radio, and if we were going to New Zealand, I'd mention the words, "meat pie," and if we were off to Australia, I would somehow put the words, "mango pie" into the conversation. Mango pie was the first thing she ever cooked on the boat, and, I cannot forget it. I just hoped the trip to Australia wouldn't be as bad.

Chapter 5

On the plane flying out of the January sun toward the warmth of Malaysia, I was just a little nervous. Just think if something did go wrong. I'd never be allowed back in Japan. My almost finished boat would probably lie rotting on its slipway for years and years. And, what about Chantal and little Radja? Well, they'd be okay. She'd go back to France and be a single mum, and that really was what her intention was in the beginning anyway. Not being able to get back into Japan, though, now, that would hurt.

I like living in Japan for lots of reasons. Top of the list after food is a total lack of acro. That's probably because they never talk about religion or politics. Or, more correctly, they never think about religion or politics. That's because they don't have either, not in a serious way. When it comes to religion, eclecticism finds its true meaning. You have a little newborn baby? Dress him like a samurai and take him to a Shinto shrine for a ceremony of Shintoism. That's a little like Druidism without the human sacrifices. Getting married? Deck yourself up like the stars in *Gone with the Wind* and have a very fair imitation of a Christian ceremony in a plastic gothic chapel complete with an authentically-robed, faux priest. When it's time for the slightly more serious business of dying, a Buddhist priest will chant a few sutras before laying up your ashes in the temple grounds. Isn't that wonderful? Ceremony for ceremony's sake without all the background noise of ideological bickering.

Jack was waiting at the airport when I arrived, looking like he had just jumped off a long boat and couldn't find anyone to hack down. But, he'd always looked like that, so he hadn't changed much. He looked slightly more cynical, maybe, like he wasn't really expecting me to come, but now that I had he was going to play with my head or something.

It was nighttime when the plane landed. The boat was a good six hours drive away, so we were going to spend the night in Kuala Lumpur. It felt good to be back in the tropics again, smelling the frangipani and feeling the warm, damp air. So far, so good. No regrets about coming yet. On the way downtown by taxi, Jack pointed out a sign on the back of a speeding bus: "Drugs Kill," it said very tersely. He let me look at it until the bus had vanished up ahead. Then he gave me a nudge and a sly little grin. The meaning was, "Hey, you into this? This is big time stuff." That's another annoying thing about Aussies. They think they're the only ones with balls.

I'm not sure what they meant by that sign anyway. Of course, drugs can kill if you take too many, but lots of things can kill you. Not least of all, Southeast Asian bus drivers. I'm willing to bet that more people are killed by their reckless driving than the number of people snuffing it on overdoses. In fact, I think more of the governments down there should have signs warning people not to ride the buses. And what about AIDS? That will kill you more surely than sniffing coke. Maybe it's time to outlaw sex? Heavy drugs are, of course, a problem, but the problem is not inherent in the drugs themselves. The real problem is the squalor, the violence, and all that money, but everybody knows the solution to that--just legalize them. Put them on a par with Asian bus driving. The Mafiosos and offshore bankers won't be very happy about that, but no need for them to worry just yet. The Pope will get married before governments see the logic in that argument so it looks like business as usual for quite a while.

Just go back to that sign for a second. I'm sure it's not out of concern for the people's health that they stick those signs up. What they're really trying to say is, "People who use drugs are anti-authority, so either you start thinking as we do or we'll stop you thinking at all." And to make sure there's no relapse in your thought processing, they'll hang you in Singapore, Malaya, and Indonesia and shoot you to death in Thailand if you falter. Quicker and less painful than sitting on top a bonfire, no doubt, but it's still the same mad dog mindset of the Spanish Inquisitors.

Jack was as intrigued as I was with the adventure. He was playing it up like we were in a movie. No talking about it in the taxi or in the hotel. Everywhere might be bugged. If you saw all the police standing around looking super efficient in their pressed, starched uniforms, swinging their night sticks almost as long as lances, you could believe even the paving stones were bugged.

Then, there were the goon squads—the guardians of Islamic Shiria law. These guys weren't so obvious as they weren't wearing uniforms, but I'm sure the faithful could spot them easily enough. It's a very weird situation in Malaya. Being officially a Muslim country with a large non-Muslim population, the government is scared to death that the true believers are going to get contaminated by the ways of the infidels. I'm not sure if these religious zealots are paid a salary or not. It's possible they just volunteer to go around checking up on the indigenous Malays, making sure they are not drinking alcohol or sleeping with someone they should not. Paid or not, the Muslim Malays take them seriously. They could get you into big trouble. Imagine being a Malay, sitting in a restaurant at a table with your Chinese friends or some other non Malays. They can be washing down their food with beer, but God help you if you stray from your Orange Squash.

We had to find a noisy outdoor eating stall before Jack would fill me in on the details, but first, I had to have a cigarette. I'd only been with him for an hour or so, and already he was influencing me in a bad way. Six months before I had stopped smoking, but watching him roll a cigarette brought back the urge. I guess it was bit of nerves, too, but I started again that night. Between mouthfuls of nasi goreng, he told me the plan. I was right about Australia as the drop off place, but wrong about Thailand

The picking up was going to be in India. Two thousand miles away in Goa, north of Bombay, up the west coast of India. That was more like it. People weren't as uptight there as in Malaya, so going there was okay with me. All these "Drugs Kill" posters were making me nervous. India was much more pragmatic about drugs. It would take a little longer than I thought, though, but it was still only the end of January, and I had time. The northeast monsoon was still blowing steady, and we were a long way off the cyclone season. We'd make an easy run across the Indian Ocean up to Goa, turn around, and get out before the monsoon winds changed in April and the southwest winds made the west coast a dangerous lee shore. I was beginning to like the idea better and better. In India, it should be easy to pick up an illicit cargo and get away. Nobody cared what you did in India, and even if they did, a little money from the back of your hand would sort it out.

What about the goodies? I was wrong there, too. It wasn't marijuana in its naked leaf state. It was hashish. Well, it's all from the same bush, and I'm not going to tell you how it's made because you probably know better than I do. I figured that it would be a little like trading in vanilla essence instead of vanilla beans. A hundred and twenty kilos. That's what we were going to pick up. I had no idea what a hundred and twenty kilos of hashish looked like, but I knew that it was about the same weight as two people who hadn't overdosed on McDonalds. It seemed enough to bother about. Jack reckoned it was worth about one million dollars on the streets of Australia, and we would be getting a substantial percentage for a delivery fee. I know nothing works out to the dot, so I was a bit skeptical about the amount we would actually receive. No matter, it was going to be worthwhile and get me back out at sea on my own boat again.

First, we had to get over to India where we were to meet up with the second half of the act—an airline steward who, through his contacts, had arranged the deal. He was to bring it all in suitcases to us while we sat innocently waiting at anchor in Goa. That was the plan, but I was sure even then that it wouldn't quite work out that way.

The next day, careening down the road, heading to Kelang, where we would change buses to Shar Alam, we were doing about Mach 2, speeding past miles of brand new hotels and golf courses and gleaming clean Lever Brothers palm oil factories. It was difficult to believe this was Malaya. Where were all the kampongs I remembered from twenty years before? The rubber plantations? The scruffy roadside markets? The happy-go-lucky Malays? It looked like the country had fallen into the same sorry state as Singapore had. They'd got the money bug. I remember back in the 60's when Singapore first caught it. Almost everyone then was living happily in kampongs, small family plots nestled among the coconut trees in beautiful wooden houses with chickens in the yards. For the Chinese bankers, that wasn't their idea of fun so they convinced the government, if not the people, that living laterally was very wasteful. People should live upwardly on top of each other so that golf courses and shopping malls could stretch and spread out. They threw up hundreds of thirteen story look-alike apartment buildings, but nobody wanted to take the bait. That's when the mysterious fires started breaking out. Every night a different set of kampongs went up in flames. It was a pretty obvious tactic, but what can you do when the media denies the rumours? Nobody got killed, and the government took credit for having all the unfortunates re-housed so quickly. Suicide rates went up enormously for awhile until all those wishing to jump from their high rise windows in despair had done so. Just in case there were any ingrates still living on the ground floors, and to make it easier to spot these dissidents, the President, whose relatives were all barbers, decreed that a short-in-back haircut would be the new symbol of acceptance for this brave, new utopia. Malaya is not quite where Singapore is yet, but it's a bigger piece of real estate.

After changing buses at Kelang for Shar Alam, a small town further up the river where Jack's boat lay, I thought maybe the first bus had gone into hyperdrive and we had gone through a time warp. Here, at last, was the Malaya I loved. The monsoon ditches half full of rich, sweet sludge. The sinus-clogging smell of tropical fruit rotting on the ground. Thick, red dust coating the trees along the narrow roads. In the taxi, bouncing down the final few miles, I finally felt that I had left Japan behind.

The boatyard was just a family kampong, really. A scattering of wooden houses nestled under the palm trees. Jack, and his pal, Andy, were staying in the only concrete building. It had one big room with outdoor loos. They were living there while the boat was being worked on. Jack must have put in a good word for me, telling Andy that as Poms go, I wasn't too bad, so we got off on a good start. I could see he was under the sway of Jack. I was going to have to deal with two of them if I was going to advance any ideas I might have about the trip. As soon as I saw the room they were staying in, I knew there was going to be some sort of friction unless I kept it under control.

Jack's other boat, the one he had bought in Taiwan and eventually sold in Israel, had always been a mess down below. Clothes were all over the place. Nothing was put away. Books and charts stuck around it any old way. It wasn't my boat so it didn't bother me. In fact, I liked it. I love visiting people whose houses are a mess because I can't live like that. It's my curse to be a Virgo.

Astrology. That's something else I don't believe in. I find it hard to credit that millions of people all have the same obsessive, compulsive disorder. But when people say Virgos are neat freaks and order-loving people who like everything in its place, I have to admit that they're talking about me. Chaos makes me nervous, and if not sorted out, makes me depressed.

When I saw the mess their room was in, I got really jumpy. Here we were going on a trip that could have serious consequences if we didn't get it right. Surely we should be thinking straight and serious about everything we did from now on. How could you be serious about anything when all your gear was all over the place? There was a compass stuffed in the sink; wet weather gear heaped in the corner; boxes of food strewn all over the bedding; and clothes, books, and food all jumbled up together around the door. I had to be careful here. I didn't want to get off on the wrong foot. These guys had been here a few months now, and before that, they had been in Singapore. So, they'd had enough time in the tropics to get a little tropo. I'd just come in from super speedy Japan and was still buzzing with higher latitude energy.

The boatyard was pretty much a clearing in the trees, which went right down to the riverbank where the boat was tied up to a wooden jetty. At first sight, I wasn't too impressed with the boat. For one thing, it was painted black. I don't like black boats. About the only good thing you can say about them is that you can see them easier in a blow when the waves are all kicked up white. In the tropics, though, it makes for an oven down below. One of Jack's ideas to defray suspicion from our nefarious journey had been to say that the boat was going to the Antarctic eventually. He had even gone so far as to name her Adelie, for the Antarctic penguin that looks like it's wearing a tuxedo.

The topsides looked too far out of the water, but that was because it was a flushed deck. Although that was much easier to build and safer in a rollover, sorry, Jack, it doesn't look nice. Because there's no cabin and no cabin sides, all the portholes have to be in the hull where they make it much harder to keep water from entering. The boat was rigged as a sloop with one heavy sectioned aluminum mast, and the stays would have held up Sidney Harbor Bridge. I would have made it a ketch with a smaller mast aft, but there was a massive wooden tiller in the way of that idea. The tiller was attached directly to an equally massive steel rudder, which was hung on pintles off the canoe-shaped stern. Double-ended boats—boats that are pointed at both ends—are a good idea in short breaking seas, but a waste of space in a cruising boat. The one good feature is that you can fit a very simple self-steering wind vane on this type of rudder. Around the tiller was a small cockpit built into the deck, where, in theory, you could sit on the deck with your legs in the hole. Apart from that, the whole deck was flush with no obstructions except for the winches and cleats. Thank God there was a strong looking safety line around the boat because there was very little else to hang on to. The companion way was through a hole cut in the deck, and the opening was a bit too big for my liking. I think hatch openings should be small and narrow, not only so you take less water down below when the waves break over, but also so you don't get your ribs busted when you're going down below and the boat lurches. If you're going to spend your time in a marina, you better go for a big hatch so you can pass the martinis up with both hands. Better still, get a marine-side apartment.

I had to admit, however, that, despite her negatives, she was a powerful, no-nonsense boat for any kind of sea. While we were checking the boat over, a short intense squall came through with some nasty look-ing lighting. With the bare steel deck flooding with rain, I wondered what it would be like at sea if we got hit. Obviously, the lightning would dissipate through the steel hull, but would we be part of the circuit? I thought I'd let Jack test that one out.

On the previous radio link up to Japan, I had gotten the impres-sion that we would be pushing off as soon as I had arrived, but one look below put that idea back a week or two. Jack had been given about $10,000 petty cash from his dealers to finance the food and fuel side of the trip, but he was obviously spending as much of that as he could smartening up his boat with lots of high quality interior woodwork. Stepping down into the saloon, I saw Chinese carpenters all over the place, banging, measuring, and sawing. I wasn't feeling very happy with the situation now. I didn't want to be gone from Japan longer than nec-essary, and there were the northeast trades to think about. In April, they would die out and the southwest monsoon winds would start to blow, bringing wet and stormy weather. I determined to give it some slack for a week, but I'd have to get pushy after that or it was all going to fall through.

Jack had always been laid back, but it just seemed his attitude should have been different. After all, we could get twenty years in jail for what we were doing. Andy agreed with me that we ought to be more serious about hurrying about, but then sided with Jack when he took the bushman's mañana attitude. It was going to be like that the whole trip. Aussies and Poms rarely see eye-to-eye on anything, even if they're good mates. Then, something even more serious turned up. Jack was contemplating having an affair with the wife of a local Muslim who was a policeman or some kind of official. Jack reckoned she had given him the eye, and he wanted to see if it was for real. God, that was all we needed. I can't imagine why he thought that would work. He'd have no head left, or at least no balls, unless we got out of Malaya fast.

I rang Chantal up on the phone that night and told her I was getting a bit hesitant about it all. I didn't get any comeback from her at first, and then she reminded me that we wanted the money. I thought, "Bloody hell! She's right. What am I thinking of? I'm here because of a message from God." I had to get Jack thinking the way I was. He was getting stuck down here. So I pushed him, cancelled most of the work on the boat and started to move all the gear they had taken off back aboard. In four days, we were ready to go. I think all along Jack had not intended to pay for the work done on his boat, but I told him that skipping out would be really bad karma. It was a good six-hour trip down the river to where it entered the Malacca Straits. The Chinese don't like people running out on their bills. They'd be after us with machetes and hatches and catch us before we'd gone too far, even if we did leave at night.

Leaving at night is what we did anyway, but he did pay the bills. Paying the bills, we decided we might as well get a clearance paper. We had to take the bus back to Shar Alam where there was a small government office, but when we asked them they said that we didn't need a paper and to just go. We did get a stamp in our passports, though.

Pulling away from the jetty with a bit of a moon still showing above the jungle, things felt good. We had the boat supplied, water tanks full, gear stored, sails bent on, engine running nicely, fuel tanks reasonably topped up. "Hey, this is going to work!" I finally started thinking.

Just one last hiccup. Jack was a bit pissed off with having paid his bills, so to make himself feel better, he brought out of his pocket a packet of small metal files that he had shoplifted that morning when we were shopping for some boat hardware. That didn't feel good. We were setting off a serious crime gig, and starting it off with a petty theft didn't seem right. I asked Jack to throw them in the river. He hesitated, but Andy backed me up. To my surprise, Jack did it. He could understand the logic of paying the bills to avoid the Chinese axes, but throwing away the files just for a feel-good wasn't too logical to him. But, he went along with the idea, and I think we all felt we might make a good crew together after that.

There was a fantastic light show going along the riverbank as we motored slowly out into midstream and headed for the sea. The bushes and tress all along the shoreline were lit up with what must have been millions and millions of fireflies, and they all switched on and off at some hidden signal. On for half a minute, then plunge back into darkness for another half a minute. What gave the signal for such split-timed synchronizing? No idea, but we took it as a good sign of success to come.

Why do we always look for signs from heaven to give us hope? Obviously, we aren't too sure about success if we are left to ourselves. Better to put your hope in some outside agent and lessen the stress level so you can free the brain to get on with working out the details. I guess that's the logic in carrying lucky rabbit tails and things. They must act like a sponge to suck up the fear. Now that the voyage had been given heavenly approval, I was free to go below and check out the living quarters for the next few months.

Going down from the deck, there was a steeply angled companionway entering into a huge saloon made larger because it was empty of furniture. To starboard was a low bench type sofa, but no table. To port was another low sofa-cum-bunk bed, and above that, another bunk. I took this bunk, as Jack and Andy had already claimed their places. It would be good at least for the trip to India with the northeast trade winds putting us on a starboard tack. I'd be heeled over towards the hull when I slept and couldn't fall out. Later, I could always move over to the bunk on the starboard side. Looking aft at the bottom of the ladder was a big box covering the engine, the top acting as a chart table and galley countertop just perfect for rolling out bread dough. To port of that was the sink and a kerosene cooker, and over to starboard was a passageway leading into Jack's aft cabin, where he kept his precious radio. Andy slept forward, opposite the head, which had draped, in place of the door, an Aussie flag. In the right forward of the boat was lots of room for sails and provisions.

It's a good job we weren't expecting any heavy weather for the first week or two. It was going to take that long to sort everything out and get it stowed properly. Of course, it's not like we were taking the boat on her maiden voyage or anything. She had already been sailed up from Melbourne, but the carpenters in Malaya had been moving things around and knocking up bulkheads and ceilings, changing this and that. It was a right mess, unfinished, and it looked unloved. Jack, hoping to finish the interior off at a later date somewhere, had brought along all the mahogany planks the carpenters hadn't got around to fitting, and these were stowed anywhere they would fit. Everywhere there was sawdust, especially in the bilges, which would have to be cleaned up or that would block the pumps when water got below, which it was bound to do someday because, before this trip was over, we were going to go down into the Roaring Forties. There was no electric light in the saloon space or over the bunks. There was a small light in the galley, and Jack had one in his aft cubbyhole of a cabin. Wiring was another job to do in the distant future. If I wanted to read, it would have to be by paraffin lamp tied up on the bulkhead behind my head, and of course, I wanted to read. What else do you do on a long boat trip? Luckily, what the boat did have was a fire extinguisher, and I thanked God it worked a few weeks later.

Apart from the fire extinguisher, the rest of the equipment onboard amounted to two sextants, one that I had brought, a digital watch for timing the sextant sights, a hand held compass for taking bearings, and the main compass, which was not even fastened down but was the type used by coastal fisherman on small boats who take them home at night. We also had the transceiver, which would be good for checking the time on the watch, but otherwise I thought a waste. We didn't have any charts with us. Imagine, no charts! There were the ones Jack had used to come up from Aussie with, and we could use them towards the end of the trip. From here to India and back to Aussie, though, we had nothing but some large-scale routing charts. Routing charts are printed for each month of the year and cover a whole sheet of paper. There is one sheet for each month that gives the winds and currents expected for that month. They don't have any details about the coastlines or sea depths. We did have a *Good Times Atlas,* so all in all, we were certainly better off than Francis Drake and company.

When you think about what those guys did back then with what they had, it's truly amazing. It's all right lying in bed reading about those old time mariners and how they went from here to there, rounded this and that cape, and came back home again. Though you might skip that part, wanting just to hear about the raping and the pillaging and how much gold they swiped. Although you wouldn't get any raping with Drake, he wouldn't allow it. If you really think about it, rounding Cape Horn, with a mast tied up with vegetable fiber, and going the wrong way to boot, with no wet weather gear, no winches, no hydraulic steering, no sonars, and no charts, it's hard to understand how they did it. Drake, the first to round the Cape, had no sextant, no timepiece, and no hot coffee. He had a compass of sorts, but no variation correction tables, no pilot charts, and no admiralty sailing directions. These sailors must have had as finely-tuned and primitive feeling for the sea, the movements of the winds, and the turning of the heavens as any sea bird. If, as they say, navigation is an art, then these old pirates were grand masters up there with Michelangelo and the rest of the Renaissance mob. That bit of art in navigating by the sun and stars has all gone now, though. Now that everyone and his mother can buy a GPS and arrive off the Needles within a meter.

W e reached the sea at dawn and found a place just up the coast off a sandy beach where we dropped anchor in ten feet of water. We intended to rest up for a day or two, catch up on our sleep, put the boat in some kind of order, and give the bottom of the boat a bit of a cleaning. There weren't any barnacles because the fresh river water had killed them all off, but it was pretty slimy and patches of weeds were growing around the water line. We jumped over the side to have a little swim, but there were so many little stinging jelly fish that we soon came out. I never did think much of the beaches and seas around Malaysia. They always seemed dirty and the seas murky and full of floating sand particles. I don't know where they take the photos for advertising all the new resort hotels they're building around the coast of Singapore and Malaya. Either they had a massive cleanup or they took them somewhere else.

Anyway, we weren't here on a pleasure cruise, and I wanted to get going and back to sea. I couldn't wait to get back to the Indian Ocean now that we were so near. It's the best of all the oceans for me. The winds are always fair. For half the year, they'll blow you east, and for the other half, they'll blow you west; from Africa to Asia and back again. The trip is a milk run in the northeast monsoon and a little rougher in the southwest winds. The Indian Ocean is a magical place, where all the stories of Sinbad come alive. It's just so full of history. Sailing that ocean you can follow the places Vasco de Gama stopped and follow the routes of the old Arab traders and Marco Polo, from the mosques and spice markets of the Malay archipelago to the endless grasslands of East Africa.

We were north of the narrows of the Malacca Straits where most of the pirate danger lay, and although there were rumors of pirates off the coast around the border of Malaya and Thailand, we weren't going near there. Pirates have been operating out of the bays and jungle inlets of Sumatra for centuries. These days, undercrewed, slow moving tankers are a favorite target. They'll take anything they can get, even stealing the nets off fishing boats. Rich looking yachts are tasty targets, too. We didn't have much to worry about there, then. These pirates, although some of them are professional and do nothing but waylay foreign boats, are mostly just fishermen who moonlight. It's like having a second job. If they see a likely boat when they're out fishing, some slow moving freighter or a sailboat, they'll check it out and come back at night. Anytime we thought we were being checked up on, we beckoned them over to come onboard and have a cup of tea. We showed them around and let them see there was nothing worth having. It's no good having a weapon onboard because the chances of getting to use it first are pretty slim. More often than not, it will get you killed first while you're hold-ing it and wondering whether to fire or not.

A few years before, further south, just off Singapore, a sailboat with a man and wife and child aboard were approached at night by a small boat whose passengers didn't look like they just wanted a cup of tea. The woman (French, what else?) came up out of the forehatch bran-dishing a rifle, and she got shot down dead. The pirates, if you want to call them that, came onboard and were very upset by what they had done when they saw the man and the now motherless child. At least that's how the story goes. I could tell you a more personal pirate story, but I shan't. There have been too many diversions already.

Most of the Indian Ocean is a Muslim lake. From the Swahili culture of Zanzibar and Mombasa up the East African coast to Somalia, across to Aden and Oman to Pakistan. There's a bit of a break along the Indian coast, but then they're back in full swing in the Maldives Islands and down through Malaysia and Indonesia. So most of the pirates, well, all of the pirates, are followers of the Prophet, bless his name.

Okay, if you insist, I'll tell you that pirate story of mine. These pirates were up the Red Sea, not the Malay coast. I had always known about pirates being in the Indian Ocean around Malaysia and Indonesia, even before I started building boats. So, I thought I'd go prepared when I did eventually start sailing. I painted my boat green, and I gave her an Arabic name. She was called *El Helal*, which in Arabic means that first slim, sliver of moon that announces the beginning and end of Ramadan when everybody gets holier than thou, at least during the daytime. Of course they party all night so fasting for a month doesn't seem any big deal. On the table down below was a large Qur'an on a special stand opened to a page that threatened hell for stealing. I also had lots of Arabic art hanging around the saloon. I didn't decorate the entire boat like that just because I thought it would make the pirates more friendly. I rather like Arabic art. One day we were sheltering from a sand storm in a very shallow cove right on the Sudan Eritrean border of the Red Sea, the heartland of radical Islam. Just after dropping the anchor, a small boat pulled out from the end of the inlet and came along side. There were six guys, two of them at the oars, all dressed like they had just come off a set for Lawrence of Arabia, and they weren't smiling. In the bottom of the boat, wrapped in a blanket, was a rifle, and I thought, "This is serious trouble." We were literally miles from anywhere surrounded by a wind swept desert and a wind swept sea. Without any by your leave, they all swarmed aboard and headed straight below. I really thought something heavy was going to happen. I didn't like their attitude. They were very belligerent and threatening, but then, one of them, the younger one, noticed the Qu'ran and tapped the leader on the arm, pointing it out, so everyone looked. They then started noticing the prayer mats and other odds and sods that a good son of Islam should have. After looking around for a few minutes, the leader looked me in the eye and asked me in quite good English if I was a Muslim. I told him I was not worthy to be called such, but I hoped one day to be allowed into that exalted band.

"You are our brother," he said, as he took my hand and patted me on the shoulder.

Tea all around after that. I was dying for a drink of whiskey just then, but that would have given the game away. We parted smiling, and before I left the anchorage, they returned bringing twenty liters of water, which is more precious than blood in those parts.

Jack and I weren't worried about pirates, but we were worried about the Australian Air Force, which had a base at Butterworth on the Malay coast just opposite the island of Penang. They fly sweeps way out into the Indian Ocean and up and down from Australia to Singapore, keeping track of naughty boys, not just for drugs but also for refugees. We knew they photographed everything and checked the photos out later. They were especially observant off the north coast of Australia from Darwin to southeast Asia and the ports from there around to Perth. They were always on the alert for boats putting in from Asia. That's why we planned to go right around the bottom of Australia's Cape Leeuwin and across the Great Australia Bite. These are some of the stormiest waters in the world, so they didn't expect anyone to be fooling around down there.

There were lots of sea miles to go before we got there, but at least we were off, putting the boat on a northwest course to scrape the north end of Sumatra. We had shopped at the local market a few days before and were well stocked with fruits and vegetables. We had bread for a week, but Jack could turn a beautiful loaf. When we ran out of flour, we had a few canned goods, nothing gourmet, but we would be living on the fish we caught and getting our protein from the hundreds of fresh eggs stored down in the bilges. Some people take elaborate measures to keep eggs fresh on long voyages, like covering them in grease and wrapping each one in paper, but I find eggs will keep fresh well over a month if just kept in a cool place. We had lots of bananas, too, swinging in large bunches in the rope locker. When they went bad, we'd mash them up and make banana cakes.

The water tanks were full, but the water was beginning to look a bit rusty. We'd have to do something about the tanks. We would probably paint them somewhere. We didn't seem to have too much fuel for the engine, though. Jack should have built bigger fuel tanks, but we were expecting good winds on this trip and didn't plan on using the engine much. The boat seemed to be going well under full main and genoa, doing about seven knots, but Jack reckoned all the extra weight from the woodwork he'd had done had spoiled the performance. He was complaining all the time about how slow the boat had become. I was just happy to be sailing again in the tropics. Coming from a winter in Japan, this was close to heaven. When I looked in a mirror, I saw how much the sun and wind had already scorched my face, making it swollen and puffed up, my nose and forehead all peeling. I'd have to take the night watches for the first week.

Speaking of mirrors—that was the only piece of equipment that could be classed in the emergency category. You know, for flashing at anyone who might want to rescue you after you'd been knocked down by a tanker or holed by hitting a container thrown off a ship in a storm. There was no life raft, although there was one life ring, tied by a thin, long string, which could be thrown over if anyone fell off while doing their toilet over the side. What we did have was a big Zodiac, a very good one. That is a rubber dinghy, but quite a few steps up from what you play in at the beach, with a fifteen horse for an engine that could shove it along at a high rate of knots. It was part of our plan to use that to zoom in and out of secret beaches. This was kept down below deck, and it could take a good thirty minutes to set it up and get it launched. The thought of having to use it for emergency situations wasn't part of our thinking.

The minute you're past Sumatra from a line drawn from the island of Whey to the Andamans, you know you're in the Indian Ocean. The water gets bluer, the skies cleaner, and always the dolphins come to meet you, like a welcoming committee. They flash around snorting and whistling, diving in and out of the bow waves while you stand on the deck and shout for joy, "It's so good to be back!"

The first time I crossed this way it took thirteen days to Galle off the south coast of Ceylon. That's a bit slow, but it's such a pleasant trip, who cares? This time, though, we were in a hurry to meet our contact in Goa, and we set all the rag we could on the single mast. We had a huge lightweight sail the Aussies call a blooper set to port. It was not hanked on the forestay like a spinnaker, but cut flatter. The genoa was poled out to windward, and the full main was set. We were flying, and the good part was the wind vane worked like a dream and freed us from having to steer.

Andy and I spent all our time reading and drinking tea and watching the fishing line while Jack shut himself up in his cubby hole and talked on the radio to his wife. Good seamanship should have made us shorten sail at night, taken in the big free-flying blooper sail and the boomed out genoa and hoist a smaller jib. If any wind shift had happened at night when at least two of us were asleep, all hell would have broken loose as the genoa would have backed full of wind, the blooper would have collapsed, and the main might have jibed and swung the boom, crashing across the backstay to the other tack. But, the weather was so perfect, the trade winds so settled, that night and day just blended into a perfect oneness. So we kept every sail up. The wind vane could handle it well and kept us on course, swinging just a few degrees either side. Anything over that would have brought the wind forward of the jib and backed it, and that would have woken us up.

It's magical being on deck alone at night, sailing with a free wind in the trade belts. The wind was over the starboard quarter, and we were making about eight knots on a course of 270, due west, heading for Dundra Head on the south coast of Ceylon. It's good to leave on a sea voyage on a new moon, and then watch the moon rise night by night as it grows through its cycle of crescent moon waxing to full and then waning again, giving a real feeling of the movement of the heavens while watching all the familiar stars rise and set in their ordered sequence.

On this trip, the stars were of added importance because the boat's compass, apart from not being fastened down, didn't have a light fixed up fore yet, and not only that, but being on a steel boat, it gave a wildy different reading from that which it should have. To get a heading to steer by, someone had to climb half way up the aluminum mast, where the interference was less, with a hand bearing compass and shout down the magnetic heading. The guy below would then check it against the main compass, which was often something like twenty degrees off. So if your heading was 270, you had to steer 290. As night fell and the first stars came visible, we could pick a star to steer by, keeping the boat on that heading. Stars, like the sun, shift fifteen degrees in an hour, so you have to interpolate the movement of the star. That's kind of like working out a shifting vector, which the subconscious can do easily, but try doing that with a pencil and a ruler. Every hour it's best to pick a new star. The North Star would have been perfect as it doesn't move. It just stays put as all the others putter around it, but that star was too far down. We were only eight degrees north of the equator, and in those latitudes the North Star doesn't shine very brightly.

You could also keep track of the course by feeling the wind on your cheeks and keeping the waves on the quarter. Getting the wind to cool my sunburned face, I would occasionally walk around the deck, lie down over the bow to watch the dolphins play as they streaked in and out, making ghostly shooing noises in a shower of phosphorescence spray, or go down below to brew a cup of tea and roll a cigarette. Heaven couldn't be better than this. It's good to be alone at times like these, but it's also good to know that someone's going to take over and let you sleep sometime. That's pleasant, too, in the trades. With the gentle constant rhythm of the wave pattern rocking the hull, the soft fluttering of the sails, the creak of the blocks on deck, it's better than a baby's dummy to get you off.

The only real worry now across to India, now that we were out of range of the Australian surveillance planes, was getting hit by one of the tankers and freighters, which follow the same route from the Malacca Straits to Suez. We kept well north of the shortest route, but still, at night, the seas to the south were lit up with the navigation lights of an endless stream of traffic taking oil to Japan and cars to Europe.

Chapter 5

After leaving Sumatra and setting what must be some kind of record for a heavy cruising boat, Jack, Andy and I were just off Galle harbor on the south coast of Sri Lanka. We had lost the trades in the lee of the island, but we didn't intend to stop there as we were still well-provisioned and didn't want any more stamps in our passports than necessary, though I don't think a Sri Lankan stamp is anything to be suspicious about. They don't grow any of the bad plants there. They don't need them. Everyone is naturally stoned all the time; their brains shriveled in the heat.

Jack thought it time to run the engine and give the battery a bit of a charge. He had talked on the radio so much, however, that there wasn't enough juice to crank the engine over. It was quite dead. Going through the motions of starting it didn't even make the engine go clunk. I don't know why Jack hadn't installed two batteries, especially as these radios use up a lot of power when they're transmitting. There was no way to crank the engine by hand, although that would have been possible with a system of chains and cogs. We definitely needed the engine. Who knows what would happen in Goa? We didn't know anything about it. We knew that we would enter a river and then have to motor around it to find somewhere to park our boat and wait. We wouldn't want to be towed somewhere where the authorities could keep a watch on us. We decided Jack should take the Zodiac into Galle Harbor and try to borrow a battery from somewhere, come back, use it to start our engine, and then return the battery. If we had ever had to use the Zodiac in an emergency, we would have been done for. It took almost an hour to struggle it up from the fore locker, put the wood flooring in, and pump it up. Then it was so heavy, we had to use the mast winch to lower it over the side and very carefully hand down the outboard motor and fix it on the transom.

Andy and I lay hove to with lowered sails outside the harbor entrance and hoped Jack wouldn't be too long. We were in too much water to anchor, and there were rocks and pilings all over. Jack zoomed off and must have forgotten himself because he hit the throttle too hard, and the bow of the Zodiac flew up in the air. If he hadn't caught himself in time and thrust it down, he would have flipped right over. It's an art driving a rubber dinghy with a powerful engine. When you first start off, you must be as far forward as possible, then open the throttle. Once the dinghy gets up on the plane, just skimming over the water, then you can go aft and sit down. When you stop, if you crash it right into slow, you'll swamp yourself and fill it up with water.

Andy and I were getting ready for a long wait, but in just twenty minutes Jack was back with a big, heavy duty battery. By some good fortune there was a Swiss yacht at anchor in the outer harbor, and sailors always help sailors. The Swiss guy disconnected his battery from his engine and handed it over. If he had known Jack as I did, he might have thought twice. He was quite safe, though, with Andy and me. No way were we going to sail off with it. Once the battery was connected up to the engine, it started without any problem and kept going when we took the battery away.

We had already loosely tied down the sails so they wouldn't come loose and flap around as we motored into the harbor to return the battery. The Swiss boat was on its own, lying off its anchor and had an awning up and washing hanging up over the rails. We had decided it was easier to pass the battery back from off the deck of the boat rather than struggling it back from the Zodiac. As we approached him, I was at the tiller and tried to drop the revs and put the boat in neutral ready to come along side, but instead of dropping, the revs soared up off the clock, and the lever stuck in forward. "Whoa! What the hell is going on?" I had to shout.

"Christ! That's always happening," said Jack as he flew down the hatch. Andy explained, a little embarrassed, "The linkage sticks sometimes."

While Jack was trying to get what was stuck unstuck, it must have been deafening down there next to the engine. I expected it to explode any minute and send pistons and con rods shooting up through the deck. Well, it wouldn't have done that. The decks were steel. They'd probably go through Jack's head instead. There was nothing for it but to go round and round in circles, really high-speed circles, with the engine screaming and kicking up a wake that made the Swiss boat rock. I think the Swiss guy realized quite soon that this wasn't a normal approach. He watched and waited patiently until Jack at last got the linkage free and we got the boat back under control. The Swiss guy got his battery back, and I'm pretty sure he had wanted us to tie up alongside and have a chat. However, our spectacular arrival had brought out the immigration launch, and we decided to leave. We would have liked some ice from that ice making plant alongside the wharf, though.

It's natural that we should lose a bit of the northeast winds now that we turned the corner of Sri Lanka, heading northeast, and were in the lee of the land, but we thought it would come back as we made more heading offshore. It was still only the beginning of March so in a normal year we should hope for at least another month of wind from that quarter, but the sea had turned to glass and looked like it would stay that way for some time. We might get a sea breeze later, but we bagged the sails and motored along our new course, waiting for the wind to come back and charging the batteries so Jack could get back on his radio.

I'd also been in contact a few times with Japan, and everything there seemed okay. I got Chantal to let my daughter, Vanesa, know her dad was okay. I knew Vanesa wasn't too happy at school in England and was wanting to get back to Japan to join us again. Chantal told her that I was helping Jack to deliver his boat back to Aussie, which, in a way, was true. I hadn't wanted to give any thought to what would happen if we were to get caught and end up in prison. I'm like that, a real selfish bugger. But, kids have their own luck, and she'd be okay with her mum.

Dropping in Galle Harbor, though, had made me sentimental about my daughter. It was here, some years before, that she had started to speak English for the first time, and we could at last talk together in the same language. She was born in Japan, and when her mum decided a Japanese stone sculptor was more fun than a English boat maker, Vanesa was only three years old. I wanted her to live on my boat with me in Nakaminato town. That's where I build all my boats. Having a boat is just great, but having a little daughter living with you on a boat is even better. Sons are okay, but they're noisy little buggers and need a mum.

Little girls are quiet and think you are a hero, at least for a few years. I had a great time back then. Taking her to kindergarten on the back of my motorbike and rowing up and down the river searching for fairy grottos. There were very few foreigners in Japan back in the 1970s, so I was the only one she ever saw. One time on a rare trip to Tokyo, she made me cross the street in Ginza to talk to a blonde lady she had seen entering a shop. Going to kindergarten and the elementary school, she spoke only Japanese. I thought she didn't know how to speak any English. Even though I spoke only English to her, she'd answer me in Japanese. She had never met any English-speaking children until we arrived in Galle Harbor. She was seven years old, and the only other boat in Galle was a boat cruising up from Aussie with two little blonde boys onboard, seven and eight. I didn't think she could swim, either, but twenty-four hours later she was swimming and speaking English. Now she could tell me exactly what she really thought of me.

We motored all that day and the next and nobody was happy with that. Without any wind, the wind vane wouldn't work and we had to steer by hand. That's a drag, sitting there all day, pushing the tiller back and forth. It really keeps you trapped down. You can't read, can't get up to put the kettle on, and can't even pee over the side. We tried four-hour shifts, but that was too long. Then we tried two-hour shifts, but that cut into sleep time. I wished Jack had bought a battery-driven auto pilot. They're not that expensive.

On the third day out of Galle, there was still no wind. Strange, that. We were now two hundred miles from any land that could have blocked the wind from the northeast. The sea was still and quiet like a bowl of dull mercury. It blended into the sky with the same color. Only directly overhead was the sky a lighter grey. Although this wasn't a sea fog, visibility was very short. We had been under engine power for the last three days, and the battery was fully charged, but a new problem was beginning to dawn on us. Fuel. Jack hadn't built in very big fuel tanks, and we hadn't taken any jerry cans with us as we thought we'd have plenty of wind. So, we could talk on the radio as much as we wanted, but with only enough fuel for another half day of cruising, the radio might become a problem, too. We needed the radio now as it was the only way we had to know when our airline steward would be in Goa.

The ham radio operator in Australia in the city where Jack's wife lived was getting to be a little difficult to deal with. He wasn't part of the deal, of course, and I think he had seen through all the double speak that we had used in talking to Lynn. He was getting a little nervous about communicating with a radio pirate as he could have put his radio license at risk. We seemed to be losing momentum with the guys in Sydney and couldn't get a firm date for the pick up. Communications are always the problem in these sorts of carry-ons. We'd have to wait until we reached India and try to telephone through to Australia, but having dealt with Indian telephones before, that prospect wasn't too encouraging, either.

If we didn't get any winds soon, we'd run out of fuel, and then we'd be stuck out here becalmed between the end of the northeast monsoon and the start of the southwest monsoons. It was only the beginning of March. The northeast winds couldn't have stopped so soon. Regardless, there wasn't a breath to stir the water and the air just hung hot and sluggish. It would have been unbearable except we were making some way over the water, keeping the engine ticking over at low revs so as to not use up too much fuel. This was getting depressing. If we didn't get out of this windless hole, we might have to call the trip off this year. In our planning, we wanted to be up in Goa by the end of March to make sure we could get away before the southwest wind started to blow. We didn't have an exact position, but we knew we were about a hundred miles off the south tip of India. That would give us about two thousand miles yet to Goa. It would have been nice to have a fix with the sextant. We could see a hazy sun up above. It was not very sharp around the edges but probably good enough to get a reasonable fix. What we needed was a horizon. In order to get an angle to work out the trigonometry for a sun fix, a sharp horizon was a necessity, but it just wasn't there. Sitting up on deck, sipping endless cups of tea, and waiting to catch sight of the horizon, we noticed a darker shape low down on the sea coming out of the humid gloom.

"Let's go and have a look at that." I suggested.

Anything to break the monotony. As we came closer, it turned out to be a small fishing boat, about thirty-foot, with a fish well aft for the catch and a small cabin forward. That boat didn't look like it should be anywhere except pulled up on the shore for a good paint job and some major repair work. The fishermen onboard were all dressed in rags. They were all handling lines, but didn't seem to be having much luck apart from a few scrawny non descript fish lying belly up in the fish well. We had thought at first that maybe we could buy some fish off of them, as we'd had no luck either. In fact, we hadn't caught anything except one dolphin fish since leaving Malaysia. Probably because crossing over to Sri Lanka we'd been going too fast.

It's strange, that, about fishing. Up in Japan they troll very slowly, barely two or three knots, and that's the speed they seem to have the most luck at, but down in Guam and off Hawaii they zoom around, well over ten knots and catch tons of the same fish. Then again, it could be the color of the lure. Most fisherman use plastic squid in all kinds of colors. I find the best lure is a piece of red cloth with the head around the hook wrapped with a strip of silver foil, but even then, in the Atlantic, I caught nothing until I turned to blue cloth. Obviously, there's a lot of skill in fishing, but lots of luck is needed, too.

In any case, we pulled up alongside and matched our speed to theirs. They said they'd been out of Colombo for three days and would go back when they had some fish. They didn't seem very worried about their meager haul and even less about the lack of visibility. When we asked them which way they thought Colombo was, it was way off our estimate. I'm not sure who was right, them or us, but they didn't have any kind of navigation aids that we could see, so we weren't going to worry about our position.

They did have lots of fuel, though. There was a two-hundred-liter barrel strapped on deck. We had to have some of that, but how to get them to part with it? We showed them U.S. dollars, which made them think a bit, but still they were reluctant. Offers of food, cigarettes and whiskey also didn't hit the mark. Then, Jack brought out the trump card—pornographic pictures. We had noticed when we sailed this way before that more than alcohol and tobacco what customs and immigration wanted was pornographic material. Not necessarily hardcore stuff. Playboy magazines would bring a quick rubberstamping of the passport. Hustler would get you off a customs search. But, these photos that Jack had were heavy duty stuff that he had stashed away. Really disgusting. We held them so they could get a tantalizing glimpse. They siphoned that drum can into our tank in about three minutes. We had to stop them in their hurry to make sure they had enough fuel themselves to make it back to port. I don't think they cared. All they wanted was that handful of photos. We handed them over and pulled away, and the last we saw of them they were disappearing down below. They must have fallen over each other. God knows when they'd get back on deck again.

The rest of that day and into the night the same grey heaviness hung around, but a few hours before dawn the next day, stars began to appear from behind this heavy grey stuff until the heavens were bright and clear. Nothing like seeing stars after days of gloom. That's better than seeing the sun in a way. Here are a thousand million points of light telling you it's going to be okay. Dawn found us just where we thought we should be. Maybe a little closer in shore than our dead reckoning put us, but that was okay. In fact, it was good. It was such a beautiful sight: the Malabar Coast, the southernmost tip of that crazy, beautiful heat-sodden land, dazzling in the sunlight as pure as the very first day. This is the place where people come to see the sun rise and set on the same day over an unobstructed horizon. Of course, being on a boat you get to see that every day, but still it must be worth the journey for landlubbers.

What is it that gives this coast such a blue sky? Like the blue of the winter sky in Provence, there was such a clarity about it. A sharp, green sea was set against the emerald shoreline. It's probably due to all the rivers and waterways that cover the land inshore all up the Malabar Coast and Kerala that keep the dust down. What a contrast from the east coast of Tamil Nadu where the heat and dust make the sky too fierce to look at.

As we got within a mile of the shore, we could see people standing up on the sea, fishing. They were standing up on the water, or that's what it looked like. Pulling closer, though, we saw that they were standing or kneeling, with a few sitting, on what looked like logs of balsa wood. There were sometimes two, sometime three, logs, each about twelve feet long and round as a fat man's leg, tied together with coconut rope. It was such an idyllic morning, like an English summer day, that I didn't see much danger in it, but I'd hate to think what'd they'd do if the wind got up. Some of them did have what seemed to be a sail made of plastic bags and sack cloth, but these were stowed away, wrapped around a stick-like mast and laying on the logs. To move around, they used pad-dles. What a laborious business. These weren't kayaks or Canadian canoes, just tree trunks with a slight rise to the bows to give some stream-lining. There must have been a fleet of twenty of these rafts—you couldn't call them boats—and most of them were manned by boys, usu-ally alone, although some had a two-man crew. We were feeling so good, we thought to share our high with them. We would give them a treat; give them some fruit. They looked like they could use it--they were thin as rakes and dressed in rags. We couldn't get them to come up close when we beckoned them, and we didn't want to chase them all over the place so we threw the oranges at them so they could pick them up out of the sea. They got the wrong idea. They thought we were bombarding them. Panic! They all started shouting and paddling away. I doubt anyone had ever tried giving them anything in their lives before.

Later on, though, we did manage to get up to one little guy, burned as black as cherry wood with arms as thin as string. His eyes were so big and round, you wondered how his face had room for a mouth and a nose. He was a happy little guy, and we swapped some fruit and chocolate for two small silver fish. We asked where he came from, and he pointed to what looked like a harbor wall just a little farther up the coast, with a small red beacon on the end. There were no ports or har-bors marked on the atlas, and the name he said made no sense, but he said it was quite deep water behind the wall, and we could get in easily. We thought to give it a go as we were running low on water. Maybe we could top off the tanks there. Rounding the end of the concrete wall, we found a small, sandy bay set back a few hundred feet in a sweeping curve.

The wall was an extension of a short, rocky arm and gave some shelter to what must have been a pretty rough spot in a westerly wind. The wide, sandy beach reached back up to the tree line, which was main-ly made up of very high coconut trees under which were dwellings made of sticks and thatched with the leaves of these trees. Right down the mid-dle of the beach, and dividing it exactly in two, was a shallow ditch run-ning with putrid green water and strewn with garbage. Not the plastic garbage of a more affluent resort, but dead dogs and fish heads. Off to the right, and almost concealed by the trees, was a huge church that looked like it was made of brick with a slate roof. We found out later that all those who dwelt on the left of the ditch were Muslims and those to the right, Christians. Apart from this distinction, everyone seemed to be in the same sorry plight. It was a fishing village and pulled up on the sand were dozens of the balsa wood crafts we had seen earlier. Hard up against the concrete wall inside the bay was a dredger, about a hundred feet long, and a small barge. There were still a few hours of the day left, but we couldn't see anyone onboard or on the jetty so we tied up against the barge and waited for someone to come. Nobody did, even though we were flying the yellow flag. We didn't expect there to be customs or immigrations about, but at least we wanted to let someone know that we were tied up in their harbor.

We left Andy onboard, and Jack and I went to find some official. There were no buildings around the jetty and no gate, either—just a wide, dusty road with the sea to one side and coconut trees on the other. The view of the coastline stretching away to the north was breathtaking. Low cliffs and rocks going down to a deep, green sea, fringed along the shore with a line of gentle, white surf. Looking down at the rocks to our left, they looked and smelled like they had a more practical purpose. This seemed to be the village's communal toilet. The smells of India are undefeatable in their insistence, but at least they all get blended together, and the final concoction is not so nauseating.

A little further along the road where it leveled off a little, there were some low buildings set back among some old flame trees, whose branches were swelling with large, scarlet flowers. There were also not a few goats roaming around, and the grass was closely cropped. In contrast to the beach, it looked more like Hawaii. The buildings were all locked up, but the signs on the doors made them seem very impressive. One read, "Superintendent for the United Nations, Harbor Development Project. Then there were "Chief Engineer," "Sub Engineer," "Minister of Works," and "Chief of Construction." You'd think they were building a port for supertankers. We did find out later they had been hard at work for the last fifteen years using up money given by the United Nations. So far, they had managed to lay fifteen blocks of concrete that formed the jetty wall. That's one block a year, and it would take at least another hundred years, at that rate, to make it a worthwhile harbor. I think the United Nations had given up on them.

Just a little further on, where the road crested a slight hill, there was a small mosque under construction. It was made of breese block and rough mud bricks, plastered over and whitewashed. The workmanship was really bad, but from a distance, it looked very elegant. Compared with the church built down on the beach, it seemed to float on the ground. The church just hunkered down, heavy and stark, with all the sins of man staining it a dark color. The church seemed as out of place amongst the slender palms as a house brick in a jeweler's window. In contrast, that little mosque at night with the full moon behind the minaret was as pretty as the Taj Majal.

We followed the road a bit more and passed a bus stop so we knew then that at least we could get to some town and a telephone, perhaps. Then the road went down to the sea again, and bang! We were right in the middle of a bunch of hippies laying around on the sand, playing music, and smoking dope. We never suspected that. It was just like Kalkuda, the hippy beach in Sri Lanka, or one of the beaches up in Goa. It's getting so you can't go anywhere without finding half the restless youth of Europe camped out on the shoreline. This was Kovalum Beach, and, I think, like all the other beaches of the world that were originally discovered by the long-hair, dope-smoking, seekers-after-truth, it has now become part of the resort holiday phenomenon. We joined them for a smoke and found that there was a bus twice a day for Trivandrum, a pretty large town about thirty minutes away. None of them knew about the little harbor down the road.

It looked like we found a way into India that nobody knew about. We could have brought in gold enough to pay a million dowries. If we could get in with no fuss, we could get out, too. This place would make the perfect Smuggler's Cove. It was quite a long way from Goa by land or by sea, for that matter, but if we could get our airline steward to bring the hash down here, then the first half of the trip would be as easy as walking out of a bread shop.

We had to contact Sydney and see what was happening. The day after we arrived still nobody was around on the dock, but there was some guy who had come to open the dock for the Public Works Bureau. He didn't seem to care whether we contacted customs or immigration or not. His worry was that because work was continuing on the harbor extension, we might be in the way. We gave him a box of biscuits for his wife and a bottle of whiskey for himself. He said he'd see if he could keep the frantic pace of construction down. We got permission to stay as long as it took to do maintenance on our water tank, which was certainly an open ended deadline.

The next day, we went by bus to Trivandrum. We managed from the post office to get a call through to Australia, but our contact in Sydney couldn't get hold of the steward. Obviously they were keeping contact down to a minimum. The airline steward had his schedule, which was to be in Goa by the end of March so there really wasn't any need for him to get new instructions, and anyway, he was off on a routine flight just then. This was such a great place—a duty free zone for hashish smuggling. We had three weeks till the end of March so we decided to try every day for a week to see if we could contact him.

Andy and I spent the time looking around the countryside, like a pair of tourists, and making friends with the fishermen on the beach. Being white, we got more visitors from the Christian side of the beach, but there was no friction that we could see between the two halves, and we were happy to buy fish from either. Jack preferred the hippie beach and would come back stoned every night, which was great, but India has a way of clouding the brain, making plans and schedules seem less than important. I didn't want to get in the situation where we couldn't make the right decision. After a week of trying to get hold of our flight attendant with no luck, we just had to go on and get to Goa. Otherwise, we wouldn't be in time to keep with the original plan. I think we made the right decision and got ready to leave for the long haul up to Goa. We made a final trip into town for some fruits and vegetables and topped off the newly painted water tanks with some pretty suspicious looking water from a tank lorry that was sitting on the jetty.

We cast off on yet another gloriously sunny day, with just enough breeze to put the sails asleep. While we had been staying in the harbor, there had always been a soft onshore wind to keep the heat down, getting a little stronger in the afternoon, and lasting until well after night. As we made our track north and west, getting away from the shore, this sea breeze increased until it was blowing a good twenty-five knots. That's about Force 5 on the Beaufort Scale. Nothing at all heavy but kicking up lots of whitecaps, and the waves were short between the crests.

If we had been going the other way, we would have had the wind astern, and it would have been a fair wind. We would have been sitting upright drinking tea as we lounged around the deck, but our course made it so we took the waves dead on the stem. Most of these we could ride through as we heeled over, beating on the port tack.

Getting a healthy shower of wind-thrown spray, but keeping our forward momentum, every seventh trough or so was deeper than the others. The sea just seemed to drop away in front of the bows into a hole. The boat, coming out of this dip, got her bows stuck in the following wave and would shudder and shake like we had hit a sandbar, and the speed would drop a knot or two. We hadn't expected such a strong sea breeze. In fact, we had hoped that the wind would be from the northeast.

We were waiting for the wind to go down after it got dark and the sea got a chance to cool down, but that didn't happen, either. In fact, darkness just seemed to make it stronger. Around two in the morning, it did ease off a bit, but then it was back again and blowing as hard as ever. It was a hot, sticky wind, and the spray that continually blew over the deck coated everything in salt crystals. The hatch had to be kept closed in this weather, so going below was like going into a Turkish bath. It wasn't even the lovely looking sea it had been close in shore. The water had turned a muddy brown, and even though we were about ten miles off shore, it looked shallow and dangerous. I wished we had a chart. I don't know why Jack hadn't got one. He knew we were coming this way. An echo sounder would also have made things less stressful. It was no good throwing a lead line even if we could have stood up to do so, which we couldn't. We were bouncing around so much, bucking like a tin can going down a drain.

We were not making any headway, certainly not enough to make us happy. The first twenty-four hours we covered fifty miles along our coast. At this rate, it would take us thirty days to reach Goa, which would put us out of our rendezvous date. Not only that, but we'd have to sail back down on the opposite tack, and if the southwest monsoon did start around April, then we would have the same conditions again. At least, we'd be able to brew tea up easier. The galley was on the port side, so with the wind anywhere to starboard, we heeled over to port. That way, you only had to stop yourself from falling into the stove. The other way around, you had to claw your way up and try to stop falling away from it, which was much more difficult.

Three days out from our secret port, and the wind was showing no signs of letting up. It was one hell of a sea breeze. I would have thought that all the lakes and rivers that lay inland from the coast would have kept the land cool, not giving the sea breeze a chance to get going. Somewhere it was really heating up to suck in all this wind so furiously. No one wanted to say they'd had enough. That would be admitting you hadn't got your sea legs yet, but after three days and nights of this, it was looking like we wouldn't reach Goa in time. There was no way we could make it with this wind. I wouldn't have minded going back to the little port with the beautiful mosque. That would have only taken a day, but Jack was for finding somewhere nearer.

Jack had got more serious since we left the hippies behind and seemed more focused on the purpose of the trip. Jack and Andy had always had more of an image of this outing as a grand adventure, living on the edge. Me, I just wanted the money. Sure, the adventure was good, too, but it wasn't my boat. I couldn't stop imagining my unfinished boat back in Japan sitting alone and uncared for. I felt that I shouldn't be enjoying this trip too much because I was being unfaithful to her, even though I was doing it all in her name.

Anyway, it was Jack's deal and his boat, so I was happy to leave it all up to him. We got out the atlas and looked up the coast as far as Goa. There was only one likely spot—Cochin. We didn't know if we were north or south of it. We hadn't taken any sights since we left. It was already getting dark on the third day out of our secret little port. We could see the land to starboard, probably fifteen miles off by now and still too far to make anything out. We decided to wait until noon the next day when we could take a latitude sight. Taking a star sight when the boat was pitching like this and the horizon was a jagged edge of sharp-backed waves would have given us a hugely unreliable fix.

All that day, the sky, like every other day, had been just a huge bowl of glaring blue, and the sun, a merciless ball of heat. So, we were very happy to see the sun go down over the horizon. Although the sky had been cloudless all day, it was suddenly banded with a bank of cloud, starting about a hand's width up from the western horizon and stretching to directly overhead and all the way to the north. The skies to the east were cloudless, and stars were coming out there. The bottom edge of this cloud, which was as black as pitch, looked like God had drawn it with straight edge . Underneath this the sky was a deep, ominous dark red; red like monkey's blood.

Silhouetted against this sinister and unnerving backdrop and thrown into sharp relief about twenty yards away on our port side was a very small open boat. It could have been a dugout made from the same balsa wood as the flat fishing rafts. There was single sail made of what looked like black, plastic sheeting. The bottom half of this rag was full of wind and pulling well, but the top half had torn loose and was flapping in shreds, whipped forward by the wind. It made the boat look like it was flying before the wind, which I suppose it was, as it had the wind behind it. In the stern was a man dressed like all the other poor fishermen we'd seen. It's not saying much to say he was soaked to the skin. Sitting huddled in the center of the boat just behind where the mast was stepped and facing forward to get shelter from the spray was a young woman dressed in a sari. The way she held herself in the stooped forward posture like she was protecting a baby in her arms, I knew this was a family. With that terrifying backdrop, it looked like they were fleeing Armageddon. What could have forced these people out here in such an unseaworthy boat?

How did they get so far offshore in an onshore wind? What desperation was behind their flight? Maybe they were fleeing from his family who wanted to kill her because her dowry was too small. I can't see anything less than love or murder that could have driven them to be out there. Whatever, it was a brave, sad sight, and I hope they got to where they wanted to go and lived happily ever after.

If we had been in Polynesia, it wouldn't have been so surprising to see that sight. Down in the south seas, both men and women do incredible journeys in small boats, but Indians don't have the reputation for going to sea, especially women. There was some king in Kerala back when Marco Polo was looking into going into the pearl industry down there, and this king, he wanted nothing to with the sea. He reckoned only mad men would venture off from the shore into the sea and a certain watery death. That's the image the sea has for Indians.

The next day we didn't have to take a sun sight to know where we were. We could see the entrance to a large river with lots of buildings just a little further inland. It certainly looked big enough to be Cochin. Just inside the river mouth, on the north shore, were Chinese fishing nets. You must have seen photos of them. They're like giant mosquito nets spread horizontally on a long, wooden arm, which they dip into the water to pull up the fish unlucky enough to be swimming over top. They are the defining thing about Cochin, ever since Vasco de Gama mentioned them way back in the fifteenth century.

Over on the south bank was something ominously modern: a cigarette boat. A cigarette boat is a long, sleek, very fast motorboat. I don't really know why it's called that, but someone told me it's what they use in Italy to smuggle cigarettes. Certainly, I had seen them in Gibraltar, where they're used as high speed smuggling boats because no government agency has anything fast enough to catch them. They mustn't have known in India that governments weren't supposed to have them because this one was parked outside the customs house and had the officious grey color of a bureau boat. That was a slap in the face. I didn't expect India to have anything as high tech as that. The image of India is sort of rural poverty and bullock carts. I kept forgetting that they had atom bombs and a movie industry. What had we gotten ourselves into here? With customs having a boat like that, they must want it for some reason. What else but to chase after smugglers? Oh well. Being India, maybe it didn't work. Still, the sight of that sleek craft dampened the mood a little. Leaving here didn't look like walking out of a bread shop anymore.

There was still quite a bit of wind blowing in up the river from off the sea, but we pulled down the sails and motored. There was quite a bit of traffic milling around: Mostly small motor launches being used to ferry people from one side of the river to the other, and some rowing boats and a few barges being towed about, full of quarried rocks. A mile or so up, the river, which was about half a mile wide at this point, split into two. To the left it seemed to go to a modern freight terminal, and we could see some large ocean freighters down there. To the right, it looked more like Asia, where the river side was overgrown with shanty buildings, derelict workshops, and small coastal fishing boats. Dead ahead and thrusting out into the river as though trying to cleave its way into the sea was a small green promontory of land, palm trees and flame trees. Set back from the river was the Malabar Hotel. That's what we could read on a big sign up on the roof. There was even a covered wooden jetty built in the colonial style. Tied up there was the most beautifully maintained, small, steam-driven launch with all the brass gleaming and crew in dazzling white. It must have been around in the days of the British Raj and probably ferried all the colonial big wigs around. Even now it looked like it was waiting for someone with shout.

This spot looked like the small boat anchorage, too. There was just one other sailboat there, flying the Italian flag. It was all snugged down with the awnings up and people sitting on the deck having brunch. They shouted an invitation for us to join them. Maybe they were there to pick up some hashish, too. I hoped not. Didn't want customs to get too suspicious. Getting closer, though, this looked unlikely. There was an older woman onboard who turned out to be the owner. When we got to know her, we realized she was a very eccentric person who just loved India. I think they'd also just come down from Taiwan where they'd bought this yacht, a forty-five foot plastic copy of a traditional European design. It looked very smart and seaworthy, but there was something missing. The boat was like a beautiful centerfold girl, flawless but soulless. All these Taiwan plastic boats are built by cabinetmakers, not sailors, so they have nothing of the seaman about them. Then, there was the older woman's boy toy and her daughter. We thought the young man was the daughter's lover at first, but Jack was happy to find that wasn't so. They weren't smuggling hash, but they liked to smoke it, and while we were there we professed a distaste for the stuff. After all, we were serious sailors preparing for a trip to Antarctica.

Isn't it amazing what you can tell people and get away with? Nobody questioned us when we told them we were on our way to England to prepare for the Antarctic. Nobody said "Why go all that way?" when Australia or New Zealand or even South Africa would have been a more logical choice to fit out for such a trip. Just five minutes looking around the boat should have made them realize that, even though it looked sturdy and strong, there was nothing onboard that pointed towards the South Pole. Except for one thing. Down below was a white board screwed to the bulkhead, and we had penned the grand and fictitious title of *Adelie Antarctic Expeditions* on the top and listed a hypothetical schedule for the trip to the ice. We anchored about six boat lengths from the Italians and waited for immigration to come. We waited for one day, which is quicker than the last port where they never came at all.

I wished we had stayed in that last port. We were only three hundred miles nearer to Goa, with still another six hundred to go. If our guy was going to come down by car or bus, he could just as easily do another day's drive. What a perfect place it had been compared to Cochin with its cigarette boats and officials who took an interest in you. Too late now. We'd blown that option and would have to play it by ear all over again. We had ten days before our date with the hashish man.

Cochin turned out to be a cool place to hang out. Immigration were friendly, and they didn't even stamp our passports, instead giving us slips of paper saying we were seamen granted privileges to go ashore. That was a relief. Now we wouldn't have to worry about Australian officials asking awkward questions about us having been in India. We did get a shock the next day when a customs boat pulled along side, and three guys in uniform climbed onboard with screwdrivers. Like immigration, though, they were totally taken in with our Antarctic expedition. They were probably in the mood for Antarctic stories. Just the week before, India's very own Antarctic expedition ship had set forth to do whatever it is they do down there. Imagine that. An Indian Antarctic expedition. No end to the surprises out of India and just one more coincidence to add to the growing list. Their interest didn't stop them from using their screwdrivers, though, and they took off quite a few of the mahogany slats sheathing the ceiling. Up with the floorboards and a look in the water tanks. They said they were looking for gold, which in India sells for way above the world standard. We brewed them a cup of tea and persuaded more information out of them. They were proud to tell us a few weeks before they had arrested some Australians for smuggling heroin. It seemed like they had been doing it for years, these Aussies, and had been caught because they'd just been hanging around in India and looked too respectable to be hippies. I can't tell you how they smuggled the heroin out. That would be giving away trade secrets. But, I will tell you that they had a lot of diving gear, and some big freighters leave from here for Aussie. Customs didn't suspect us, I don't think, but they gave the impression that Cochin was a big smuggling base, and foreign boats coming in and out were kept under surveillance.

I wasn't going to sleep very well after hearing that. It was obvious that we were going to have to get clearance before leaving so we would have to get the cargo onboard after clearing which would mean that we would have to do that between here and the river mouth and after passing the cigarette boat. I couldn't figure out how that was going to happen. We had to get hold of our hash man before we could worry about that.

All the arrangements to meet up with our contact had been made long before in Aussie. He should have been at the hotel in Goa on the 20th of March. He had arranged to take some leave between flights so we would probably have a few days to play around with. Then again, it would depend on his contacts in India, too. We had no idea who he was getting all this stuff from. It's not like you could buy a hundred and twenty kilograms of hash on the street corner, but that wasn't our job. We had to get it out of India and into Australia. We hoped he was going to be at the hotel before the 20th so we could get hold of him and tell him where we were. After we were done with customs and immigration and were told we could take down our yellow pratique flag, we could go ashore using the hotel jetty as a landing place. The first thing we did was to put a call through to the hotel in Goa, but there was no Mr. X staying there.

So, we set about enjoying life at anchor, drinking cold beer at the Malabar Hotel and talking with the Indian guests who we'd imagined were all smuggling something either in or out. Most days we were invited for breakfast to the Italian yacht. I suppose you could call it a yacht because it looked quite smart, all polished brass and varnished wood. Looking over at Adelie, she looked like a sturdy factory girl next to a model from Vogue. The Italians had been in port long enough to have organized everything in the grand manner. Fruits and vegetables were brought along side by rowing boat, the Italian lady standing on deck and pointing at her choice. Another boat arrived with a tailor. He was allowed on deck to show his wares and measure up their sun baked limbs. Then, the dhoby man would come with his baskets of freshly laundered bedding and clothes. I liked this guy from the start. He spoke good English, and obviously, was quite educated. Maybe we could use him somehow. We'd have to get to know him better.

Jack wasn't interested in that, though. He was only interested in the lady's daughter who was just his soul mate. She came across as quite a heavy lady, having lots of opinions on the state of the world, and she didn't like to be talked down to. Jack was going to have to work hard on her. In fact, Andy and I hardly saw Jack after arriving. Those two were always down below deck, playing Italian opera and talking philosophy.

So, it was up to Andy and I to suss the surroundings out to see how we were going to get our cargo aboard if it ever came. We took buses all around the place trying to find a likely spot around the river mouth where we could transfer the dope. Around Cochin, there are so many rivers and waterways to cross that getting from one place to another would take all day, and it was not looking good. The most likely spot was around the Chinese fishing nets, but there were always people around, even at night. They were just ordinary people fishing or bathing in the river so they probably wouldn't have got too excited if they saw someone in a Zodiac pick something up, but with that custom boat across the way, I didn't really want to take the risk.

Three days into our stay, we had got friendly enough with the laundry man to get him to row us over to the other shore where he lived. He took us to his home in a dusty part of a village where everything was made of sun dried bricks. His wife was dead a few years back, and he lived with his eleven-year-old daughter who he insisted go to school. We met her, too, and she seemed like she was well looked after. Same for his house, which was nothing but a dark room with no windows, but the floor of dried mud was swept and clean, and the few things he had were arranged with some order, just like a good sailor. He did his laundry outside in a big communal tank, along with some others doing the same work. It looks like hard work doing laundry the Indian way, dipping the clothes in the water, swirling them around above your head, and smacking them down on a stone to break out the dirt. I didn't think he'd say no if we offered him some money to do an easy job. We couldn't ask him right out just then because we still didn't know ourselves what was happening, but by beating around the bush a little, we thought he'd do whatever we asked when the time came.

With only a week to go to deadline and no contact yet with Goa, we began to worry again. Well, Andy and I did. Jack was still off in Italy somewhere. Now the Italian mother was starting to ask questions about what we were doing in Cochin if we were off to the Antarctic. She knew her winds, too, because she kept saying that we should be off or we'd be into the southwest monsoon season. Jack put her off with all kinds of vague answers, but I'm sure she thought we were up to something. Maybe she just wanted us away from her daughter and out of the neighborhood. Although, one night she must have been glad we were around.

It was around midnight, and Jack was ashore with the daughter somewhere. Andy and I had just gone to sleep below deck on Adelie. We were woken up by the mother's boyfriend shouting and screaming, and the woman joining in, both really loudly Mama Mia-ing for all they were worth. Andy and I rushed on deck and saw right away that a barge full of stones towed by a small tugboat with a too-long tow line had misjudged his turn as he came out of the south part of the river making for the freight port. The barge had clipped the Italian yacht at midship just below the water line. Maybe just clipped it, but still there was a fist sized gash running up half way to the gunwales. I've never seen panic like that. They were just jumping up and down on deck and screaming they were sinking. They were, of course, standing on the same side as the collision and forcing the hole even further down into the water. Jack had the aluminum dinghy ashore. He was at the hotel wooing his lady. We could still see it tied up at the hotel jetty. The Zodiac was still stowed down below so there was nothing to do but to jump in and swim across.

I didn't think there were any sharks around, but you never know. They often get up into river mouths. I knew there were dolphins because we had seen them--pale, whitish river dolphins who must have put their sonar to good use in that mud-colored, oily water. Swimming in tropical waters at night always makes me feel uneasy. You never know what's going to come up and grab your legs.

It look less than a few minutes to reach the boat, and when we got there, we were able to pull ourselves up on deck and get them to release the boom and swing it out to starboard and away from the side with the hole. With Andy and I and the Italian guy hanging off the end of the boom as it swung out over the water, we managed to get the hole above the water line and shouted for the owner to plug the hole up. She was too panicked to think straight. Luckily, Jack had heard all the shouting and was coming back. We managed to stop the hole by screwing down a plywood patch with layers of newspapers underneath. It worked so well that they were still sitting like that when we left. I'm sure they must have had a better repair job done later. The strange thing is, nobody would take responsibility for the accident. Even though we found out who was piloting the tug and the company who owned it. At least the barge company didn't try to claim damages from the Italians. They probably would have done that in Hong Kong. The favorite trick there is to cross your bows when you're under way. They come so quick and close that it's not possible to avoid hitting them, and then they claim damages from you.

We were heroes for a few days, and, thankfully, they stopped asking unkind questions. The next morning we placed a call through to Goa, but the hotel was still insistent that the guy we wanted was not staying there. It didn't seem to worry Jack too much. He was more and more into his Italian fantasy and left Andy and I to worry about everything else. Which we did. We still had no plan how to get the stuff onboard. Jack thought we could just take it off the hotel jetty, but that would have been pretty foolish. There were always people around day and night on the landing: Hotel guests, sitting savoring the cool night air; hotel workers goofing off, and the hotel ferry boat's two man crew who slept on the thwarts. We had also been told by customs to check out with them before we left. That meant going over to the customs house where the cigarette boat was. Whether they bothered to come onboard to check or not, we didn't know, but it wasn't worth the risk. Or, so at least Andy and I thought. We also had to provision the boat but wanted to wait until the last minute before doing that. We didn't want to have a load of fresh fruit and vegetables going bad on us if we were delayed by our contact being held up.

On the 18th of March, two days before our planned meeting, the hotel in Goa finally told us that Mr. X had a reservation for the 20th. We asked the desk there to make sure he called the Malabar Hotel as soon as he arrived. On the evening of the 20th we were all sitting in the Malabar hotel—we had even got Jack to come along—waiting for the call to come in. When the hash man did call, we couldn't all sit around and listen to the conversation. Jack had to disappear into a soundproof box where all phone calls had to be made and taken.

When he came out about ten minutes later, he didn't look too unhappy so we guessed things were going okay. It turned out that our Mr. X had arrived in India quite a time ago and stayed at a different hotel. He got the hashish from his contacts and had hired a boat and got taken all around the harbors and backwaters of Goa looking for the Adelie. He must have been in a panic, too, stuck in India lugging a hundred and twenty kilos around with no one to take it off his hands. He must have been so relieved to find us that he wasn't upset about us not being in Goa as planned. He said he'd take a long haul bus and be in Cochin in two days. Well, this was it. So far, we had done nothing against the law. We had told a few tall stories, stretched the truth a little, and entered and left the country without a by your leave. All in all, as innocent as you. But, now there's this guy coming with a hundred and twenty kilograms of hashish, and it's all for us. If he's caught, so are we. Reality was changing quickly. It was getting to be immediate. Before, I could think about when I got back to Japan, when I finished my boat, when I was sailing on my own, as my own skipper. Now, my world was compacted into the very pressing present. If anything went wrong now, I wouldn't have a future, except for a long time in an Indian jail, or even longer in an Aussie one.

Chapter 7

here were two days to go before meeting Mr. X, and Andy and I spent them buying food and filling up the water and fuel tanks. We were keeping in with the dhoby man, hiring him to bring out the water and fuel in the jerry cans. I had mentioned to Jack about using him to get out the hash after we had cleared customs, but Jack wasn't too keen on that. It was pretty frustrating trying to get him to come up with a better idea. I didn't even know if the dhoby many would have been willing or not. I hadn't asked him yet.

Eight o'clock at night, two days later, Andy and I were sitting on the jetty in the chairs provided by the hotel, drinking beer. Behind us was a party of Indian businessmen sitting at another low table. A taxi pulled up at the head of the steps leading from the jetty up to the hotel. Some guy came down, stood at the water's edge, and hollered for the Adelie "Jesus!" I thought. "What's this guy doing?" Here we were trying to be so low profile, and this guy was shouting over and over the name of our boat. "That's him," said Andy. Andy had met him in Aussie when they were arranging it all. "For Christ's sake," I told Andy. "Go and stop him shouting and bring him here."

He seemed a nice guy. Typical airline steward, he was trim and well dressed and speedy as hell. Maybe he was on some other drug than hashish. In India, Caucasians are probably less suspicious or conspicuous if they're dressed in gaudy hippy rags rather than business suits. If anyone asked, we'd have to say he was our Antarctic expedition sponsor. I thought we could sit down and have a drink, but the taxi was still waiting. He had booked into a hotel on Willingdon Island across the bridge from here about thirty minutes away. Jack was off somewhere, so I thought he should send the taxi off and wait around until Jack came back. We went up to see the taxi man who was standing at the back of the car with the trunk open. When we got nearer, the over ripe mango smell of hashish nearly blew my head off. In the back of the trunk were two very large, leather suitcases, so large the trunk wouldn't close properly. They were bulging at the girth and tied around with some old rope. "No! We can't unload that here, now. No way!"

I got the taxi driver to close the trunk as good as he could, and we all got into the taxi and got the driver to take us back to the hotel on Willingdon Island. The trip down from Goa had taken two days with these suitcases strapped down on the roof of the bus in the blazing sun. The bus had been stopped twice at police checkpoints when they crossed state boundaries. I guess the odors of India are so powerful that the people grow up with their sense of smell destroyed.   How could anyone within a half mile not know what was in these? At his hotel we unloaded them and took them up to his room. It was only a small, local hotel so there was no big foyer with lots of people running around.

"We better open the window and let these bags cool down." I said, taking the lead. "You stay here, and I'll find Jack."

Later, on the way back again downtown I told Jack that I couldn't see any other way to transport these to our boat than to use the dhoby man, and we had better do it the following night. I was happy he had agreed. He'd been acting very strangely lately, but the fact that the stuff was here, ready to be picked up, had changed him and made him take it all seriously again.

The next morning, I waited until the dhoby man rowed out with some laundry aboard, and I invited him onboard. I was a little uneasy about asking him to help us. He seemed such an honest, ethical kind of person. He was a Christian, like a lot of people in the state of Kerala. I suppose Vasco de Gama had brought that along with him when he came to open up the trade route with Europe over five hundred years ago. Then, of course, Francis Xavier had followed him a little later to finish the dirty work. Christianity wasn't bludgeoned into them, though, like it was in so many other parts of the world. They wouldn't have gotten away with that behavior in India. As a result, Indian Christians always seem more gentle and less in your face. I don't know if it's true or not, but they also seem more intelligent. That's probably because in India there are so many crazy aspects to religion that the simplicity of Christianity seems easier to accept. Given a choice between that and a god with eight arms and an elephant trunk, it probably seems slightly more intelligent to take the one whose only peculiarity is a virgin birth.

We weren't asking the dhoby man to do anything unethical. Well, not according to his ten commandments. All we wanted him to help us do was to get two suitcases full of hashish onto our boat. In fact, when I outlined the plan to him, he accepted so fast that I thought he misunderstood, but he had a young daughter to educate and the hundred rupees we offered was a good month's salary. He was a pragmatist, thank God.

Jack had gone off to bring Mr. X back to the boat, and after they arrived we finalized the plan. We thought we'd leave at midnight. Obviously it would be dark, and there would be fewer people around. Leaving at that time was not so strange for a boat. We could always plead winds and tide.

Half a mile from the riverbank on the south side, almost opposite the Chinese fishing boats, there was a small storehouse of some kind where small boats would unload during the day. It was also about half a mile up from the customs house on the same side but still in view of it. The dhoby waller and our Mr. X were to be waiting there with the suitcases in the laundry man's rowing boat. When they saw us pull away from the custom's jetty, they were to row out into the stream and wait for us to come up to them. The Indian chap and our man went off to find a place where they could arrange to meet that evening and transfer the suitcases from a taxi to his boat. We weren't to see them again until after midnight.

We had some more shopping to do. We thought it would take four to six weeks to reach Aussie so it was quite a bit of food to take. We had lots of fruits and vegetables, but dried food was a bit of a problem. They're not into canned food very much, but we could get lots of chutney and water crackers. Chutney and crackers for breakfast it was. Rice, of course, but you have to be careful when eating Indian rice. It's full of very small stone particles from the stone thrashing floor. If you don't eat really slowly, you'll get a mouth full of cracked teeth. Cooking rice takes a lot of fresh water, so we took more spaghetti, which could be cooked in at least half salt water. We took lots of eggs, still covered in dirt from the farmyard. We tested every one for freshness by seeing if they would sink in a bowl of water. Even so, one turned out to be bad. I hate the smell of rotten eggs. It puts me off food for days. Good way to slim, that. Rotten egg aerosol spray.

Because by this time we were all pretty nervous, we were smoking cigarettes like mad. We bought a whole bunch of cheap cigarettes, and Jack, in an effort to quit, got some beedies, some kind of thing with dried leaves rolled up a little thicker than a match that tasted just like a dried leaf dipped in cow dung.

More important than food, maybe, we had to get some large rubber tire inner tubes and meters and meters of coconut rope. We thought to put the hash into the inner tubes, and then wrap the tubes with rope to make them look like boat fenders. We could go into port with them hanging over the side, leave them fending off the boat from the jetty wall as customs came aboard. Eight big truck tubes should be enough, but we'd need some rubber for patching up the slits we would make getting the hash inside. So, we got ten tubes and lots of rubber glue. Of course, we didn't buy them new. We bought the tubes from a truck repair shop and the rope from a boat chandler. Have you ever seen coconut fiber rope? It's rough and as course as sandpaper. If you ever had to slide down a coconut rope, you'd strip your hands of flesh. It's quite strong but chafes through in seconds if stretched over a sharp edge. When it's wet, it stretches; when it's dry, it shrinks. Manila rope made from hemp is equally useless on a modern sailboat but smooth as silk compared with the coconut stuff. It was only for decoration, though, to make the tires look more seaman-like.

That was about it. Water cans were topped off. We had extra fuel in jerry cans on deck because we expected to do a lot of motoring. The northeast monsoons should be ended around April, which is usually a transition month with no wind at all. The fuel would help us to get well below the equator and out of the doldrums. We could get far enough south to pick up the southeast trades, which would then take us on a port tack heading as far south as the Roaring Forties, where we could turn east, run down the fortieth parallel to Cape Leeuwin, and then south across the Great Australian Bight to Wilson's Promontory, the southeast tip of Australia.

We went to give back our shore passes and let immigration know we were going. There was a small immigration kiosk used by seamen located right next to the Malabar hotel, and we had to go through here every time we went to town. There was usually a sleepy bunch of guys on duty here. There was obviously another main port entrance somewhere. This was the largest port on this coast, home to the Indian Navy and freight depot for the whole west coast. There must have been another entrance from the sea, further up the coast. Probably at Ernakulum, which is part of Cochin, but the whole of Kerala is crossed with waterways. To go anywhere, you're always crossing and re-crossing some river, canal or inlet. By luck, we seemed to have fetched up in the sleepiest part of the whole complex. Immigration took our slips of paper back and put no stamp in our passport. We promised to let customs know we were going. Then we rowed our dinghy back to Adelie to get ready to get underway.

Jack disappeared for dinner on the Italian yacht, and Andy and I spent the time stowing away all the provisions, lashing down the fuel cans on deck, and getting the sails ready. Getting on for eleven-thirty that night, Andy and I started the engine to get it warmed up and checked the throttle linkage. We didn't want it slipping full ahead just as we approached our pick up. We got some mooring lines ready for tying up at the customs wharf and pulled up enough of the anchor line until it was just hanging up and down. Jack seemed to be having difficulty getting away. Nobody would believe we were leaving at midnight. Maybe Jack had been smoking more than the beedies. He didn't seem concerned that we had to meet these guys within the hour. Andy and I stood on the stern of Adelie shouting for him to get over quick, and the Italians were shouting back that tomorrow was soon enough and what's the hurry? Finally, Jack did get away and rowed over. More time wasted hauling out the dinghy and securing it on deck. Then, we pulled up the anchor, lashed it to the windlass, did a farewell circle around the Italians. They must have thought it really strange, this frantic, last minute haste to get away.

Navigation lights on, we motored over to the customs wharf. We were still this side of the law, but when we left, we'd be on a collision course with the meaning of legality. We pulled in just behind the cigarette boat and made fast to some rings set in the cement of the jetty. We had not seen this boat leave the landing since we had been here, but we had seen someone working on it and heard the vroom of the engine, so we knew it could go if it had a reason to. We went into the customs house. The lights were on, but nobody was at the desk in the front office. There was an open door leading off the room, so we peeked inside and saw some guy in uniform, sleeping. Nobody else around. God, we had no need to stop. We could have just kept going. What to do now? If we wake him up, he'd probably get mad and make things hard for us, maybe even tell us to wait until morning. If we tried to sneak off, though, and back out now, he might wake up when we revved the boat engine, come out to investigate, and follow us with even more interest. From the customs jetty, we could see the lights from the storage shed and our guys must be already rowing out into the stream getting ready to meet us. We went back into the front office.

"Right," we thought. "Let's do this proper."

We banged on the table and shouted for some service, and straight away the customs man came out, smoothing down his crumpled uniform. I don't think that he had been sleeping too deeply. He was all smiles, too. We told him we were leaving and asked him if he wanted to check the boat, but I think he just wanted to get back to sleep. He wrote down the time in a ledger, wished us a good trip, and went back to his charpoy. Still the sight of that speedboat in custom colors stopped us from feeling too elated. That thing could catch up with us even if we had three days head start. We still had to be careful about being noticed. We pulled away from the jetty and headed for the river mouth. We loosened off the lifeline that went around the deck at hip height. From there we could reach down and pull aboard the suitcases.

As we approached the storage shed, we could see a single electric light upon a pole casting a pool of dim orange light onto the concrete jetty. There were two Indians sitting on the edge fishing, and a few feet off from that was a small boat with another guy sitting with a line in the water. There was just one other small rowing boat with two guys in it, and that must be ours. They were very close in shore, only about two boat lengths out. It looked like we would have to pass them on our port side, but that would have put us in full view of the people fishing. I'm sure they wouldn't have got too excited about seeing us hauling anything aboard. Indians only get excited when they see cows in china shops. We didn't want to take even that tiny risk, and at the last moment, we pushed the tiller down to take the dhoby man's boat to starboard, putting us very close in shore to the jetty, but at least our dhoby man and Mr. X would be hidden from view. We were only going about two knots, which, when judged against the jetty, made it look like we were stopped. When we brought the rowboat along side, however, we seemed to be going way too fast. We should have prepared this better. We hadn't even thought for them to have a rope ready to pass the stuff up to us. The dhoby man was standing up trying to hang on to our gunwales, but even at two knots he was getting dragged along and was in danger of falling over. The steward was hanging on with one hand and trying to lift a suitcase up with another. The sides of Adelie were very high and he could only get the suitcase about half way up. The bow of the rowboat was starting to move away from Adelie. The gunwales of the rowboat, which were only about two feet from the water when stable, were dipping lower to port and threatening to swamp the boat. "All this for nothing," I thought. "A hundred and twenty kilograms of good hashish on the bottom of the Malabar river. Back to Japan worse financially off than ever." Then, Andy, with a super human spurt of strength, got two fingers bent over the side around the suitcase handle. There was no room for any more fingers because Mr. X was holding it, too. Andy heaved it up on deck. The next one was easier. We had learned from our mistake, and Jack had got a rope around the handle. Planning was good in the big picture, but bad on the details. We were so happy to have it aboard and heading to the open sea, we shouted back to Mr. X to double the fee for the laundry man. I hope he did. I'll never know. I never met either again.

*Y*ou would think that there would be some kind of sandbar across the river mouth, but it was just a smooth transit into the open ocean. There wasn't even any swell, and the wind that had been blowing so fiercely when we had arrived seven days earlier wasn't anywhere about. In fact, it was breathlessly calm, so flat and still the stars were reflecting off the water in the moonless darkness. We headed out under full power to get some mileage between us and the land. We didn't think anyone would come after us now. We were pretty sure we were out and free, but you never know. Someone might have seen us as we struggled with the suitcases in front of the storage shed. Those few guys sitting there fishing on the wall could have reported us. We didn't think they would, but we didn't want to take any chances and we kept powering away at full throttle until the lights on the land had disappeared. Then, we turned south and, keeping at full power, headed towards Australia. We kept the suitcases on deck up against the gunwales so we could heave them overboard if we were chased. We felt pretty good, and we didn't even mind there being no wind. We were making good headway, just slicing through the water with the phosphorescence streaming out behind us like a stream of sparklers, and the dolphins shooting across the bows leaving their ghostly jet trails shining deep down into the dark water.

We didn't want to start spending our money just yet because that cigarette boat back there could have found us as easy as anything on such a calm, waveless night with no other boats in sight. We would have stuck out on their radar screen like a donkey at a wedding. At the speed they could go, they could give us a day's start just for the fun of it.

When the day dawned, and the sun started coming up, already hot and promising to be getting hotter, it was still flat calm, and there was nothing in sight—no ships, no land, no birds. None of us had any sleep during the night, and we were all pretty tired. All the adrenaline had wiped us out, but someone had to steer. When there's no wind and no electronic motor-driven steering aid onboard, then it's sitting by the tiller and holding a course. What a bore. You can't read, can't walk around the deck, can't pop down below to put the kettle on. Taking a leak over the side takes planning and coordination, trying to hold the tiller with one foot while stretching out over the safety line like a ballet dancer striking a pose. We tossed a coin for who would take first watch. I was on second, so I could get three hours sleep.

Four hours is a normal watch on a boat, but it's too long to sit in the blazing sun. After that length of time set trapped to the tiller, even in the cool of the night, it makes you quite bad tempered. Two-hour watches would only give the other guy four hours sleep, so we made it three hours, which was still too long for me. It's okay when you're sailing around the islands and headlands and have something to look at, but when all you have in front of you, stretching on forever, is this endless flat blue sea, it's worse than watching endless reruns of the Teletubbies. When we were underway with a good wind, and the weather vane was kicking in well and keeping us on course, then we didn't keep watches. Whoever was awake kept an eye on things. Trying to get the boat to self-steer in these windless conditions, we tried endless combinations of bungee cords tied to the tiller and fastened down to port and starboard, but the best we could get was a two minute respite. Not enough to make a cup of tea in one go. We put the main sail up before leaving Andy alone on deck, more so he could get some shade from the sun than to steady the boat. Three hours later, after a sweat-driven sleep, I was still sleeping on the port side and was getting a full blast of the sun on the black hull just inches away from my body. Up on deck, Andy only had his head in the shade of the main so we rigged up an awning over the back of the boat to keep the sun off, but it didn't cool down the air any, and it was getting unpleasant to breathe. Three days and nights like this with not a change in the weather, and we were beginning to pray for a bit of wind.

We didn't have that much fuel left, either. Maybe enough for six days cruising. We had cut back the throttle after the first day's mad dash but were still making five to six knots. We took our first sun sight since leaving Cochin, and it put us twenty miles south of Cape Comeran, not too far from where we'd handed over our pornography. We felt we were totally safe now and struggled to get the suitcases off the deck and down below. We would put it into the inner tubes when it wasn't so hot on deck. We still had many weeks to do that. We were keeping to the original plan to get as far east as possible before crossing the equator to pick up the southeast trades which would blow us down on the port tack into the Roaring Forties.

It was going to be a problem, though, if we didn't get any wind soon. We were hoping for the first squalls of the southwest winds to push us over towards Sumatra, but the sky remained empty of any kind of clouds. The sun came up as red as a cherry, heaving itself up until it was a shimmering peach and then sliding back down over the west, disappearing over the western horizon but not taking any of the heat with it. Morale was high, though, and we were planning our attack on New South Wales. I had always thought that getting the stuff out of India would be the easiest part, but I wasn't too worried about getting it into Australia, either. I don't know why. Maybe because Jack had a plan. He made it sound such an empty, desolate place where we intended to land, and nobody would be expecting drug runners down there. I was even beginning to think about buying things for my boat, still sitting up on its chocks in Japan. I could start dreaming about the final fitting out and bringing my daughter back from school in England. If there was a dark spot on the horizon at that time, it was thinking about her stuck in England. I knew she didn't enjoy being there, and I wanted to get her back to Japan and rejoin the boat. Although I wasn't sure how she would take to this French woman in the long run. They didn't seem to be hitting it off too well after a good beginning. Still, she liked having a little brother, and once we were sailing again, just the four of us, it would be fine, I hoped.

I had been in radio contact with Chantal since we left Cochin and let her know that we should be having mango pie again in about four to five weeks. She told me there was no problem on her end, except her visa would run out in two months so I better be back then because she had found that she couldn't renew it without me sponsoring her. We'd also got Chantal to phone through to Jack's wife in Aussie to let her know we were safely on our way. The radio contact there was getting too suspicious and was afraid he'd get his ham radio license taken away for talking with pirate broadcasters.

The fourth day out from Cochin we were forty miles south of Galle Harbor in Sri Lanka and well below the shipping lanes. The sun was still fifteen degrees above the horizon to the west. It was one hour before sunset when we came across a fishing boat heading north making for Galle, or more likely Madurai, which is the fishing town ten miles to the east of Galle. The boat was about the same size as the one we had come across on our way up to India, but this one was much better conditioned and seaworthy looking. We shouted over to them, and they wished us good luck. They were still a speck on the northern horizon when from down below came a horrible, angry bang. A ferocious clank. Just once, and the engine stopped dead. I was at the tiller at the time.

For some reason, even though the engine wasn't turning over anymore, I kept hold and tried to keep a course until the boat's forward motion finally stopped. We'd had no wind at all since leaving Cochin, and the sea had been glassy calm, but the noise of the engine clanking over and the disturbance the boat made to the sea as we motored forward gave the feeling of being inside a bubble of activity cut off from the world outside. The moment the boat stopped dead in the water, the bubble broke, and the outside void rushed in.

We were now in an unimaginably huge, silent calm where directions were meaningless. When you're underway steering down a course, the empty sea is made meaningful. The course becomes your landmark to steer towards, but now all landmarks had vanished. Within minutes a feeling of panic and despair set in. I could hear Jack down below ripping off the engine box to get at the engine. Every sound that had been masked before now seemed alien and out of place and very loud and clear. I think we knew immediately that we had broken the connecting rod that turns the crankshaft, but we kept trying to start the motor. We just didn't want to admit this final predicament.

We only had enough fuel for another few days motoring so sometime, if we didn't have any wind, we would have had to shut the donk down. We could have motored a few days just to catch fish and keep up morale, though, and we wouldn't have felt so hopelessly abandoned and stranded. And, what about the final stage of the game when we approached the rocky coves of Wilson's Promontory on the stormy tip of New South Wales? The engine could be essential for maneuvering in small, narrow inlets.

If this had happened one hour before, we could have probably got a tow from that fishing boat back to Sri Lanka to get the engine repaired. We consoled ourselves by telling each other that if we had seen one, maybe there were more, and with hope being the strongest of human illusions, we got ready to meet the next Sri Lankan fishing boat returning to land. In fact, so much did we believe this that we hung a hurricane lamp in the rigging so they wouldn't run into us in the dark.

By noon the next day still no fishing boat had appeared to tow us to harbor, and a sun sight showed we had moved nowhere, or possible had moved slightly to the west, toward the Maldives. Now that the boat was stopped, and there wasn't a ripple to break the surface tension, little long legged insects appeared, just like the ones we called water boatmen on the ponds in England, or Japan for that matter. Where did they come from? Quite amazing. Skirting around way out on the ocean. They had no wings, so I couldn't imagine how they had gotten here. Then, there was our very own traveling aquarium. Three or four sucker fish that had been sheltering under the stern since we had left Cochin were now flitting in and out of the shade of the hull seeming very upset. They must have thought their host was dead or something. There were also a few small crabs that lived on the algae growing around the water line. You could have sworn they were conscious, thinking animals. They would dart out to check any piece of floating jetsam and come scurrying back if it seemed too great a distance. Some lovely green blue dorado seemed to like the safety of the boat, too, but they were too deep down to spear and wouldn't take a lure. With no wind on the boat, it was hot, hot, hot. The deck, where not in the shade, was like a skillet on a slow burner. We actually tried to fry an egg on the side deck, but it didn't do anything but turn a milky white. Decks on a boat on the tropics should be all white if you want to keep cool, but that's bad on the eyes, so Jack had opted for a light grey, and now they had got dirty, they absorbed more than they reflected.

Spending time down below was out of the question. We constantly swashed the decks with buckets of sea water and took turns swimming around the boat with someone on deck looking out for sharks.

Even the dolphins didn't come around anymore. We were far too lazy a play pal for them. And, no wind, no birds. Sea birds need a breeze to get them going. They don't spend their energy flapping around like land birds. Although, occasionally you might find a tern or something that had slogged its way through the heat-heavy air and would chirp away, probably having found a cooler layer. You'd start looking for it just above the mast, but eventually you'd spot it maybe a mile away, high up, so absolutely still and quiet was the air.

Two days later, our tow to Sri Lanka still hadn't come and we were definitely not moving. Orange peel thrown in the water the previous day was still there the next. According to our noon sight we seemed to be making a little way towards the Maldives, so maybe we were in the equatorial counter current. At this rate it would take a half a year to get there. It looked like we would have to put in somewhere to get the engine fixed, and we decided to pack the hash into the tubes so it would be easier to hide from any customs search. They'd have to be in the inner tubes anyway when we got to Aussie because there we intended to bury them for a time until we could get back by land with a van.

It was too hot to do the work down below. Too hot on deck, too, really, but at least we could wash down the deck so that no evidence would remain, like little pieces of hash in the floor cracks that curious custom dogs could sniff out. We spread a big, blue tarpaulin on the fore-deck and emptied out the suitcases. A hundred and twenty kilograms of hash all wrapped in one-kilogram plastic packets. Mr. X. reckoned the stuff had come from Afghanistan, not India. So, in a way, I reasoned, we were helping the Mujhadeen kick out the Soviets. Although I doubt that rationale would impress the Aussie authorities. Probably be okay if we'd been selling Afghan guns and other people-maiming things, but helping them run a non violent exchange of money for drugs was a very unsociable thing to do. We should have been giving them the money directly to buy the guns. Or, better still, just give them the guns. Then, we would have been doing what governments do and would have been socially acceptable.

Does it sound like a lot of hash—a hundred and twenty kilograms?

Probably not to some warlord up in the Golden Triangle, but it sure made a mountain up on the foredeck of the boat after we had taken it out of the plastic wrapping. It looked a bit moldy, full of white streaks. It was nice and squishy and looked like cow patties mixed with a bit of lime. I can't smell a mango to this day without thinking about that mountain of hash. If it smells so much like ripe mango, shouldn't it share, somewhere, some of the same genes? The sight of all that dope was a bit unnerving for me. I had just spent the last three years in Japan, in a place where drugs are not a thing. There's some grass around, not very good, left over from when there were fields of hemp grown for rope-making during the war, but that's about it. The Japanese just aren't interested. I didn't say no to a joint now and then, but I was no fan of hashish. It made my head feel heavy and my limbs like lead and brought on a feeling of anxiety. Just the fumes from that great heap of sun-heated dope made me feel panicky, but Jack and Andy, especially Andy, who had been living in the bush with a bunch of hippies for the last few years, were going to sample the goods.

Jack had brought along a little kisaru with him, and they filled it up. Suddenly, it was like I was all alone on the boat. They had gone off in their heads somewhere. Things were definitely beginning to break down. I couldn't smoke any of this stuff. I was paranoid enough. It would just put me over the top. These two had been living in a different headspace than I had been for the last few years. I'd just come out of a totally normal existence. My reality had been work and bread-earning, talking and interacting with people who considered themselves well beyond the fringes of any alternative society. Jack and Andy had been living in the tropics, cut off from a normal world. They were used to a more flexible reality and could accept the strangeness of the situation easier than I could, half-trapped still in a Japanese mindset.

I had to keep my head focused on doing something. Reading was about the only thing there was to do, and there weren't too many books. I had to take every sentence really slowly and savor every word. An hour of that at a time was all I could take. Then, I would wander around the deck, take a swim, try again to get a conversation going, which was getting more and more difficult. Nights were the worst. They would go on forever. They were not much cooler than the day, and the nights made the world close in, and the feeling of loneliness increased to unbearable heights.

It's better to be physically alone than with two guys who are stoned all the time. At least then you can talk aloud to yourself and shout out your frustrations. There was beginning to be an atmosphere of distrust growing among us. They couldn't understand why I wouldn't relax and get stoned with them. Day after day, the ennui dragged on. A week later the dope was still sitting out on the foredeck. At least I had covered it up by then, more to keep it out of mind than to protect it from the sun.

Every day I was taking noon sights, and we were very slowly drifting west. The Maldives were still too far away to offer any hope. The rate of drift was not enough to make the spirits rise. Ten days out from Cochin, and I was getting desperate. I had a time frame. This was okay for Andy and Jack. A month one way or another wouldn't affect them, but I had a woman up in Japan whose visa to stay in the country was running out. Truth be told, I probably worried more about my unfinished boat, though. Had the shelter I had rigged up over the unprotected topsides held up? Were the supports against the hull strong enough to keep it from toppling over in an earthquake? Had anyone stolen my power tools I had left below in the cabin?

You can't imagine the feeling of total helplessness being becalmed. There's not a single thing you can do to control your fate. The situation is hopeless. You're abandoned and forgotten. You're going to be there forever. The wind will never come back. Jack and Andy seemed to be handling it well, though. Maybe because they're Aussies and used to great open spaces, but for me, almost straight out of tiny Japan and brought up in even tinier England, this vast open space was almost too much to take. It's different when you're moving. You're in control and you cut it down to size, taking great bites out of the chart every day. If the shrinking world isn't enough, you begin to worry what would happen if you got a toothache, or even worse, appendicitis. Every little twinge in the gut, even a little itch just below the navel that only needs scratching, brings out the panic of anticipated pain. We had quite a lot of multi-spectrum antibiotics onboard. Jack had somehow got them from a doctor in Aussie. We had the idea that massive doses of these would cut down the inflammation of any rotten appendix, but still it was a frightful prospect.

We had started to go through a futile period of taking sides. When we first became becalmed, Jack was for trying to get to Sri Lanka or the Maldives to get the engine fixed. I wanted to keep going even without the engine, but a week later the positions had changed. He wanted to keep going, and I wanted to get the engine fixed. It was impossible to get a consensus. Jack would get Andy aside to give him his views, and then, later, usually when Jack was asleep, I talked Andy into agreeing with my ideasonly for him to change back again when Jack got hold of him. It was just silly, really. We weren't going anywhere. There was nothing to push the boat one way or the other, so I don't know why we were so driven to come to some decision. It was more than frustrating; it was eating me up. Because they were stoned most of the time, it was even more frustrating for me. I wanted to get at a decision all the time I was awake, but they only talked about it between joints. It was just crazy to get so worked up about something we had no control over, but if we could have all agreed on what we would have liked to do, if it were possible, then we could have had a certain sense of purpose and direction. We just kept flip-flopping from "Let's go on" to "No, let's go get the engine fixed."

Two weeks of this playing with my head, and I was getting close to the edge. You know how they talk about going over the edge when you go crazy? I know what they mean. I came to this edge one day. I was down below at the time. I had just gone down, and nobody else was around. Jack was back in his aft cabin, and Andy was zonked out forward somewhere. It was the hottest part of another flat calm day of hopelessness. Out of the blue, I suddenly came up to the edge of insanity. It was literally like that. I could see it in my head, but my whole body tensed as it loomed near. It wasn't like a barrier I could go through. It was a definite edge that I was going to fall over, and I knew if I went any nearer, I would go over. I also knew I would never come back. I don't want to say it was terrifying, that adjective is used too often, but I don't know any other word. It was pure terror. I was going into another reality with no way back. The neurons and synapses in my brain had been so abused they were threatening to rewire themselves in some utterly bizarre way that would leave my body in this reality, but God knows where my mind would be. I had to force myself to stop and pull back. I did this physically, too, walking slowly backwards and trying to stop any thought that came into my head. I went up on deck very slowly and refused to allow thoughts to germinate. Just look at the sea. Look at the mast. Look at the bucket on the deck. That's a rope. That's a tiller. That's an empty cup of tea. I just looked at things and named them, not dwelling on anything beyond the name, just bringing them back into the reality I was familiar with. After awhile, this edge to insanity I had almost fallen over receded, and I felt okay again. In fact, I even felt slightly more optimistic now that I had escaped from that. I went to read a book, hoping to keep open the usual passageways that my brain chemicals took. I knew I had to keep away from dwelling on our situation or these chemicals might spill over again.

Long before, when I was twelve years old, I had another strange experience with the chemistry of the brain. It's still very clear. It was early morning on a school holiday in summer. I was just a normal kid, physically and mentally secure, or at least I thought so. I was playing with some toy soldiers on the dining room carpet making them scale the legs of a chair to attack the troops on the top. Suddenly, just like that, I was out of my body. It was very weird. I could see myself still down on the floor playing away, but my mind, or whatever it was, was perceiving all this from its usual standing height. My mind and body were definitely two separate things. I was a little afraid but more embarrassed. I thought I had some strange illness that I should be too ashamed to talk about. Before I could panic, I was back in my body, and that's where I've been ever since. I kept my secret for years until I read that it's quite a common phenomenon. About a third of people have this weird trip at some time in their life. It is a gentle experience. So gentle you don't know it's happening until it has. One minute you're in your head, and the next you're out of it. It wasn't the gut wrenching terror I had just faced of having my brain chemistry ripped out by the roots.

If the vastness of the ocean can unhinge the mind, then the searing, empty spaces of a desert must be able to do it, too. When you're stuck out there with no hope of rescue or aid, there's a feeling of complete abandonment. You can see nature for what it is, terrifyingly self-sufficient. It just doesn't care a damn if you are around or not. There's a vast and empty void behind our usual understanding of reality. There are so many things knocking at our senses all the time that we never get to see it. All those sights, sounds, and feelings clogging up the passageways in the brain make a barrier that's hard to find. Unless, like I'd almost done, you come across it by chance and then, being unprepared, you fall into it head first. And, you know what happens when you fall anywhere head first.

To handle the emptiness that lies behind the illusion of reality, you have to train the brain. Then, maybe you could get to rappel down into it. You can't say train the mind because the mind is only the thought made lucid by the working of the physical, biological brain. Some monks are supposed to be able to do this. Not your average Bidhisattva charlatan that crowd the roads of India but a really serious contemplative person who studies this nothingness. This nothingness that scares the hell out of anyone who comes across it suddenly without warning. I reckon that's what happened in the deserts of the Middle East. Moses, walking in the desert sun, suddenly sees the desert for what it is—a very unfriendly place and far too big for him, and his neurons panic and start to leap across the wrong synapses. He feels the void behind the senses and begins to panic, but he manages to hold on. He's desperate for something to anchor him in reality. What someone really needs in this situation when the world is just too enormous and indifferent and the void behind too terrifying to contemplate is a dad, or the voice of one. The trick is to get your neurons to conjure one up before they start short-circuiting. It doesn't matter if the voice is from a burning bush or from the top of a rocky mountain. Once you have your dad around you can be sure of staying safely in this reality. You can even go around and convince the rest of us that it's your father who is the savior and the guardian at the gate of the void. I don't think I would have liked to hear my dad's voice right at that moment, though. I don't think he would have been very happy about what we were up to. He wouldn't have promised me any land of milk and honey.

What we did get, though, soon after my cliff hanging experience was even better than the promised land. It was a breath of wind. Not much of a breath but enough to fill the light genoa and give a knot or two over the water. It was out of the north, so I don't know where that had come from, but it was all we had needed—the voice of God—to make us pull up our socks and get on with it. We decided to head west and make for the Maldives—three-hundred and sixty miles away. Sri Lanka was nearer, but with the wind from the north, we'd have to cover twice that distance as we tacked east and west trying to get north. They might still remember our strange arrival just a few weeks back and given us a thorough going over, looking for maybe not drugs, but guns. Guns for the Tamil Tigers was a hot issue at the time.

Now that we were under way, morale came back. We were a team again, all the bickering and hard feelings forgotten, or at least shoved on the back burner. Jack put his pipe away, and it began to feel like a summer cruise. We even used some of our precious electricity to play music while we began to get the cargo sealed up in the rubber tubes. I don't know how many times we played Men at Work, but it seemed to hit the spot and just suited the buzz we were on at that time.

We made a short slit in the side of the tube and pushed the hash inside—great big handfuls at a time from the heap that had been lying on the foredeck for the last two weeks. It seemed a lot more now than when the suitcases were first opened, and it had been compressed in the plastic bags. Now it was all fluffed up and crumbling. After the tire was full, we sealed the gash with a rubber patch and wrapped the tube with a coconut rope. It looked like a poor man's fender, and one or two hanging over the side would probably have fooled somebody, but eight looked a bit over the top. They were heavy, too, so they sagged down where the rope tied them to the lifeline. No, we would have to use them as deck furniture, like beanbags. They were good to sit on, but a bit scratchy with the fiber rope. With the breeze came some life back to the ocean. Not much, but enough to show us we were not alone on the planet anymore. The suckerfish showed up again, taking station just under the stern. We hadn't seen them for a week and thought they'd gone off. Then, a sea snake swam past, a thousand miles from any land, just gliding under the surface, sometimes putting his head up to have a look around. We saw two whales blowing up ahead and hoped to sneak up on them. It looked like a husband and wife team. I don' t know why I thought that, but one was smaller than the other, and they were swimming so close together. Come to think of it, maybe they were just courting. They were the ones with the big box for a head. Before we got up to them, they must have sensed or heard us. They looked back and saw us, their eyes opened wide, and I swear they said, "God, no! Not humans again." Then they dove out of sight. Twenty minutes later, we hadn't gone that far, and the larger one surfaced again, off to port, two hundred meters away. He was looking away from us when he came up, and he slowly scanned the horizon until we came into view. He did a double take, just like a bad comedian, or a good one, if it comes to that. He flashed his flippers in the air and went off to tell his mate it wasn't safe yet. If whales aren't conscious beings, than neither are we.

We were now at four degrees north and about seventy-nine degrees east with about three hundred miles to go to the Maldives. We'd have to go to the capital on Male Atoll to find some mechanics, but we were having worries about going there with all this hash onboard. Even if we got in without it being discovered, we would have to spend some time getting the engine fixed. That meant mechanics would come on deck and all kinds of curious people would be around. It was a risk, and we thought we should drop it off first on some uninhabited island. We knew there were over a thousand islands making up the Maldives so finding one shouldn't be too much of a problem. I had been here before and knew that the south part of South Male Atoll had lots of small, un-peopled islets. I also remembered that the bottom of the atoll was about three and a half degrees north, so that's where we were headed.

Jack had managed to find a ham radio operator living in Perth and got him to phone his wife and explain the situation to her--how the engine had broken down, how we had been becalmed for two weeks, and how we were now heading toward the Maldives, maybe a week's sail away. We hoped this little breeze would last. It wasn't much as far as winds go, but it was a long way better than nothing. With a little equatorial countercurrent going our way, too, we should get there in a few days.

We were still a long ways off starving. We still had plenty of dried goods aboard to last for another few weeks, though we were getting a bit fed up with chutney and crackers and just could not catch any fish. Eggs, we still had, and onions, but the potatoes were beginning to sprout. The fruit had all gone, but there were still some bananas gone black and soggy but good for making cakes. Our main diet consisted of oats mixed with powdered milk and water. We always used a baby formula milk. It was cheaper and dissolved easier in water. It also seemed to have more goodies in it. Water--we still had half left of what we'd left Cochin with, although it was looking a bit suspect. I wouldn't have liked to check it under a microscope.

*R*unning down a low-lying coral island and making landfall on a high island are two different things. An island with a high elevation like the Seychelles can be seen up to sixty miles away. If you see it at sunset, you still have all night to sail towards it without fear of running into it. A coral island, though, isn't visible until you are almost on the beach. Well, a bit of an exaggeration, that, but you don't have much more than five miles unless the palm trees are really tall. I have seen written in a British Admiralty pilot book that these islands are visible for ten miles. If you're standing on the deck of a warship, fifty feet about the sea, maybe they are, but we were standing practically on the water. Of course, when we got nearer, we could go up the mast or at least as far as the spreaders, but in any case, I don't like arriving at coral islands any time but in the mornings, with the sun low down and behind so the shallows and corals lying just below are easily seen. Usually this means juggling with the sailing time some days before, slowing down a bit so as to get there when the light is just right.

Now, with GPS, you shouldn't have to worry like that, but we only knew exactly where we were once a day—at noon. The weather was good enough for us to take star sights at dawn or dusk, but I never really trust my star sights, and if our readings put us in a different place than the noon sights, then we'd be really screwed. Well, that's only half true, really. With the sky as clear as this and the horizon sharp and crisp, we could have got a very good star sight position, which we could have used, but it didn't seem worth the bother. There are only a few hours between a noon sight and an evening star sight. If you were going twenty knots or so it might be worth a check, but going as slow as we were, even going in the opposite direction, would not have put us that far out. Taking morning star sights was just too much hassle. If you're coming off a watch, all you want to do is sleep, and if you're waking up to go on watch, you're much too groggy. Any excuse to get out of taking a star sight. It's a bit of a hassle. First, you have to find three stars, kind of equally spaced around the horizon and not too high. Getting the sextant angles and timing them is no big deal and kind of fun to do, but working out those figures is stomach churning. All those declination and star sight tables and almanacs to flip through. Check this column. Go to that page. Back to another column in the other book. Check out another list of numbers, and on and on. Not on your life. Unless it really was a case of that, and then we'd probably do it. I don't think Captain Cook would have admired our laissez-faire attitude.

From here on, from noon to the next, it was all navigating by dead reckoning. That was pretty hit and miss, too. We'd judge the speed by checking the wake and figuring out how fast we were going, or in our case, how slow. We did have an autometer when we left Malaya. It was the type that had a small brass propeller on the end of a long line and spun around as the boat moved through the water. This spun the line that turned some gearing in a little housing secured to the aft of the boat. The gearing attached to a dial that showed the miles run, so you could time it every hour and get your speed. It was not one of the best ideas man ever had. The box it comes with has two spare propellers, probably enough up in northern waters, where sharks aren't as ferocious, but we had already lost two by the time we got to Sri Lanka. The flurry of wake the prop makes while spinning in the water is just too appetizing. We could guess our speed faster and just as accurately by a glance over the side so we put that instrument away.

Steering a straight course was a bit more difficult without an adjusted compass. With Andy up the mast as far away as possible from any metal interference, we could check the main compass once a day. With a hand bearing compass giving us 270 degrees, with three degrees off for variation, our main compass said 285, so that's what we steered. It didn't really matter. The Maldives stretched for five hundred miles from north to south so we could hardly miss them even if we wanted to. We were aiming for, more or less, the dead center of this huge, sprawling archipelago, looking for one little uninhabited island to stash our load for awhile.

We thought we should start to pick up an island around eight or nine o'clock in the morning, but it was nearer noon when the first dark smudge appeared on the horizon dead ahead. I guess we had been a little too optimistic in our speed. There was no doubting where we were now. On the first island we spotted were tall coconut trees, and there seemed to be a lot of them. It was about a mile long, which was pretty big by Maldives standards, and it would certainly have people on it because the big islands would have drinking water. On the small islands the water, even in the center of the island, is too brackish to drink because any well dug there is not far enough from the ocean to get the salt filtered out.

What we wanted was something was very small and easily recognized when we came back to pick up our cargo. The big, very light-weight blooper sail had done a great job for the last week keeping full and pulling even in this very light breeze, but it wasn't a good sail for maneuvering. The front of the sail was free, not hanked to the forestay, but just pulled tight at the mast head and the foot pulled tight at the bows. We changed to the big genoa, which was clipped on to the forestay and made it easier to tack to the wind. Now that we were getting into coral waters we would need to be able to twist and turn to dodge the hidden coral heads.

We must have been somewhere around the bottom of South Male Atoll, which from top to bottom covers less than sixty miles. So, we turned south, bringing the breeze behind us, and gradually lots of little islands came into view, strung out like beads on a chain. We were looking for one with a unique shape, one whose coconut trees made a really recognizable pattern. After about an hour of coasting down the chain of islands, we had to bring the wind to starboard to keep the islands on our beam. We must have reached the bottom of the atoll, as we were now bearing more west than south. We were entering the channel separating Male Atoll from Felidu Atoll although the islands on that atoll were too far away to make out. There was one island to the west of us, and we couldn't figure out where that fit into the scheme of things. It was quite large, too, and had what looked like a low white building on it, but it was too far away to see clearly. It must have been part of the Male Atoll, and we must have cut the corner of the atoll somehow, but strange that we had not gone through any fringing reef of coral.

There in front of us was the perfect treasure island. It was just big enough to have a crown of five closely spaced palm trees. In the center was one tall and straight, the two on either side bending away gracefully to form a five part fleur de lis. There could be no missing that when we came back, and it was too small to be visited for any other reason than for hiding contraband. So, I don't think there would be any casual visitors. We would have to keep an eye out on that white building. I can't imagine anyone coming over to check out a sailing boat, but you never know. Everyone's so paranoid these days.

We dropped anchor in a few feet of water, not more than fifty feet from the beach in fine, soft coral sand. Not a sign of coral anywhere so there must be a huge gap in the outer reef somewhere, and we were now inside the atoll. We would just sail back on the same course, past the long island we first sighted. Keeping everything to port, we would be funneled north to Male town. These little coral islands of the Maldives are really something special. I don't know why that should be. They don't look any different from coral islands in the Pacific. Maybe it's the light or the freshness of the air, but they seem younger and fresher than the Pacific islands. Maybe because the distances are not so great as in the Pacific. By the time you sail to anywhere in that ocean, it's taken so long, you already feel old and jaded when you arrive. Because of the huge ocean surrounding them, they have a daunting feeling, a feeling of being lost beyond reach. The Maldives, though, are only a few days sail away from India or Sri Lanka. They don't feel so shut off and lonely, although most of the islands are just as unvisited and deserted. More than anything, I think, it's the light. At this time of year, anyway, during the northeast monsoon or the transition period. It's the kind of light heaven must be lit up of. It's like a mix of that rare English summer morning light, the summer light of Provence, and the winter sky over the Pacific coast of Japan. It's just so clear and pure. It makes you feel so alive, but at the same time, it's the sort of light I'd like to die in. Figure that one out.

Talking about dying, these little coral islands remind me of the death of two scrawny little chickens. A bit of a diversion, this, but we're still in the Maldives and very near this island, too, I think. It happened three years before, and I was never sure, even then, where we were.

I think I mentioned getting to Sri Lanka with my seven-year old daughter onboard. There we met up with a boat from Australia with two young boys. These guys were leaving in a day or two to cruise to the Maldives before coming back to Sri Lanka. Vanesa, having just met for the first time children of her own race who she could talk to in her dad's language, begged to go with them. No way I wanted to go, but I indulged Vanesa and agreed, leaving my younger brother on the boat to look after it while we were gone. I think the reason the mum and dad wanted me to go along was because they weren't getting on so well. In fact, it soon became obvious that there was definitely some kind of drama in process. He said he was an ex-U.S. Marine, she was out of England, and they were settled in Aussie. I don't really know if he was an ex-Marine, but he had the attitude of one: Men should be men and boys knocked into little Rambos. If ever I was to lose my marbles, it should have been on that trip. We'd gone over on the very last of the northeast monsoons and expected to come back on the southwest ones, which we naively thought would arrive sometime the end of April, but they were late that year, too, and we ended up marooned there for two months.

The chicken saga started about two weeks into our trip. We called in at Male town to go to the market to get some fresh fruit and veg-etables. At the market, someone offered us two live chickens. I asked who was to kill them if we bought them. Of course, the Marine said he'd do it. Trained to kill men, a couple of chickens wouldn't dent his con-science. They bought the chickens. Just as we were leaving the market, the atmosphere of the crowd seemed to change. There was a growing panic in the air, and people were beginning to leave in a hurry. Someone told us cholera had broken out on the island, and everyone was hurrying to leave Male and get back to their own little islands. We followed the rest and hurried back to the yacht, throwing the chickens in the dinghy, which we towed behind. I remember the little shock of horror imagin-ing dying of dehydration and diarrhea out on a little boat under the mer-ciless sun. None of us had had a cholera inoculation. It was something you never thought about. Cholera is something you got in Africa, back in Livingston's day. We scattered with the rest of the boats going every which way. Sailing dhows mainly but also quite a few motor launches were all packed with these frightened, fleeing people. We went south to find a deserted island to lay up next to until the southwest winds arrived.

We motored around for two days with these two chickens still scrabbling around in the bottom of the dinghy. Poor buggers out in the midday sun. We weren't even feeding them because we expected to eat them any day. The dad's attitude was changing. He was starting to get more macho and demanded to know why I wouldn't kill the chickens. The atmosphere was getting really charged. He was starting to suggest that any man who wouldn't kill a chicken must be some kind of wimp. The atmosphere got worse and worse, and aggression was in the air. I realized I had to kill one of these chickens or there would be no living on the boat. He was already making innuendos to my daughter about the Pom who couldn't kill a chicken. Five days later, we were lying at anchor, off an island like the one we were at now, a little bigger perhaps, that took ten minutes to walk around. It had the same sort of surreal atmosphere these islands all have and the same stunningly beautiful light.

It was about mid morning, and I thought, "What a beautiful day to die. Right. Let's do it now. Let's take the chickens to shore and execute them. Get it over with." It had gotten really out of hand. It was only a chicken, but I was so worked up about it, it was like I was off to commit seppuku. I'd heard the best way to kill a chicken was to pull the neck with a sharp twist, but I wasn't sure I could work that one properly. I might end up pulling and pulling and just stretching its neck while it squawked louder and louder. It turned out the Marine had never docked a chicken that way, either, so it was going to be a beheading with a long, rusted machete. We all went ashore, the kids, jumping around, went with mum to round the island. The marine and I tied the chickens up to a palm tree near a fallen log in which we left the machete notched. We hadn't talked about who was going to kill his first, and we both took off for a little stroll, going different ways. When he was out of sight, no one else around, just me standing out there on the burning sand, I thought, "I've got to do this now. When I turn around, I'm going back, grab a chicken and cut its head off, no hesitating, no thinking about it." God, why was it so difficult? We eat animals all the time. Someone has to kill them, but I had worked myself to such a pitch about the horror of ending a life. It was a huge barrier to get over. "Right, I'm going to count to ten, turn around and just go do it," I said aloud. I would be like a robot, like an automat. I did that. I turned round, strolled back, grabbed the nearest chicken, held him by the neck laid him flat along the palm log and brought down the machete just before the horror of the act flooded back to my brain. Too late now. Its head was resting on the soft white sand. But, it wasn't dead! It was squawking and flapping. In a panic, I thought I'd missed. But, no, there is its head on the sand. Why is it still alive? I shoved the headless neck into the sand, but it still flapped. Everyone was going to come back and see what a mess I'd made. It made me think of Mary, Queen of Scots, when the executioner had botched up his job, too. It stopped squawking and flapping after awhile, and I realized it was just reflex action. The kids had come back just to see the end of it when I was holding the headless corpse in the sand. The boys thought it was great fun, but Vanesa, thank God, was much more sensitive about it and was very quiet. Fancy finding your dad red-handed, a cold-blooded killer. The mother shouted at me for having tied them up close together so that the one still alive watched its own end. I didn't care. I was elated. Not because I had killed it, but because I was through the rights of passage. Not that I wanted to be accepted as a Marine, but I had done something I didn't want to do, I thought I couldn't do, but knew I had to do, and it was over. I won. I went to find the dad and handed him the bloody machete. "I just killed mine." I told him. When I saw the look in his eyes, I felt so sorry for him. He looked so forlorn. I realized it was all a posture with him. He didn't feel like doing it any more than I did. But, I couldn't let him off the hook. It would be worse if he'd known I'd seen through him. So I went for a swim to wash the blood off and let him get on with it. Only the boys and their dad ate any of the chicken curry that night.

Back in the present at Five-Tree Island, as Jack and I had named it, we'd staked out our claim and were busy ferrying the tires of hash ashore and digging a hole as far up from the water's edge as we could, just below the top of the island, which made it about one and a half meters above sea level. Even in a strong southwest blow, I doubted the waves would get this high up. Although we couldn't see it, there must have been a fringing reef around the atoll somewhere, and then, there was the whole of the atoll to break any high waves. Jack might not have had too many aids to navigation on his boat, but he'd thought of one piece of important equipment for a lark like this—a spade. It was the sort of shovel you'd get in an Army/Navy store--collapsible and used by marines to dig latrines and bury bodies. He'd been thinking ahead to Australia when he'd bought it because that's what we were going to do there with the hash. Good bit of forward thinking and was really necessary in this soft coral sand, although I suppose a frying pan would have done as well. Have you ever tried digging a hole in soft coral sand? The sides keep collapsing and instead of getting deeper, it just gets wider. Finally we managed to get a hole deep enough to stack in the eight tires, two to a layer, and covered them up with sand. The top layer was about three feet down, and I doubted the turtles would even get down that far to bury their eggs. Then, we paced the spot off from the nearest palm tree, just like in the book, *Treasure Island.* By the time we finished, it was late afternoon.

We didn't want to sail at night. Following a chain of islands with reefs around wouldn't have been a good idea at night, so we decided to stay at anchor for the night and leave early in the morning. That should get us to Male in one day's sail. We thought we'd sleep ashore and have a barbeque. In the Maldives they had one good law--no spearguns. It's to stop people shooting each other and to keep the fish stock up, but we didn't think they'd begrudge us one fish. We'd have liked a coral trout, but just near us there was no coral. We settled for a travelli and baked it over dried coconut husks, dipping it in an onion and lime sauce. It certainly beat chutney and crackers.

We always intended to take a sun sight to check the position of the island, but we hadn't bothered when we arrived, and with this and that, we never did get around to it. We did take a morning sight just before we up anchored which gave us one line of position but that only told us we were somewhere on this line running from the north pole to the south pole. If we waited another two hours or so, we could have crossed it with another line of position because the sun would have moved. We could have crossed the previous one at right angles, giving us a reasonable fix, but we were in a hurry to be off, and the five palm trees were such an arresting sight that no way we could not find it again.

The northerly breeze was still holding. It had been puffing away for a week now, never more than ten knots. It was not enough to ruffle the surface of the water but enough to keep us going. The island stretched away northwards, and with the wind from that way, too, we had to tack off on a close reach bearing away from the islands at about forty degrees. Now with our forward speed adding to the real wind, we were feeling quite a comfortable blow. The sea was flat and calm, too, so we sliced away at it, cutting through it at six knots. Just before losing sight of the islands, we'd have to tack back towards them, so it was about twice the distance to Male for us than it would be for a crow or frigate bird. Not the sort of sailing to write home about, but it was quite pleasant with the blue sky and tropical sun. The dolphins were doing their line dance on the horizon. The brilliant white little terns and parrot birds were flying around. Everything was putting on a show for us. I really like to watch the frigate birds, about the size of seagulls, which look like Stuka Bombers, those World War II German dive bombers with wings shaped like a W. The birds are jet black except in the horny season when the males have a bright red bulge around their neck. These are the pirate birds of the tropic seas. They fly up high, hovering for ambush and waiting for another bird to catch a fish. Then, they scream down, scare the other bird into dropping its catch, which they scoop up as it tumbles free. Sometimes the victim bird won't let go, especially if it's a gannet, and the frigate bird tries to tear it away, and both birds will fall tumbling, locked together, beak to beak. The frigates rarely lose this tug of war.

I don't know how many times we tacked in shore, but we were getting close to the top of the atoll. There were more reefs around, and we had to be careful not to run aground on any of the coral heads that lay just below the surface. The sun was past the zenith so it was now in our eyes to the west, making it difficult to see the different colors of water, which would show up as light green for shoal water, going into dark blue for deeper parts. After tacking off with the sun now behind us, we could see that we had sailed into a trap of really shallow water with lots of coral heads scattered around. It probably wouldn't have done much damage to us because we weren't going fast enough, but it could have been embarrassing to get lodged up on a reef, with no engine to back us off. Trying to find a way out of this maze, we came across a small boat with two young kids diving for lobsters. We had just seen one of the boys surface with a beautiful big one harpooned on his three-pronged spear. Fresh lobster, that would hit the spot. We were going slowly enough to glide right up next to them and ask what they wanted for it, but they didn't want to sell it. It was for the tourist market where they could get top dollar. Then, we saw it was a female. Even from up on our deck we could see the bright orange egg sack under the lobster's tail, and in the bottom of their boat, they had a couple of other very small ones. If they carried on like that, there wouldn't be any lobsters left in a year or two, although they'd probably be able to retire on what they got for the last, fat female. I don't suppose we could complain about trying to make some fast money, but at least our trade was sustainable. It didn't matter how much hashish we sold, there would always be more, but taking female and baby lobsters was like cutting your own throat. At one time, the seas around the Maldives must have been swarming with these creatures because Muslims don't eat anything that feeds on carrion, or at least they shouldn't according the rules of their faith. These guys pointed us towards a channel leading out to deeper water, probably to cut short the lecture on ocean conservation rather than to be helpful.

Two more tacks brought us to the north end of South Male Atoll, and we could make out the radio masts on Male Island. We had made good time, rounded Male Island by late afternoon, and dropped anchor off the north side just outside the little harbor. We sat there with the yellow quarantine flag waiting for someone to come out.

It was going to be a heavy slog to pull up the anchor and chain that was hanging up and down in ninety feet of water. There was a small mechanical windlass on the foredeck but more for ornament than anything else. We always pulled up the pick hand over hand. There's not much of a tidal range in these islands, about one meter or so, but the currents are quite strong in the channel when all the water in these huge lagoons is slurped up by the lunar spring tides. It rushes out very fast, so we hoped someone would come soon. We were already getting swept past the harbor mouth. You really should have enough anchor line out to equal at least three times the depth, but we didn't have anywhere near that amount, and the anchor was just bouncing along the bottom as the boat was dragged along in the current.

I would think anyone living on such beautiful, quiet, sun-drenched island would be as calm and mellow as a contented cat, but the three guys who came out to officially welcome us to the Maldives were as uptight and aggressive as New York cab drivers. They'd come out of the harbor in a powerful little launch dressed in olive green uniforms without any insignia on the sleeves. They could have been anything from immigration men to the local postmen. The short-nosed submachine guns they carried probably made them army. They came alongside and shouted at us to move over to the holding zone near the airport, which was about two miles away on another island to the northeast. We explained that our engine was broken, and we had come to Male to get it repaired and wanted to enter the harbor. They didn't like that. Nobody was allowed in the harbor, but we insisted, and they got on the radio to someone who eventually gave us the okay. First, though, they insisted on searching the boat. I don't know what they were looking for, but they stomped all over the place in their heavy combat boots, opened every cupboard, looked in every nook and cranny, and even poked in the sail bags, but they seemed mainly interested in the canned goods. We had some tins of corn beef and they took ages reading the labels until they were satisfied it wasn't made of pig and wasn't from Israel. They didn't want any pork products or anything from Israel to contaminate their island. They also let us know that pornography would get us into a lot of trouble. God, that was a first. I'd never met an official who wouldn't kiss your boot for a naughty picture. They better not find any drugs either, they told us. Out of the three no-nos, I think pork was probably the worst. The tourists locked away on their little fortressed island resorts could get pork and alcohol, but the contamination was kept to a minimum and under control. If the tourist industry were ever to die off, these resort islands would probably be under quarantine for hundreds of years until they were purified enough for good Muslims to live on again.

We were glad now we had dropped off our goods. I would not have fancied spending much time in a Maldivian jail if these sort of guys were the jailers. They don't really have jails in the Maldives. They just put all the bad guys on an island farthest away from anywhere. Even so, a coral island only seems like a paradise if you are free to come and go when you want, but to be incarcerated on one, knowing that the wide world is going on out there over the horizon without you, that's a terrible fate.

Probably the worst thing about tourism on any small island group is not the destruction to the reef, the stolen shells and broken coral, nor the pollution from the hotel sewage, but the way that contact with the outside world has messed around with the islanders' way of thinking. They probably didn't know if they were happy or not fifty years ago, but they must have been contented. Now they've seen that there's a wider world out there and an airport to get there, too, they just aren't satisfied with a few yards of sandy beach anymore. The saddest case of this I've seen is in the Marshall Islands. It's the same sort of coral atolls but located in the Pacific. The Marshall Islands include the infamous Bikini Atoll, which was blown up by a hydrogen bomb in the 50's when all the big powers were playing tic-tac-toe. Can you imagine that? How stupid can you get? Living on this tiny little ball in the vastness of space, and it's the only one we've got, and they start blowing the best pieces up just to see if they can. It's like going into the best room of your house and smashing up your grandmother's collection of priceless Ming pottery just to see what will happen. No, it's not like that. It's infinitely more stupid. Anyway, the Americans, who were the villains in this particular case, felt guilty afterwards, and so they should have, but it was definitely not a good idea to salve their conscience by giving the islanders a bunch of supermarkets and drinking dens and the money to spend there. Now these islands, which are off the tourist track and should have been doubly idyllic, are where at one time not too long ago they fished and swam in the lagoons and played with their children in the sands and watched their beautiful sunsets. Not anymore. The parents drink and fight all day, and the kids hang around the video store lounging and glowering in aggressive takeoffs of L.A. gangs. And don't try diving off the reef. It's covered with the tattered remnants of throwaway nappies and McDonald wrappings.

The Maldives aren't that bad yet, but the sense of claustrophobia fostered by contact with the bigger world got to one guy here just before we arrived. It must have been gnawing at him for quite awhile. Here he was stuck away on a speck of sand, and all of the outer world was awash with women and wine. Unlike the other poor frustrated islanders, he had the means to get at it because he was the treasurer. One day he just up and went and took all of the money in the treasury with him. There are definitely some good perks in being a politician.

The entrance to the harbor was not more than a boat length wide and at high water only had a little over six foot in clearance. I suppose in the old days it had been the break in the reef that surrounded the islands. Now they had built up the harbor wall on top of the reef and enclosed the lagoon into a reasonable, safe mooring for small boats. Any cargo ships were unloaded outside in the channel and the goods ferried in by lighter boats. The three guys with the guns were not too happy about it, but there was no other way for us to get inside without being towed. We thought we might try and go in under sail, but we were already swept way past the entrance by the current, and the tide was still falling. It would have been dark before we had tacked back, and there would probably not have been enough water over the entrance at that time. They towed us in and not too soon. We touched once or twice when the bottom shallowed out at places. We found a place to anchor in just ten feet of water. We were warned not to go ashore that night, and first thing in the morning we must go to immigration.

We just wanted to get rid of these guys. Not that they made us nervous, but anyone in uniform with a gun was bad for morale. We hadn't told them we had come from India, and they hadn't asked. So, we were going to stick with a story of drifting across from Malaya. Talking about an Antarctic expedition seemed a little out of place here. What we really wanted to do was to get to a telephone. God, it was hot in that harbor. It wasn't even seven o'clock in the morning when we woke up the next day, but the sun was already high enough to bake the decks, and without an awning up, it was trying to blister the paint off. There wasn't a breath of wind stirring inside the anchorage, although we could see some dhows under sail on the far horizon. The bucket of water scooped up to cool the boat off was almost hot enough to make tea with. Being only about six feet deep now at low tide, the harbor water was heating up nicely. It was quite clear, and it was like being anchored in an aquarium with schools of little blue fish scurrying about. There were some suspicious looking objects floating around, too, which was only to be expected with about two dozen dhows crowding inside the harbor. Our pump-operated toilet masticated everything into an unrecognizable mess, but the dhows were obliged to do without any mod-cons. It was a far cry from Aberdeen Harbor, though, in Hong Kong where you can almost walk on the water there's so much offal about. I guess that's why most tourists go there at night.

During the night some dhows had come in from distant islands and had moored alongside us. The crew was squatting around on sacks of dried fish, which spilled out of the open hull. They were cooking breakfast on a charcoal stove. The smell of sundried fish was overpowering. It smelled like a thousand dirty dogs just coming out of the rain. By the time we left Male, though, we didn't even notice the smell anymore. It's just everywhere. On the shore, near the landing, were large single story warehouses, every one packed sack upon sack with this foul smelling stuff. It's the only export from the Maldives going to India and the gulf states, and before the tourists arrived, it must have been the only way to get hard cash. It's not bad to eat after you get used to it. You tear a strip off and dunk it into hot tea, and if your teeth are up to it, it's a good nutritional snack. No match on chocolate and biscuits when you've got the munchies, but it suits a sailor's life.

After our breakfast, which was the last of the rotting bananas--it was too hot below to cook anything--we got the aluminum dinghy overboard and headed ashore to check out immigration. The town itself, seen from the water, looked like an ancient Baghdad in miniature. Flat-roofed, whitewashed houses with the golden dome of the matchbox size Sultan's Palace poking up behind. Over to the right, more out of town than in, was the minaret of the mosque. The predominant color of adornment along the windows and doorways was a light blue which gave a cool, refreshing feeling to the place. But, that's all it was, just a look of coolness, because it was hot—so hot you couldn't even sweat, just a slight moistening of the eyelids. It would have been nice to go native and walk barefoot along the sandy roads of the town. That was going to take some conditioning, though. Our feet were still too civilized for this rough, hot roadwork. We hadn't been given a time to go to immigration, so we thought we'd check out the engine shops along the waterfront first. That was an easy one. There was only one. As mechanic shops go, it was by far the cleanest I had ever seen. In fact, there was nothing inside the place to give away what kind of shop it was. A few posters for Yama outboards stuck on the wall, and that was it. We weren't feeling too hopeful when Mr. Muhammed Aquine, the owner, came out from the back room to answer our call. How were we going to get anything done here? I was beginning to think the whole point of coming to the Maldives was futile. They might be able to repair a broken fuel line but a broken connecting rod, I doubted. He didn't seem surprised to see us. He had us all sit down along a large wooden office desk and had someone bring in lemonade. Then, he told us the name of our boat, the date of departure from Malaya, and all the symptoms of our engine failure.

For one frightening minute, I thought the game was up. I thought the Aussie Coast Guards had surveilled us somehow, and I expected armed men to charge in through the back door and arrest us. But, then, if he knew all about us why didn't those guys yesterday know it, too? The Aussies wouldn't ask an engine mechanic to arrest us when there were other guys around with guns who could probably do it better. The answer is that there are some people, not too many, its true, but a few who could be called super efficient, and one of them works for the Perkins outlet in Singapore. When Jack had managed to contact his wife on the radio, he had let her know what had happened and asked her to contact the dealers in Singapore, which she did. I can't remember the guy's name, but if I could, I'd put him down as my choice for Man of the Year. When he knew we'd probably end up in the Maldives, he had contacted the only company here capable of doing major repairs and had them ready for us, and not only that, everything was to be covered by the guarantee. Things were not looking too bad after all, although we would certainly be here when the monsoons arrived. That would be okay. We could take off on a starboard reach to get as far south as possible before we caught the southeast trades and then tack down through the Roaring Forties. The only problem was that it looked like we would be stuck here for maybe a month if we had to get a new crankshaft sent up from Singapore. The mechanic here thought that was very likely. And then, what about our million dollar's worth of tires buried in their shallow grave? How would they handle it if the monsoon came with heavy storms and high seas? These islands are very fragile and they can disappear overnight in a good blow.

I was also worried about Chantal back in Japan with our little boy, Radja, and her visa about to expire. Then, I had an idea. Why don't we get our women to come out here? Then, they can come with us to Aussie and be part of the subterfuge. Good cover story: The last family voyage together before taking off to the frigid waters of Antarctica. We'd think about that for a day. There was a cable and wireless office just back from the waterfront, and we were going to call later that day. We still had to get to immigration and get clearance to be in the Maldives, so we arranged for the mechanics to come out to the boat, later, after lunch. We went off to find the man with the rubber stamps.

Almost everybody in the Maldives gets along fine working indoors with an electric fan, but if you're government, you have to have air conditioning in your office. In a town with no five star restaurants and no roads for your Mercedes, having an air conditioner is one symbol of your elevated position.

What is it that makes customs and immigration people all over the world indistinguishable from one another? Is it some slight similarity in the genetic code they all share or is it because they have a job where they can control people without the threat of violence to themselves? It's a lot less stressful than being a policeman, for example. It was like I'd met the man behind the desk a thousand times in other countries, and the minute he asked for our clearance papers from Malaya, I knew we weren't going to get our passports stamped that easily. We explained over and over that they stamped our passports out from Port Kelang in Malaya. They didn't give us any clearance paper, we told him, but he wasn't having that. He put his foot down right at the beginning, and official pride wouldn't let him change his mind. He was adamant. No paper, no stamp. We weren't really worried about this. It's international law that we can enter for repairs and stay until they are completed. He couldn't make us leave, but at the same time, we didn't want any hard feelings that might make him vindictive, then maybe suspicious, and then who knows what he'd do. He could make it difficult to get our women over, too, if that's what we decided we wanted. We definitely would not be free to go to the tourist islands. There was one island I could see from the harbor, about fifty minutes away by Zodiac, where I hoped to go for a cold beer and a pork chop.

He was sure we must have the clearance papers somewhere. We must have misplaced them among our other documents, he said, so we promised to go and have a thorough search. When we got back to the boat, the dhow that had been anchored along beside us was now unloading against the harbor wall so we could search around free from the horrible stench, but there wasn't much to search.

The boat had only made three port calls since leaving Aussie — Singapore, Malaya, and India, and the only clearance papers were from Singapore. It would have been difficult to doctor that document. It was all in English, with SINGAPORE written large across the top, and all the dates and places were typed in. We had intended to go back later and say, "No, we couldn't find it," and hope that he would relent. It was Andy who found the Malaysian express bus ticket. As bus tickets go, it was a beauty. It was the size of a sheet of B5 paper, all written in Malay and had no drawings of a bus with wings, thank God. The only word that made any sense was the name, MALAYA, written large across the top. It was worth a try. If we wrote the name of the boat on that line on the bottom and a flourish of a signature off to the side, it would surely pass. We wouldn't have to say this is it. We could say *maybe* this is it. That way it would be the immigration man's decision.

We got back to the office just before he left for lunch, so that probably helped. You can't keep a Maldivian from his two-hour siesta. He took it with hardly a glance and with an air of, "I told you I was right." He covered it with a rubber stamp so big it almost covered the whole sheet and effectively disguised it beyond recognition. Even the Malayan bus company would have been hard-pressed to recognize it. With an equally big stamp in our passports, we were free to remain and travel, unhindered, for ninety days.

Just before letting us go, though, he felt obliged to point out a notice pinned to the wall. This had obviously more to do with customs than immigration, but it seemed like they were both in the same office. Maybe that's why the guys in the boat had no insignia on their jackets. They couldn't decide which branch of government they belonged to. Starting at the top of the notice, it ticked off the things you couldn't bring in. Alcohol was prohibited, along with pork products and arms of any sort. Then, strictly prohibited was anything coming from Israel. At the bottom, written in larger letters than the rest, was "Most Strictly Prohibited: Pornography." In fact, that was the only injunction the immigration man voiced aloud. No pornography. So, where for the three guys in uniform, pork was the greatest evil, for this man, it seemed that pornography was the voice of the devil. I couldn't understand the reason behind no pornography. Sex—that's all they have in the Maldives for entertainment. It's all they talk about. What did the government think the people did at night? Sit on the beach and count their toes? All right, drugs and alcohol maybe could cause a bit of strife, but pornography?

When I was here before in the cholera scare, before we got too freaked out to visit people at all, there was one island we stopped at where we were invited to a festival. By the light of the moon and a few hurricane lamps, we sat in the sand and watched the most sensual and erotic dancing. Ten young women, aged twelve to fifteen, dressed in fine white linen that clung where it shouldn't, whirled and swayed. They held aluminum pots and kettles under one arm and beat the time with their fingers. That imagery doesn't do anything to convey the reality, but I tell you, if you had put Janet Jackson or Madonna in that line up, they would have looked like a couple of nuns at a Vicar's garden party. When we were told their ages, I thought it a bit young to be dancing like that. Then we learned that most of them were married. And, out of the fifteen-year-olds, most of those were divorced and wearing out their second husbands. Don't think this is a second Bangkok. It's all kept strictly in the family here. These are lovely looking people, the Maldivian's. The men are all fine-featured and well-built, and the women are all slim and beautiful in face. On a diet of coconut and fish, though, you can't expect them to last too long. They have to start early or miss all the fun. I did hear that the life expectancy on the islands as a whole was just over sixty. That's including the capital, Male, where they have a much better choice of diet, with imported fruits and such.

We assured the immigration man we had none of these evil items onboard except a couple of bottles of rum, which yesterday's boarding party had sealed up with a couple of bands of lead, not to be broken until cleared outward bound for foreign parts.

You can probably do without alcohol in Male Town, but you can't do without sunglasses. My eyes were already feeling prickly and smarting, like having a welder's flash. Everything is so white and glaring. The buildings are all whitewashed and the roads between them fine with sand. The sun just bounces off everything and stabs you in the eyes from every angle. I'd lost my last pair overboard somewhere between Sumatra and Sri Lanka so I was going to get me a pair. Not an easy thing to find in Male. The natives don't need them. They all have fine black eyes not troubled by the sun. I found a pair at last in a little shop selling shark teeth--not just the teeth, the whole jaws, most of them from small reef sharks but a couple from tiger sharks that are big enough to throw the family dog inside. That must be a new industry, too, fueled by the tourist trade. I couldn't imagine a Maldivian wanting to hang a set of shark teeth up on his living room wall.

Just across the narrow lane from this display of dental ferocity was a little tea shop, which it turned out made the best samosa this side of Mombasa and became a hangout for our stay on the island. We could stay in here and watch the few passing tourists on leave from the resort as they prowled around, looking for local treasures to loot. There were a few cars running around on the two miles of highway on the island, but they didn't look quite as out of place as these tourists from the north countries walking around half undressed with layers of soft pink flesh bulging out from around the straps and chords that kept their flimsy clothes from falling down. They looked like nothing less than a walking slab of uncooked bacon.

I remember one time just having spent three months in the Red Sea, in Arab countries, where the most flesh you ever get to see are the hands and faces, and sometimes, the bare feet. I had left Port Said and was sailing along the south coast of Crete when I thought I'd just drop in to get some more fuel, there not being much wind about. Not wanting to go through the hassle of immigration and the official entry procedure,

I chose a small harbor where it would be easy to pop in and out without anybody knowing. This is what I did, and tying up the boat in the little harbor, I took a walk into the town, thinking I may as well buy some provisions at the same time. At the end of a small street, there was a little supermarket, which I entered. What a shock! It was almost like a physical blow. The place was packed with almost naked European tourists. There was one tall blonde guy walking towards me, with only a jock strap no bigger than a shoelace on. Fat pink arses and drooping tits all over the place. No way I was going to buy my packet of sausages with some guys pubic hairs not two feet a way. Why do they do it? I'm not into putting people into burkhas, but at least when they go shopping, they might have the decency to get dressed properly. No wonder the Arab and Muslim worlds are shocked at how we carry on.

A lot of these tropical islands and places around the world, and especially in the Pacific, were really spooked out by the European missionaries in the nineteenth century, forced to wear dresses and trousers; discouraged from having sex in anything but the church's sanctified position; and generally stopped from whooping it up except for on Sundays, when they could let rip with a lung crushing "Onward Christian Soldiers." Now, they've got the great grandchildren of these people coming back to tell them they've got it all wrong, and its okay to walk around mostly undressed and do it with who you want and in which way you want, and God doesn't mind you getting drunk and dancing like a fool. These islanders must think the Europeans have found a new god. But, they haven't. It's just another manifestation of his schizophrenia. Anyway, they don't have to worry about another reversal in their way of life. In another few generations, there won't be any islands left to have a life on. European inventions will have brought them the final indignity as their coral islands slowly sink under the weight of industrial smog.

Before that happened, we had to retrieve our buried treasure from its fragile hiding place, and to do that, we needed our engine repaired. When we got back to the boat this time, after being cleared to stay, the mechanics were already there, tied up alongside in their sturdy little open-decked work boat. We had kind of hoped the problem wouldn't be too bad and could be mended in situ, but they soon declared it had to come out and be taken into shop. As the depth of the water alongside the wall was only about four feet, we would have to haul it out using our boom as a davit. It probably didn't weigh more than half a ton, but the halyards and backstays weren't really designed for this type of lifting, and it was a bit of a nail-biter as she was pulled up through the hatchway and swung out overboard to be lowered to the workboat.

Finally, in the workshop and stripped down, the findings could not be worse. It was a busted connecting rod and the whole crank shaft would have to be changed, which meant ordering one from Singapore and getting it sent out, hopefully by air, but even so, it looked like a long wait. This model of Perkins engine is made for tractors and agricultural machinery, as well as for boats. When it is altered to make suitable for use in a boat, the oil sump is changed for a deeper one so the amount of oil is increased. When they had done this at the dealers in Singapore, they hadn't changed to a longer dip stick or to a longer pipe on the oil change pump. After every oil change, quite a large amount of oil was left at the bottom of the sump, and in time, it took on the viscosity of syrup, which was too much for the crank shaft to paddle through and so broke the connecting rod. This meant ordering a whole bunch of parts from Singapore. We'd have to have new piston rings, too, as well as a crankshaft, so it looked like we were going to be here for a long time.

I didn't really want to spend that much time here. The Maldives are beautiful islands to while away a short holiday, but I didn't want a holiday. I wanted to get back to Japan and get on with my boat. I didn't really want to bring Chantal and little Radja out, either. That would mean that there would be nobody in Japan to look after my boat, at least nobody with a real interest in her. There was a friend looking in every now and then to check the shoring and make sure the covers were in place, but still I worried about her. That her is the boat, not Chantal. Chantal would have to leave anyway to renew her visa, so she may as well come here. Jack, then, wanted to have his wife out, too. Andy, with the wisdom of youth, thought it all a bad idea. And, afterwards, when it was too late, I agreed with him.

Chapter
12

e wanted more money. Staying in the Maldives for a month, provisioning the boat again for the trip to Aussie, plus bringing the families out, would entail more expenses. We were going to ask for another $10,000 from our sponsors, and if they refused, we could always threaten to leave their goods buried for them to pick up.

Western Australia is three hours behind the Maldives so we figured to telephone at about five in the afternoon to catch Jack's wife at home. It's more efficient and a better line from the Maldives than from India, but actually getting your hands on the telephone is a little more difficult. The cable and wireless offices were in a small compound surrounded by high walls and a huge steel gate. Was that to protect the radio antennas from an insurgent mob? To keep control of what information goes in or out? It's strange, but during that cholera scare of a short while back, there wasn't a bit about it on the radio, even though we could see the funeral pyres burning the bodies on the outer islands.

A guard did let us in after we rang a bell at the gate and led us into a hall surrounded by one man telephone booths. After filling in the forms with all kinds of irrelevant information, one of us was allowed into the box to take the call. Jack, of course, as it was his wife who was going to do all the work at their end. We couldn't be sure how much of all this was being listened to, but he got his message across, and she'd contact the Sydney syndicate. If they agreed to the money, she'd sort out Chantal's ticket and get everybody over. I didn't want Chantal getting the cash for the ticket. No knowing where she'd end up. Jack's wife had already been contacted by the Sydney boys, it seemed. They wanted to know what was happening and to pass on some ominous news.

The airline steward, after leaving us in Cochin, had gone back to Bombay to take up his duties on a flight to Sydney via Hong Kong. It looked like he had tried to make himself some pocket money and had stashed a kilo of our hash into his flight bag. He was caught in Hong Kong and given three years in prison. That news really put a damper on things. Here was someone involved in our scam actually doing prison time. Was the whole deal falling apart? Nothing really seemed to be going right. Here we were stuck in an oven of an island in the middle of the Indian Ocean with very little money, our salvation from penury lying uncharted beneath two feet of unstable sand, and the prospect of an ocean voyage crossing Bass Straits in the middle of the southern winter. I didn't believe it then, and I still don't believe now that man controls his fate. So, we just have to let things happen as they must. I couldn't back out now even if I had wanted to. I didn't have the financial freedom, and anyway, we were still a team in this together, although that sentiment was to undergo some modifications.

What to do for the next few weeks? I spent one day watching three men digging a well, although it actually took them all the time I was there to get down to the brackish water thirty foot below the sand. They first built a circle of coral blocks about six feet in diameter cemented together with a mixture of lime made from crushed coral. They built this on top of the sand, and when this was all set hard, they scooped out the sand under the whole circle until it dropped down to ground level again. Then they built another circle on top and scooped out the sand again, the whole cylinder sinking slowly down. I was sure it wasn't going to work, but of course it did. The last day there was one guy right at the bottom digging out the now water sodden sand from under the original circle and making the thirty-foot shaft sink to its final depth. After all that, I don't think they were very happy with the water. I think they had built it too near the sea.

Most of my spare time, though, I used to watch the boat builder. The sailing dhows of the Maldives are the most beautiful boats anywhere in the world. They have something of a Viking long boat look, although they are planked rather than lapstraked. They have lovely, deep, sweeping shear lines and are double-ended and broad-beamed, just like the Viking ships. With the lateen sails set on the long booms, they're very efficient sailing boats that can tack closer to the wind than we could. The Vikings were formidable sailors as it was. If they had had the lateen sails instead of that square bedspread they used to set, where couldn't they have gone? These island boats are all made entirely from coconut wood, except for some of the frames which are made from a hardwood imported from India. They have no written plans, no line drawings, for the building process. Using just a piece of string and an axe, they can craft a piece of art like you've never seen. Starting from the keel and stern post, which are fashioned from the heart of a coconut tree that has been felled and let dry for two years, they then build up a few feet of the rib frames, plank it all up, and then build up more frames, framing and planking at the same time, unlike in the west where a boat is fully framed first and then planked. You wouldn't think a coconut tree would be very good for anything, but when cut down and properly dried, it's a perfectly good wood for all kinds of uses. It looks like Honduran mahogany except the grain is rougher. It planes well and takes a varnish, but they say a boat made from it will only last twenty years. Well, that's almost a lifetime here. I would sit and watch for hours these dhows as they crossed the horizon. There was always one in view somewhere transitting the atolls. On days with no wind, they'd just sit there all day making a picturesque backdrop for the tourist brochures. Their cargo would almost certainly be coconuts. If there were no coconut trees, there would be no people here. I'm surprised they don't worship a god of coconuts. They should have great big images of coconuts and sacrifice tourists to them. Because, if the coconut goes, so do they.

People say there are more uses for the coconut than days in a year. You get copra, which is a dried meat of the nut, to make vegetable oil to cook your food in and slick back your hair with. You can make toddy and arrack and sugary syrup, eat the young shoots as a vegetable, weave the leaves into baskets and mats, and thatch your hut from the husks. You get choir to make rope or stuff your mattresses and pillows with. Slithers of dried husks make toothbrushes and pan scrubs and make a great, slow burning firewood. It would be a pretty tough existence without the coconut tree here. It not only does a good job of filling your belly and quenching your thirst but caters to the higher senses too. There's nothing like the rustling of palm leaves in a gentle trade wind to drift you off to sleep, and you'd have to look hard to find anything as romantic as palm leaves shimmering in the full moonlight.

I knew it hadn't been a good idea as soon as Chantal came through the customs gate. Andy and I had taken the Zodiac over to the airport and tied up at the ferry jetty. That was before they blasted anoth-

er island and leveled another whole bunch of reef to make the airport runway long enough to bring in the northern hordes direct from Frankfurt and
London. At that time, everyone arrived from Sri Lanka.

She's a speedy woman, Chantal. What do you expect? She's
French. She bubbled energy out like water through a hose. I could forgive
her, of course. I knew how she must feel being set free from Japan where
she couldn't communicate very well and winter was still trailing its ragged
edges. Now, suddenly, her world was all sunshine and light. She came
through the barrier talking and gesticulating to everybody in sight, dragging
little Radja behind. She looked good, though. Maybe too good. I'd have
to see about changing her image. It's okay if you're going straight to the
tourist resorts, but life in the mainstream meant thinking about how the
locals saw you.

Poor Andy. He had never met anything like this before, and he had
a headache before we were even outside to where the Zodiac was tied up.
She just didn't stop talking, and I knew then that she wasn't going to sail to
Aussie with us. Jack's wife arrived a few days later and brought things
under control a bit, but the boat was getting a little cramped now with five
adults and a little baby aboard. Chantal and I got to camp out in the fore-
peak with Jack and Lynn in the back cabin. Andy slept on deck. It wasn't
a bad arrangement but wouldn't have done for a major ocean crossing even
if we had all been on the same wavelength, which we weren't. In fact, sometimes we weren't even on the same radio. Chantal was just too French for
everybody. Aussies are very provincial and having this sexy European
woman around who wasn't impressed with their macho posturing and
wanted her say in everything was all too much for them to take. So, after
three weeks of fractious living, we came to a consensus. The women would
go ahead to Australia and wait in Perth. I was quite happy with that. Not
that I wanted to get rid of Chantal. We were not having any friction ourselves, but I was getting worried about my little boy. I don't know why. I
don't know if they even have the disease in the Maldives, but I couldn't get
over the anxiety that he could contract leprosy. I'd heard a report on the
BBC world service about the drug, dapsone. They reckoned the disease was
growing resistant to it, and that leprosy was on the increase. There he was
walking around with his head not two feet above the dirt roads, breathing
in all the dust that had accumulated for centuries. We had already taken

him to see a doctor about an eye infection, and I didn't want his nose dropping off from leprosy in the future.

We were getting toward the end of May, now, and the monsoon still hadn't arrived. There had been one night of a fierce squall that had dumped tons of water on the deck. We managed to channel that along the scuppers into the deck caps to fill up the tanks, but that had all gone, and it hadn't rained since. Five people living in harbor take up a lot of water with showers, cooking and washing clothes. When we didn't have any rainwater, we were getting water from the local mosque, the lovely little whitewashed building with a not very high minaret surrounded by a low white wall with bougainvilleas and a large shade tree in the garden. It was one of the most pleasant places in the whole of the town. There was a deep well in the garden, and as it was in the middle of the island, the water wasn't too bad. I wouldn't call the water sweet, but it wasn't brackish. It tasted like the water you buy for car batteries and left your tongue feeling dry. But, it was cheaper than bottled water, which was selling at $10 a pop. The muezzin, the guy in charge who climbs up the tower and chants the morning prayers, was a great guy. He had the red hair and beard of a pilgrim who had been to Mecca and the gentle manners of a true believer. It was him we asked if we could use the well, and he didn't seem put out by a bunch of infidels taking his God-given rain, although he preferred we leave the women at the gate. I don't think he, himself, thought they might pollute the well, but the people coming to pray might. Most of the islanders didn't seem to mind the abuses to their culture when it was out of sight on the other islands but not in the heart of their capital. It was a slow job filling up a twenty-liter jerry can. The well was quite deep, about thirty feet. There's quite a technique to dropping a bucket down so it ends up with the mouth of the bucket hitting the water, flipping over and filling up. The muezzin even lent us a wheelbarrow to ferry the jerry cans from the wharf.

The parts arrived from Singapore. The engine was ready for putting back, so it looked like we could be out of the place by the end of May. Even though the monsoon hadn't started yet, we could get going under power. So, the women decided to go off to Sri Lanka, where they'd have to wait while Chantal got a visa for Australia. We probably would have set sail long before they arrived in Perth, but we could contact them on the radio. It was about this time that we'd been thinking of a Plan B. Dropping the stuff off on Wilson's Promontory on the south coast of New South Wales still seemed the best bet, but just in case something went wrong, we thought it might be possible to approach the coast just north of Cape Leeuwen, although it would be a lot more tricky. There were no sheltered coves on this stretch of coast, and in winter lots of cold fronts passing through. Nasty little northerly squalls. Going across the Great Australian Bight would be even stormier, but there would be good shelter when we got there. One advantage of going to western Australia, though, is that we would have Jack's wife there who could possibly come down to the beach and could whisk the stuff away by car. For that, we'd need some good weather; a nice calm night when we could use the Zodiac to get the goods to shore. And, we'd need some way to be in contact.

We didn't have any VHF or walkie-talkies onboard, but there was some kind of boom going on just at that time in the Maldives, and everybody was wanting to have one of these hand held radios. I think the maximum range for these was only about ten miles, but that was good enough to let your wife know you were coming and give her time to get rid of the neighbor. There were lots of shops selling electronics in the islands; more electronic than food shops. Lots of Indians were coming over by plane and bringing their families, supposedly on holiday, but loaded up with electrical things bought duty free in the home country. They got off the plane with suitcases filled with radios and VCRs and lugging televisions and even washing machines for a holiday in the sun. They were making huge profits and bringing very doubtful benefits to the people. Did they ever think how much water these washing machines would waste? And, what were people doing buying TV sets? There wasn't even a TV station on the island. The VCR, of course, was bringing Hollywood to the place. There was no cinema, but for a few pennies you could sit in someone's living room and watch the sex and violence. Every second house, it seemed, was moonlighting as a movie theater.

We could buy a decent pair of hand held radios. One for Lynn and one for the boat. We thought if we did go for Plan B, we could get Lynn on the ham radio first and set up a time to use the walkie-talkies. It all sounded a bit vague to me, and anyway, I didn't like the idea of radios at all. It's too easy for people to eavesdrop.

There wasn't any need now for Lynn and Chantal to stay anymore. We wanted to get the boat ready for the long haul to Aussie. So, we took them both over to the airport in the Zodiac and off they flew to Sri Lanka to connect up to a flight to Perth. Chantal was off the boat, but a long way from being out of the story.

We thought the trip to Australia should take a month, but we gave ourselves six weeks, because it would all depend on what kind of winds we found. The monsoon still hadn't arrived, but there was a lot more cloud cover now and even a few, short squalls so it couldn't be that long in coming. The engine was coached back in place on the boat, and it fired up the first time. There was a little worrisome leak of diesel fuel from somewhere around the fuel pump, but it didn't look too serious.

Stocking the boat up with food was a little more of a problem. There were lots of imported dry goods from South Africa, most of it sort of luxury food like shortbread biscuits and tin butter. We found some corn beef and huge cans of Jacob's Cream Crackers. Vegetables were not easy to get, but we found lots of small red onions and South African apples. We also acquired some hard, semi-polished rice and a few bags of flour for bread. It wasn't like we were off on a summer cruise, so we didn't care too much about what we couldn't get. All of us were smokers at that time, but decided it would be a good chance to quit, so we bought no cigarettes. It looked like we were ready to go. Food stocked, water tanks full, fuel tanks topped off, and rigging checked.

All we needed was to give the hull a scrape under the water and knock off some of the barnacles. I didn't fancy doing this in the harbor. Although the water looked clear enough, we'd been flushing our toilet for a month now, and God knows what the other boats had been doing. We decided to move out and anchor in the channel for a day or two. We had to do this anyway because we could only get out in spring tide when there was enough water under the keel. We went out on a full moon and anchored further up the channel in line with the mosque where the depth of the water was not so great, but it was still forty feet. We spent the day scraping the bottom and knocking the skin off our hands and knees. Diving down under a boat, trying to hold on with one hand and operating a scraper with the other is the hardest job I know. It's not too bad with an air tank, but we had only one aboard, and that soon ran out. With the strong current to fight against, too, it was a slow, exhausting job. There wasn't a slipway on the island that could haul us out. We couldn't get near enough because of our six-foot draft. The local dhows only draw four feet and there was no beach suitable or tide high enough to beach her, so we had to do it the hard way. We had to do it because the bottom was really dirty and would have knocked at least a knot off our speed, if not two. I hate barnacle cuts. They smart like hell and take ages to heal. Finally, it was time to go, eight weeks after leaving Cochin and four weeks after arriving in the Maldives. We were two months behind schedule and heading for a coast of winter storms. We went to clear immigration and bid a final farewell to the engine shop. They had been really good to us.

Trust the immigration man to spoil everything. This time it just had to be bloody mindedness. It just didn't make any sense at all. He wanted us all to have cholera shots. Why now when we were leaving? Cholera inoculations take ten days to be effective. So who did he think he was protecting? The women hadn't been asked to get shots when they left or when they arrived. "No, we don't want cholera shots." We told him. I didn't want someone sticking a needle in me just before I left for sea for a month or more. I'd had one years ago, and I remember it knocked me down for days. But, just like when we had arrived, he was insistent. No shot, no clearance. "Right, we'll go back to the boat," we said, "and think about it and come back later." Back at the boat, it was still only ten o'clock in the morning. If we left now, we could be at Five Tree Island just before the sunset. We were sure the man wouldn't have known we left before we cleared the islands, and even if he knew which way we were going, he couldn't do too much about it. Let him keep his stamp. We were only pandering to his officious vanity when asking for clearance in the first place. We did know there was a light surveillance plane that did a daily run around the atolls, but that was more for checking up on boats in distress like dhows adrift without engines or people marooned on waterless islands. I was sure they wouldn't strafe us just for fleeing a cholera shot, but then again, there's nothing like the wrath of an immigration man.

We started pulling the chain up hand over hand, expecting at any moment to be hailed from the shore. It was hard going, we were pulling it up link by link, and it was getting heavier rather than lighter. We put the chain up on a mechanical winch, and using the hand lever, pumped away until eventually—eventually—we pulled up the anchor. Caught in the flute was a thick, black cable as thick as a wrist that seemed to snake away toward the airport island. We decided we better not cut it free or we might shut down the place. Now we knew why we'd stayed in place all this time without the boat dragging. We couldn't have gone anywhere without taking the runway with us. By the time we got that free and let it fall back to the ocean floor, we were in danger of not having enough time to reach our island by nightfall. That could be disastrous, hanging around at night in waters full of coral heads and strong currents. We had already burned our boat, so to speak. If we decided to drop our pick and wait until the next day, then we'd have to go through all that with the immigration man again.

We still had seven hours of daylight left, although the last few hours would not be very good for spotting coral lying just under the water. The low angle of the sun would make the surface dark and all one shade. The sun would also be right in our eyes as we would be coming in from the east. Still, to go and collect a million dollars was worth a small risk. So, we hoisted up the main, and keeping our heads low, just in case the immigration man was about—didn't want to catch his eyes—we glided out of the channel, rounded the corner of Male Island and set a course to the south. We were going to keep all the islands of Male Atoll on our starboard until we arrived at Five Tree Island.

We never thought our goods wouldn't still be there. It had been a month now since we had buried the hash, and apart from that one fierce squall, the weather had been hot and fine all the time. Whenever we talked about our stash it was to worry about whether any sea water had seeped through the patches and maybe ruined the stuff. We never thought anyone would have dug it up. But, now, when we were finally on our way to pick it up, we couldn't help thinking that someone had accidentally stumbled across it and let the authorities know, who were now waiting in hiding to see who would come and claim it. Maybe they were lying and waiting on the island we had noticed just to the west of our island, the one with the low-lying white building on it. I could just see that. They'd wait until we started digging then scream across in their high-powered Zodiacs to catch us red handed. I hadn't seen any official looking Zodiacs but you can't take chances with a government that feeds its tourists pork and lobsters while not letting on that its own people are croaking from cholera. The people are lovely, but the government is pretty devious. They're definitely into control, so I'm sure they had something better than heavy, wooden dhows to zip around in. Once we had cleared the island of Male, we got the genoa up and were on a run. The wind from the north was still quite light but good enough to give us six or seven knots. We thought we might have to use the engine, but it wouldn't have helped much. We wouldn't have gone any faster, so we left it off.

We were still a bit worried about the old iron donkey. When we ran it in the morning to clear the channel, it was still leaking fuel from somewhere around the fuel pump. We'd have to check all the nuts and bolts sometime. But, not now. It was too glorious to be on deck with a fair wind, smooth seas, blue sky, and the prospect of adventure. If only I had had a pack of tobacco to roll a cigarette, I would have been near to heaven. Giving up the nicotine was getting to be the hardest part of this trip. Maybe we should have gone into it slowly. Taken at least one pack to get us through the first few days. Another thing about stopping smoking, in just two hours since we'd left Male, we'd already munched our way through half a dozen apples and a box of raisins. With the three of us going cold turkey at the same time, we'd end up chewing our shoes. It's not like we had that much food aboard. We caught a beautiful dorado in the early afternoon and were keeping it to fry in butter when we arrived, but the prospect of a good fish dinner isn't really so good when there's no tobacco with coffee to follow it.

I wanted a box full of fancy biscuits and a fistful of sugar. Jack still had some of his Indian beedies left, but that was like smoking a soft drink straw and actually made the craving worse. A smoker will try anything to quiet the urge. By four o'clock that afternoon, we had the large island where we had first made landfall in the Maldives on our beam to starboard, so we still had a few hours of light left to find the island with the five palm trees on it. We could see lots of little islands opening up to the south, but none of them looked like ours. We were starting to panic. There was no reason it shouldn't still be there, but we hadn't taken any sights to determine exactly where the island was. Although we had looked at lots of charts borrowed from the fishermen in Male, we had no idea where it really was but had a clue that it was south of the long island, whose name we couldn't ever determine from the charts because everywhere had looked the same.

I suppose now with GPS to help in surveying and determining the position of the hundreds of islands that most of them are put down in their right places, but the charts the local fishermen used, when they used them, were way out of date and full of corrections like, "This island was reported by HMS Bennett in 1958 to lie fifteen minutes north of its charted position," or even, "this island was reported to have disappeared in 1967." We were thinking we might have to heave to and wait for the morning's first light. That wouldn't have been a problem, really. The weather was still playing along with us. We hoped it would change as soon as we collected our cargo and blow like hell from the southwest to get us across the ocean. Then, we could pick up the southeasterlies, which we hoped to ride down to the Roaring Forties. The only problem was that there were no lights on any of the islands, so we couldn't judge the strength of the currents. Our only point of reference was the large island, which was already getting out of sight to the north of us. If we did heave to, the first thing we would have to do in the morning was to find it again to give us some kind of starting point.

There was another anxious moment when a small, twin engine airplane flew over going south. I couldn't imagine that they'd send an airplane to look for us just because we'd refused a cholera shot. But, when governments are using taxpayers' money they can waste it on all kinds of fun things to do.

We could see an island with three trees, another with one—that was a pathetic one—and finally, just when we had about given up for the day, there it was. What a beautiful sight. Five tall palm trees in a perfect formation. And no mistaking it for there was that other island off to the east with the low, white building.

There was a beautiful sunset behind the Five Palm Island to welcome us back. Perfect! We could recover the tires under cover of dark, rest up under anchor until dawn and be off before anyone knew. It had been a month since we had been here and buried our hash under the coral sand. Nothing seemed to have changed. The island looked the same height. The beach looked the same width, so no major storm had come to turn it all around. We didn't even wait to put the dinghy in the water. As soon as the anchor was down and biting, we dove in and swam the short distance ashore. There was one rude shock. Halfway up from the water's edge to the place marked "X," there were the remains of a fire. So somebody had been here. No way to tell how long ago from the charred sticks and coconut husks. It could have been yesterday or two weeks ago. Maybe a Cherokee could have told you, but it wasn't important. The people who had lit the fire weren't here now, and the sand over our stash looked undisturbed. It must have been some fishermen cooking their lunch, but it was upsetting to think our island had been violated. Just think if they had found that hash. They could have retired all the fishermen on the Maldives on the profit from selling it to the tourists.

We scooped the sand away with our hands, attacking it like a bunch of dogs, until we determined it was still all there. Then we went back for the dinghy and more calmly began to ferry it back to the boat. When all eight tires were stacked on the deck, the sand washed off, we checked for any seawater seepage. One tire had a patch that had come unglued at the edge, and it looked like some water had got in. I guess at spring tide, when the water is highest, the sea must have filtered through to the level of the tires. Jack and Andy weren't upset about this. It was a good excuse to open up the tire and assess the damage, and, of course, have a little smoke to make sure the goods were okay.

I didn't want to go through that again, having two stoned out shipmates, but I could see the logic, and I was interested to know if the hash was still good. After knocking off a couple of little pipes of it, they reckoned it was probably even better than before, but that was maybe because they hadn't smoked any in a month. Anyway, it was all going to have to be dried out on deck again when we had the chance, and that idea I didn't like at all. The breeze that had been blowing all day had died out during the night but was back again with the sun in the morning and still from the north.

This was getting to be serious. We were at the end of May and the southwesterlies should have been here by now. This northerly wasn't bad for us, though. All we wanted to do was to get to the latitude of south Australia where we could pick up the westerlies that always blow down there. According to all the weather charts and the experience of centuries of sea farers, the way from here to there at this time of year was to follow a long, reversed figure Z, going east and south with the south monsoons, to pick up the southeast trades on the east side of the Indian Ocean; then, on a port tack, hard on the wind, on a reach down to forty degrees south, where the westerlies should drive you east again. We decided to get as far south as this little breeze would take us. If we got stuck in the doldrums, we could motor through them.

Never include engines when discussing a routing plan. We hadn't run the donk since Male and we didn't need to now as we pulled up the anchor to leave. We had the main up and hoisted the genoa to fall off on a run with a clear passage to the south of us. Two hours later we had crossed the channel between the two atolls, and the first island of the Felidu Atoll came into view. We thought of making our departure from here and head out to sea, giving the rest of the Maldives a wide berth. We could make out a building on this island, so obviously it was inhabited, and Jack had just discovered that he had about ten dollars of Maldivian money left. Maybe there was a store on the island. Maybe we could buy some cigarettes. Just a couple of packs to help us over the first few days. I don't think any of us were looking forward to weeks at sea without the nicotine. It's not just the nicotine drug you're on, but cigarettes can divide up the day on a long passage. Dividing it up into so many cigarette intervals makes it seem less long. Some days at sea, especially when you're not going anywhere fast, seem to stretch on forever. And a four-hour watch at night can seem like the age of the earth. It's not too bad if you can think that in one more hour you can have a smoke, and then an hour after that, and then another, and another. You get through in quantum bursts rather than one long slog. The last twenty-four hours had been murder, and a little diversion to do some shopping would be a kind of celebration for our successful pick up.

There was a barrier fringing reef all around this atoll, but from the north the passage was wide and deep, and we sailed right up to the beach before dropping anchor and swinging round, bows into the wind and the stern a few yards from the beach. We'd have to tack to get out, but the passage was wide enough, we might even do it in two tacks. There wasn't anyone around. No boat on the beach or bobbing in the water, but then, there wouldn't be. The north end was too open, and any boat would be around the south of the island. The building we had seen was all locked up, but it was probably used for storing copra. The island was thick with coconut trees. It was difficult to tell how big the island was, but it seemed to be quite large, so there must be a village or settlement somewhere.

Two men appeared from the trees but didn't stop. They looked in a hurry and dashed off. That wasn't a very friendly sign. Maybe they'd gone to warn the authorities to call out the militia. We found out soon enough that they'd only gone to get the village chief, at least we'd supposed he was the chief. Anyway, he couldn't have been immigration because he wasn't holding a rubber stamp. He was friendly enough, but we couldn't understand a word he said. This was the first place I had been since leaving Japan on this trip where nobody spoke English. I had just assumed everybody here spoke English. I never gave it a thought that they had their own language here. I looked it up later, and the official language of the Maldives is Dhivehi, which is what they spoke when their ancestors first arrived a thousand years ago. I would have thought that with their intense Islamic culture and their historic ties with Arab seafarers, they would have spoken Arabic. It would have been great to have a chat with him, getting some info on the winds and things like that because whatever else he was, he was definitely a seaman. But, what we really wanted was some tobacco and we didn't need any words for that. Next to the universal sign for "I'm hungry" rubbing your belly with your mouth falling open, there's nothing easier than the sign for "I'm gasping for a cigarette." He was a smoker himself so he grasped the importance and took us to a hut that had been hidden by the trees. It must have been the island store. Either the people didn't have that much money or there weren't that many people on the island. It was a tiny place with only a couple of shelves on one wall that held no more than a dozen tin cans of corned beef, half a dozen bottles of Coca-Cola and one or two packs of water crackers. It looked as forlorn as a Moscow supermarket. We couldn't see any smokes either, but he saved the day when he opened an old picnic icebox. No ice in there, of course, but there was a recently opened carton of Senior Service cigarettes and lots of boxes of matches. I guess they were kept there to keep them dry or maybe to stop the hermit crabs from eating them. We asked to buy six packs, and we felt a little guilty taking almost the entire stock. God knows when they'd get to Male to buy more. As a special treat for Jack we let him buy a Coca Cola with the last of the Maldivian money. If Jack would have walked a mile for a cigarette, he would have walked all the way back for a Coke. He was really hooked to that corrosive stuff, so he was set to go cold turkey on two habits. There was going to be a bunch of grouching on this boat before long, but for the first few days it was the high of a life-time.

You can keep your fame and fortune, this is the life. Sailing free over the ocean, the wind in your hair, the sun on your back. Well, maybe you don't have to forget the fortune. After all, that was what this was all about, but it definitely beats the old nine-to-five. It's just not the sailing, which is good enough, but cocking your nose at authority, doing something illegal. That sounds a bit pathetic, I know. But, when you think about it, how all your life is surrounded by rules and regulations, from getting up to going to bed, it's just one round of "you can't do this," and "you can't do that." "You can't eat crooked bananas," and "Put your seat belt on," and "Don't forget to wash behind your ears." Sometimes you just want to say, "Sod off." But, this is the life. Nearest thing to being a pirate without all the bloodshed and mayhem. Who doesn't dream of the life of a buccaneer? Even the local banker, when he gets his little week-end runabout, the first thing he does is buy a little Jolly Roger flag. He's too embarrassed to fly it from the masthead, but it's there somewhere, stuffed into a drawer and ready to fuel the fantasies after a tot of rum on a Saturday night.

Talking of real pirates, it's strange how all those cutthroats and bandits have been popularized and feted. Even the schoolteacher teaches with pride the coming of the Anglo Saxon pirates, although I think he was wrong about that. I don't think they were pirates, rather just dis-placed people looking for a bit of land to farm. The Vikings. Now, there were a bunch of pirates, if ever there were. They were a horrible bunch of rapists and murderers, cleaving people's heads with double-edge axes, chopping, stabbing, and cutting in a drug frenzy; burning houses; spearing children; and dragging off the hapless survivors into slavery. Because they went over to their killing fields by boat, then all is forgiven, even celebrated. But, the Huns and the Goths and all the other dark tribes of history who went about their raping and pillage on horseback and never got their feet wet, they sort of got left off the Most Popular Historical People list. The ones we think of as real pirates, the ones who ravaged the Spanish Main, weren't that much better than them, but they're up there with Robin Hood and King Arthur in the popular imagination. Even Walt Disney made them look good and turned them into role models for all their brainwashed fans. You only get this adulation if you do it all by boat, under sail. If you try upgrading and start running around in powerboats, then you lose your credibility. It's just not cricket. The pirates of the South China Sea used to be a colorful crop of seamen as blood thirsty as any and just as romanticized. They're still at it, but now they streak around in motorboats and have a reputation no higher than a street mugger. Not every seaman was cut out to be a pirate. For the more squeamish who couldn't stand the sight of blood, but found fishing for a living a bit too much like hard work, there was the honorable trade of blockade running and smuggling. When I was a young boy, stories of smuggling told of a very romantic world. I loved reading stories of sailors who dashed across from France loaded up with tobacco and brandy and chantilly lace, outracing the cutters of the customs men to land their cargos on a dark and stormy night in some lonely cave.

Today, smuggling has become a dirty word. You hear "smuggler" today, and you think of some hapless Caucasian tourist busted at the Bangkok airport for stuffing heroin into a suitcase, or for the ones with a little more imagination, into their bellies. I cringe at the words "drug smuggler." I prefer the word, "contrabandisto." That's how Joseph Conrad described himself when he was smuggling arms around the Catalina coast, and I can't see why we couldn't lay claim to that noble term. Weren't we pundits in the trade? We were keeping all the tenets of the guild. We were crossing the sea under sail to find a deserted cove and put down our cargo on a dark and stormy night. I hoped in our case it wouldn't be too stormy. Contrabandistos we were, and it made me feel better. This kind of euphoria lasted just as long as the pleasant weather and the cigarettes. Three days.

Chapter 14

We had just smoked our last cigarette with our morning coffee when the black clouds that had been moving up from the horizon in the south started to pick up speed. The northerly breeze, which had been with us for so long that we thought it would last forever, was soon pushed back. There was no contesting this southerly wind. It came leaping at us, churning the sea up in its way into short, hissing little whitecaps.

We'd been used to such a peaceful, quiet world for so long, this sudden onslaught was a rude intrusion. We'd put the boat on the other tack as soon as the wind hit, thinking it was just a local squall. We'd left her under genoa and full main, thinking to leave it set like that, blow out all the cobwebs, and have a little rush for half an hour. It was soon obvious, though, that it wasn't going to be a short-lived squall.

The seas were getting rougher and waves were building up like they wouldn't do in a squall. It was time to take in the genoa, clip on the smaller jib, and reef in the main to balance her up again. The waves were already breaking over the bows and were heeling us hard over as we steamed along on the wind on a starboard tack. It's always an anxious moment just before the decision to reef down is made, when the wind has got up so much that the boat is pressed to the limit, and you realize that it is probably going to get worse.

Each time the weather calls for the sails to be reefed, you have to decide how to do it. Every time could be different so there has to be a plan. Should we drop the main and continue with just the headsail? Or, wouldn't it be better if we used just the main, or should we just change the headsail? Should we put in one or two reefs on the main? If we were going to drop the headsail, wouldn't it be better if we put the boat before the wind so the main would blanket the wind from the jib so it would come down easier? Once the plan is set and put in action, then the mayhem of flailing ropes and wildly flapping sails begins, slipping and lurching on a wet deck, clawing down the headsails and trying to stuff them into a sail bag or lash them to the side rails. Then, get out to the end of the bows, with the boat rising and falling into the troughs of the waves, getting dipped into the ocean, like a witch on the end of a dipping pole, to clip on the staysail jib. There was an added danger on Jack's boat, too. To save money on winches the staysail had a block with a two-to-one purchase fastened to the clew. Before the sail was set, and the sheet pulled in, it flailed around like a cat with its tail on fire, right at head height, so I got a black and bloody eye from that before everything was under control.

It's a great feeling, then, though, when the boat is back all snug down again, still on course, everything battened down, and the wind and sea now working with you and not threatening to tear you to pieces. Now you can go below and brew up a cup of tea, have a cigarette, and watch the white caps flash past the portholes. We didn't have any cigarettes anymore, so that moment was ruined. I began to realize that this was going to be one long slog. At least the wind vane was working, keeping us on course, so we didn't have to be on deck steering. This was the first decent little blow we had had on this trip. It didn't get up to a full storm, and in fact, it wouldn't have rated much more than a small craft warning, but it was enough to show up what needed fixing before we hit the real storms of the southern oceans, like leaking hatches and loose deckware. Not to forget the precious cargo, which had been left on deck until now. So, out in the rain again to pass it down below. And, while you're up there, fill up the water tanks with all that delicious, sand-free water. And you'd better unshackle the anchor and haul that down below, too. You wouldn't want that to get loose. It might still be the tropics, but it's cold running around on deck in pelting rain when all you're wearing is a pair of shorts. You may as well take the opportunity, though, and have a wash and do some laundry. There was a good chance you could tempt fate to turn off the rain if you did decide to take a shower. I don't know how many times that has happened. Dashing topside in a squall, getting all lathered up, and then the rain stops, so it's a rinse down with seawater, which leaves you sticky and scratchy. Fate wasn't playing the game today, and a stormy day became a stormy night.

We were well south of the shipping lanes, which skirt the bottom of Sri Lanka. Apart from poking our heads out now and again, there was nothing to do but lie in our bunks and read. Only Jack, in his tiny aft cabin had a light. So when it got dark, Andy and I either went to sleep or lay there left alone with our thoughts. We were on the starboard tack, heeling over to port, so there was no chance of me getting thrown out of bed. My bunk, on the port side had me rolled over, pressed against the hull and I could hear the hissing and grumbling of the water as it slipped past and the slaps and thuds when we hit a wave head on. Topside and down below was as black as pitch at night, but at least we had some shelter from the seeming chaos outside. It was like being in a womb while your mum was jumping on a trampoline, and just as safe, unless we hit a whale or a container that had fallen off a ship. The biggest problem was the damp. Only a few days of this constant rain, and the humidity down below was almost at saturation point. Clothes, bedding, towels, everything that could soak up water did, until all was sopping wet. One problem was that Jack had used a lot of teak wood down below because it's cheap in Malaysia. These days, people think that's the wood to use in yachts, but it's far too oily and cannot absorb moisture. I've sailed on boats that used only unvarnished cedar down below, and they were as dry as bones because they could absorb the water in the air and then later dry out naturally, ready for the next wet spell. I was already planning to use Japanese Red Cedar down below in my boat.

We hadn't had any contact with Lynn or Chantal since we left the Maldives, so we didn't know if they had arrived or not. They would have had to spend some time in Colombo getting Chantal a visa but that was some weeks back now, so we would try to set up a radio link in the next few days. We would have to find another friendly ham radio operator in Perth. Our last one didn't seem too keen to continue being the messenger boy. Can't say I blame him. Ham radio freaks are a very serious lot and scared to death the watch dogs will take away their licenses. I wouldn't have cared if we used the radio or not. In fact, I didn't see the use for it. We weren't arranging to meet another boat at sea where it might have been useful. We were going ashore on a yet-to-be decided spot where the winds and seas could change the plans from day to day or even hour to hour. And, of course, anybody in the whole wide world with a receiver can listen in to you. Even speaking in code and gobbly gook can't hide the fact that something a little not quite right was under way, but for Jack a radio was some kind of toy. He liked the idea of extending the drama of the situation, setting up clandestine radio contacts to keep the plot bubbling so that there wasn't just the excitement of the pick up and get away or the excitement of the drop off with a long, uneventful sea cruise in between, but a continuous heightening of tension in between through contact with the shore bound members.

Probably the main reason that I didn't want any contact with Lynn was that I had a feeling Chantal and little Radja would not be there in Australia, and I didn't want to hear that just now. I hadn't known Chantal all that long but long enough to know that she was her own boss, a young woman of her time who did what she wanted when the whim struck. And, she loved Sri Lanka and the freedom of the beach life and all her stoned out friends. Although she swore she'd be waiting in Aussie with my son, I knew the magic of Sri Lanka could be very powerful. I wanted to believe they would be in Australia or the next few weeks would be very hard emotionally. My young daughter was in England, my little son was in Sri Lanka, and I was in the middle of the Indian Ocean. I had the feeling that maybe, suddenly, things did not seem right. Maybe I shouldn't be doing this? But, then I thought of that fateful letter that started it all, and surely, this had been started for me. Then, again, fate can be a fickle dealer, and what had at first seemed a trump card might turn out to be a joker.

Certainly the weather seemed to be stacking up against us again. The southwesterly winds that had set in so boisterously were beginning to lose their punch. The low black clouds that had come along to keep the winds company had started to break up and let the sun through long enough to take a sight and get a fix. Not too bad, it had been a good wind. It would have been even better if it had kept up. A bit boisterous now and then, but on a starboard tack and heeled to port, the living hadn't been too hard. Everything was on the port side—the galley, my bunk, and the head—and gravity kept you in place either pressed down on the seat in the head or against the stove in the galley. Heeled the other way wasn't going to be such fun. We must have been on the extreme eastern edge of the southwest monsoon, and it was giving out fast. Another two days, even with all the reefs out and the genoa back up, we weren't doing better than three knots, which equals about sixty miles a day. We were heading into the doldrums and it was time for the iron donkey to be turned on. Since the southwesterlies had started to blow, we hadn't seen much of each other. Jack and Andy had their little stash of pilfered hash and sort of disappeared for most of the day and night. There was no consensus on anything because the wind vane was kicking in, and there was not much for anyone to do. Whoever got hungry first, cooked, which was no big deal. There was either rice or corned beef stew or spaghetti and sauce. If it was time to shake out a reef, whoever was around at the time did it. Noon usually found all three of us around the engine box chart table, not to see how far we'd come, but how far we had to go. If we had managed to get a sun sight that day, we could usually console ourselves by saying our dead reckoning was off when we looked at the dismal few miles we had come. But, if we had a reliable fix, there was no way of getting around how far we still had to go.

When the wind had died down to hardly a whisper, the decision to turn on the engine was a whole crew affair because then we'd have to steer. The wind vane couldn't hold a course when the boat was under power. The boat under sail could look after herself. If someone now and again checked the sails and made adjustments to the sail to keep it properly trimmed, we could go for days without setting a deck watch. You can't be quite so cavalier when you have to steer by hand. You soon get pissed off if you think you're doing more time at the tiller than anyone else. Keeping a crew contented is more of an art than navigation.

This was a big occasion, turning on the engine. We hadn't run it since using it to leave the Maldives. The battery could use a top off, too. With next to no electrics on the boat, it should have been fully charged, but I had heard Jack using the radio now and again. He hadn't said that he had contacted anyone, and I didn't want to ask. He was obviously intent on using it, so wind or no wind we'd have to turn the engine over to keep the power source up. So start the check list. Propeller shaft clamped off; cooling water inlet valve open; fuel cock open; main switch on; press the starter. God, what a racket. Putting the engine on while alongside a dock in a harbor seems natural enough. You're still tied to the earth, and noise is part of that world. Turning on the engine on a sailboat in the middle of an ocean is different altogether. After weeks and days when the only sounds you hear are those of the planet sloshing around, and then suddenly, bursting into life, this alien clanking, thumping, whirling din is unnerving.

The fuel leak that hadn't seemed that bad before was now squirting out. Worse than that, it was flowing out. It was coming out around the injection timing pump. But all the pipe connections were tight, and there wasn't one single place where it was leaking from. It seemed that the whole of the pump had just turned porous like a sponge. We tried everything and checked everything to try to get it to stop. But, after an hour, with the bilges awash with diesel fuel and the cabin floor all slick and slippery, we had to turn it off. If it had been a single point for the leak, we could have collected the fuel and poured it back into the tank. It was coming from an undetermined place, though, sseeping out from somewhere, spreading all over the engine and finally dripping into the bilges from the bottom of the oil pan. We tried again over the next few days to fix the problem. The wind was down to almost nothing, barely keeping the wind vane working, which made for constant adjustment and sail trimming. We really wanted the engine to get us out of this place, but it wasn't going to happen. No matter what we did, the leak got worse. The engine mechanics in the Maldives must have done something to the pump when they set the timing after replacing the crankshaft. We couldn't even run it now to charge the battery.

Ironically, we weren't much better off now than after the connecting rod had broken almost two months before. A couple of degrees farther south, but food supplies were not much better. We had already eaten up all the fruits and vegetables, except for some onions and garlic, which sometimes we ate raw just for the vitamin C. There weren't more than two days eggs, which we kept for baking. Flour, we had a stack of, but without milk and butter, it wasn't much use. Jams, sugar and tea, we had enough for another few weeks, but now, with no engine to get us out of the doldrums, how long would it take?

When we left Male, we had ten boxes of South African assorted biscuits. We still had six left, and we determined to have a box a week, one very Sunday, from then on. It was not much of a goal to work towards, but it kind of divided eternity up into a more manageable time. Six more boxes to go sounded less threatening than six weeks. We decided Jack had better get on the radio while there was still some power in the battery and let the women know what was happening. We managed to pick up a ham radio operator in Perth, and without giving anything away, we asked him to contact Lynn with the telephone number we gave him and to tell her we would probably be way over schedule.

I was happy enough that we wouldn't be in radio contact. Now I could believe Chantal and Radja were in Australia waiting for us, and the radio messages would not be intercepted with someone putting two and two together. I preferred us all alone, our whereabouts unknown until we could sneak up to the back door and drop our cargo off with only us aware of when and where. Why hadn't Jack arranged things better if he was so concerned about talking over the airwaves? It was difficult to understand Jack's thinking sometimes. Surely, Lynn should have had her own radio set rather than relying on total strangers to pass on messages. He should at least have another battery because he knew how much power transmitting takes. I knew he had put the boat together on a shoe string, but maybe a little less teak work done in Malaya and a few more gadgets and aids to navigation would have made more sense.

If we had stayed north of the equator, we might still have been in the full force of the southwest monsoons, and we could have at least have made a lot of easting. It wasn't too bad, I suppose. Not like when we were becalmed after leaving Cochin. There was still a small breeze blowing that was coming from all over the place. It was keeping us busy, changing tack, but at least we were moving. Some days only covering twenty miles, but as we pushed further south, we picked up over forty miles on a good day.

The doldrums can be a grey and miserable place, but it's also very beautiful sometimes. This is the zone between the weather patterns of the northern and southern hemispheres where the winds take a break and let the sun soak up the ocean, turning it billowing miles high in huge masses of brilliant white clouds, multiple rainbows all around the horizon, rainbows within rainbows, painted in colors like those in a child's story book. It makes you wonder where God gets all his backdrop designs from. Imagine having to come up with a new color scheme and a different cloud formation everyday. And, all those sunsets and sunrises, not one ever the same, day after day, for billions and billions of years, and having to do that for all the other billions of planets that must be up there. The only time He gets a break is when its perfectly cloudless up there, which is pretty rare, at least at sea. Sometimes it looks like it might make it, but always, just before sunset a little grey appears, hovering over the horizon. A tiny blob of cloud. It's that contrived touch of imperfection to bring out the beauty of the whole.

Maybe your idea of the doldrums comes from Coleridge's *Ancient Mariner* where ships were stranded for weeks and months, and sailors died off from starvation and scurvy. That might have been true when sailing ships had heavy canvas sails that needed a fair amount of wind to give you any push. Those ships would have been rolling, sickeningly because, although no wind would have blown for weeks locally, the ocean is never still. Always from somewhere there's a low ground swell coming through, the remains of a far away storm that will never arrive. These swells cause more damage to riggings and spars than when underway in a gale. First, the lurch to one way, snapping any wind and shape out of the sail, then a thunderous clap of blocks and booms as it lurches back the other way. Lots of old sailing ships have their masts torn out by this short and savage motion. Shiver me timbers! That's exactly how it feels as the boat passes through this sideways oscillation and pauses upright while everything onboard--mask, rigging, sails, even the frames of the hull--shiver and shudder before starting on the next gutwrenching roll. On sailboats today with lightweight genoas and spinnakers that weigh not more than spider webs, it's possible to keep some wind in the sail. Putting as much weight on one side of the deck as possible to keep it heeled over helps to stop the boat rolling and spilling the wind out of the sail. Canvas sails just snap and flap about and spit out any wind on every roll of the hull. Sailors used to wet the sails to try to keep them stiff. That must have been a Herculean drudge, dredging up heavy buckets of water from the ocean and getting them high enough to douse the sails, especially after all you've eaten is salted pork and hard tack biscuits for the last few weeks and your ship mates are spitting out their teeth before dying off from scurvy. I was beginning to feel for these old guys. It must have been tough in those days. The boat we were on was a long way from a top of the line modern sailboat. In fact, put us in a marina anywhere in the world, and they wouldn't want us moored outside their clubhouse, but compared to the old wooden sailing boats, we had it made. If the engine had been working, there wouldn't have been any comparison at all.

Any similarity would have been in the food locker. I didn't think we were going to lose any teeth to scurvy anytime soon, but we were all beginning to worry about what we would eat if we didn't pick up some speed soon. Panic was probably setting in. Our only conversation now was around food. Pretty basic, too. All we seemed to want was fish and chips. Aussie style, though. We weren't that desperate yet that we dreamed of English cuisine.

Another thing about slow gliding around the tropics was what to do all day. We had already read every book onboard about three times over. I had taken some coconut shells along thinking to do some carving on them. I'd seen a lot of this kind of stuff in places like Sri Lanka where they'd carve in palm trees and such on polished coconuts. Some of it is quite amazing, very intricate, especially that from the Seychelles. I would be following an old tradition of sailors, especially the whalers who carved beautiful designs on whale teeth. They must have had sharper tools than I had, though, and definitely more patience. Two days of scraping and sanding got me half a coconut, which could be recognized as a bowl. That wasn't much of an achievement. Any coconut cut in half looks like a bowl. Cutting it in a design was the hard bit. Another day trying showed up a glaring lack of talent and a new respect for the hustlers who sell these trinkets on all the tropical tourist beaches.

Knitting and crocheting was another way the old sailors used to pass the time, but there was no wool onboard our boat, and the last time I had crossed knitting needles was when I was a young boy and my mother taught me how to make a scarf. I remember that. It was six inches wide at one end and about two inches at the other. Never could figure out what happened to all those stitches.

There was no way out of it. I would just have to mope around deck all day with the occasional plunge in the ocean to cool off. We used to trail a rope behind the boat, about fifteen foot long, with a knot at the end. The idea was that you could grab hold of this if you fell overboard while taking a leak or whatever. It was fun to hang onto this if the boat was only doing a knot or two. Anything over that, and it's hard to hang on. Standing on deck looking over the stern doing three knots, it looks like you're hardly moving. In fact, you could walk this fast. But being dragged through the water at that speed is a real power trip and takes all your strength to hang on. Maybe if you were really desperate, you could work yourself along and back to the boat. But, at normal cruising speeds of five or six knots or more, I think you'd be lucky if you save more than just your arms. At any speed you're very tasty bait for a shark.

One box of assorted fancy tea time biscuits down and five to go, and we were at six degrees south, the same longitude as Cocos Keeling Island. The wind, or more like breeze, was now steady from the southeast, but not from what we thought were the southeast trades. We thought they'd be full on by now, blowing about twenty knots. But everyday was a struggle to get another degree south, which means we were doing just over two knots. We were falling into the routine and the boat had fallen into the rhythm of the slow southerly process. Jack spent the day stoned out in his little aft cabin. I don't know how he did it, it was so hot in there. Andy spent his time halfway up the mast sitting on the spreaders. He was the only one who never complained, never ranted at the weather, and didn't seem to care how long it took to get there. I guess I was the one like a caged bear, pacing the decks and fretting about the wind. Even Jack didn't seem too concerned about all the delays. It must have been all the hash he was smoking that was mellowing him out, but he must have been getting anxious as the nearer our arrival in Australia came. After all, it was his territory, and the authorities would be harder on him than on me if we were caught. Also, the success of the whole trip really depended on him now. He knew the place. He had to make all of the decisions about where to drop the stuff off and things like that. So, like being in a dentist's waiting room, I guess he didn't mind waiting a little longer. But, me, I wanted to get back to Japan and get on with building my boat. It was already five months since I was away, and I was getting worried about it. But, for the moment, fate didn't seem to be interested in what I wanted. Or maybe it was, and it had a different strategy.

Why is it that in this reality that destiny is so much out of our control? If, as in quantum physics, the observer can affect the experimental results, why can't we effect the results in our life by just thinking about it? Why couldn't I just sneeze and bring on a breeze? That should be possible according to chaos theory.

No matter how much I tried to influence the weather, the seas stayed calm and the sun stayed hot. With the full main and the feather light blooper sail hoisted taut on its forerope, it was a comfortable jaunt to windward. Slowly, day by day the boat ticked off another degree of latitude on a southerly heading, but not in the best of directions. The wind was from the southeast, so we obviously couldn't go that way, which was where we wanted to go. At best, the boat could go about twenty degrees to the wind in these light airs. If we put the wind to starboard on the starboard tack, we would make toward Sumatra. As it was, we had the wind to port on the port tack, heading to South Africa. On the downward leg of our little Z, we had to stay like that until we got down to the latitude of the westerlies, where we could turn east and trace off the bottom of the little Z to Australia.

We just cracked another box of biscuits and were down to eleven degrees south when the southeast trades finally found us. They came in like they were sorry to have delayed us. It was the day after we had munched that last box of assorted, so it must have been a Monday morning when I woke up on the cabin sole where I had been sleeping. I could hear the boat thundering along, and we were heeled well over as I struggled to get up the hatch to the deck.

Andy was sitting at the tiller. I don't know how long he had been there, but he seemed to be enjoying himself, sitting with the tiller pulled hard towards him. The wind vane couldn't handle so much sail. There was far too much weather. The boat was being pressed right over. The port scuppers were under water and the foredecks streaming with solid green ocean, but Andy thought this was a buzz, tearing along like a dinghy in an around-the-buoy race. The wind couldn't have been blowing hard too long as the seas hadn't built up yet. If something wasn't done quickly, we'd be in trouble. I was just about to suggest that it might be a good idea to drop the headsail when the sail exploded.

It just disintegrated with a cracking boom. It was there one moment—a huge spread of red and blue Dacron full of wind trapped and straining to get out, transferring all the captured energy into pulling the boat along with it like a lion on a leash. But, the lightweight cloth of the blooper sail was no match for this blow. It didn't just rip or tear. It just disappeared. After the explosion, all that was left were thin, short streamers of Dacron fluttering furiously from the forestay. You could almost feel the relief of mast and rigging after it had gone. The boat came upright with a sigh. By now, Jack had come on deck and wasn't very happy with Andy for not getting it down sooner, which I thought was a little bit much. It would have been a struggle to get it down by himself. There were no self-furling sails on this boat. He might have been shouting for a hand for hours, but no one could hear him. We were definitely getting too slack. Leaving the big headsail on in this wind was just asking for trouble. With any luck, we wouldn't need such a lightweight sail. We hoped to be in the westerlies, and the westerlies in winter time would want something a lot stronger than the sail that had just blown out. We hanked on the number two jib that was made of a stronger material and only two sizes up from a storm jib. As we didn't have a storm jib onboard, though, I guess it was only one size up. With a reef in the main to balance it all, we got underway again. It was a hard slog to windward now. By noon the winds were blowing thirty-five knots. These are what are called reinforced trades. There was no anemometer onboard, of course, so we made an estimate of the wind speed from the state of the seas and past experience. It always seems to be blowing harder when you're going into the wind than with the wind behind you. It actually is a little different because the boat speed over the water makes its own wind, which must be added to the true wind speed. Whereas the other way around, you take off the boat speed from what it's blowing. It doesn't mean that you're going to go any faster this way, though, as you have the waves coming at you. If the seas are not too bad, you can go up and down over them, like so many speed bumps. But, if the waves are short and steep, you are obliged to crash through them with the bigger ones hitting like a giant fist, setting the hull shuttering and the masts and sails staggering like they want to throw in the towel. All the time, in the background, you hear the constant whistling and shrieking of the wind in the rigging like a crowd of demented soccer hooligans baying for more violence.

Oh, how I wished we were going the other way, with the wind just a little over the quarter to keep us safe from jibing. Everyone would be happy, especially the boat as it would be much less punishing for the hull and sails. With the main boomed out and jib eased free, she could surf down on the crest of the waves, and the dolphins would come to sport in the bow waves while we could sit up right on deck and drink our tea in peace.

We'd always known we'd have to straddle this trade belt, but we'd hoped the winds wouldn't be blowing so hard. By mid-afternoon they looked like they were settled in for a good long blow. The sky was cloudless, a deep, cold blue, and it seemed to have expanded, it was so full of wind. It wasn't a malicious wind, and like I said, if the boat was going the other way, it would be like taking the puppy for a walk. But going to windward was no fun, the boat heeled over tossing and jerking and the constant cold wet spray flung back from the bow waves. Going to windward, there's a feeling of being trapped, being shackled down, and you can't even dream of arriving. It's so apt to say you're sailing free when the wind is behind you. You can feel free when the wind is behind you. Your spirits feel free, and you can anticipate your destination. But, going to windward in any kind of wind, anxiety reigns. You fret about the rigging holding out; about the sails tearing; and your shipmates getting swept overboard. Everything becomes a chore: Climbing out of the hatch; trying to cook on a stove uphill; trying to stay in a windward bunk; or wrestling gravity to operate the head. All this is accompanied by the sounds of crashing crockery, tumbling books, sloshing water in the tanks, the wind, and the battering of the waves on the hull. Apart from all that, it was a very beautiful day. The kind of weather the old salts used to call Neptune's wash day, the sort of weather my mother would have prayed for on a wet and soot-flecked Monday morning wash day. It would have lifted her heart to gaze windward over the ocean, to see the lines upon lines upon endless lines of brilliant white sheets napping in the wind. We were going to have to see a lot of these wind-borne white caps on our way through this trade zone. There could be twenty degrees of latitude to go through before they gave out. That's 1200 miles, and we were vectoring through so it would be much farther than that. It could take us two weeks in these conditions. That seemed like a life sentence. It was going to be a toss up for which cracked up first—the boat or us. As the boat was made of steel, and we had barely enough food to keep flesh on our bones, it didn't look like much of a contest, but surprisingly, it was the boat that started to come apart first.

It was only two days after the trade winds had come in with such a punch that the wind vane for the self-steering was blown away. We'd noticed the first day that the half-inch think stainless steel rod that connected the assemblage to the rudder was bent slightly. No mean feat to bend a stainless steel rod. It shows what strength the wind was. During the night, it must have buckled more until it was at an angle where the wind could pluck it out of its socket. The wind vane had been doing its job well, and nobody was on deck to wave it goodbye. A sad end to a good shipmate, and we were really going to miss it. With the jib off just a little, the vane had been set to keep us a point further off the wind to ease the angle of attack so we didn't have to smash so hard into the oncoming sea. Now, with the vane gone, the slacked off jib was pulling us back hard on the wind, heeling us over even more, the bows rounding on the seas at a steeper angle, the leech of the sail, the trailing edge, flapped and flayed like a spastic hand as the sail's aerodynamic shape collapsed. Now we had to winch in the jib sheet to give the headsail its shape back, ease off the main a fraction to balance it, and tie the tiller down to windward. There was no way to set the sails and tiller to give us an easier ride. It was either a full on bash to windward or steer by hand. Nobody was interested in steering, not with every second wave breaking right over the boat. On the plus side, our course was now more south of east, so we wouldn't have so far to sail back west. We could shorten the bottom leg of the Z. That's when we'd really miss the wind vane, when we were down in the westerlies. Without any self steering gear, we'd be forced to steer by hand once we got down there and brought the wind astern. That was nothing to look forward to. True, we wouldn't have spray in our face or the deck running with water all the time, and we'd be able to sit and walk upright, but the rudder was made of steel and had negative buoyancy. That meant it didn't float, which made the tiller hard to handle. The tiller was made of solid oak and was massive and lethal. It was a rib crusher if you lost control coming off a following wave with the boat trying to broach as it careened down the hill. Well, we'd think about that when we got down there.

Maybe we could do something with bungee cords to take some of the strain off, but for now we'd have to concentrate on getting through the next two weeks. Thank God Jack had a sail repair kit onboard. Almost from the first blast of these strong trade winds, the sails had started to come apart. Not tearing—the sails weren't that old—but the stitching would come undone along the seams of the panels, especially on the leech where they were constantly fluttering.

Two days after the wind vane was plucked from its housing to make its slow and spiraling descent to the ocean floor, something much more worrying happened. Luckily, Jack was on deck at that time and noticed right away that the rudder was hanging strangely. The rudder was attached to the boat with two sets of pintles. The male parts, made of three-inch long, one-inch diameter steel rods, fit into sockets welded to the hull. The top lug on the rudder had sheared off. If it had been the welding that had given way, that could have been understandable, but, the weld was good. Incredibly, the one-inch steel rod had snapped. How's that possible? It must have been a hidden flaw in the steel, because there's no force I can imagine that can break in two a piece of steel that thick. This was really serious. If we lost the rudder, we would be in a really bad state. The bottom pintle was under tremendous force now. There were all kinds of sideways bending pressures that it wasn't meant to deal with. If there was any plus side to this happening is that it hadn't happened at night with no one to notice it right away. Another few minutes, and I'm sure it would have gone to join the wind vane. A quick shout from Jack—it's funny how you know which shouts are important—and we were all on deck and had the sails down before we knew why we were doing it.

With the sails off, the boat was dead in the water, and the pressure was taken off the rudder. Dead in the water didn't mean the boat wasn't moving, though. True, we weren't going forward, but now we were bobbing up and down on the waves and being thrown from side to side so violently that we had to crawl around on all fours, hanging on to whatever was handy, like riding one of those mechanical rodeo bulls they have in Colorado pubs. We could have streamed a sea anchor if we had had one. That would have brought the bows into the wind and the coming seas, but, there wasn't one onboard. Dropping the anchor on a short scope might have done the same trick, but getting that up from down below would have been a task to defeat Mr. Incredible. I suppose we could have tied a mattress or something to a mooring line and let that pull our head into the wind. That seemed a bit drastic, though, at least until we determined what the real damage was.

It was Jack's boat, and he had made it, so it was up to him to get over the side and see what was happening to the bottom pintle. Stripping off and getting into the water was easy enough but holding onto the rudder under water and trying to check out the fitting was almost impossible. The stern was high out of the water one minute and then crashing down, almost swamping the rear deck, the next. Two nasty cracks on the head were enough to get him out of there. Not a very satisfactory inspection, but it seemed okay. At least the pintle was still in its socket and turning freely. If the boat had had a transom stern, it would have been more difficult to come up with some way to hold the rudder against the stern and have it able to turn, but the mooring cleats on this double ender were very near the centerline of the pointed stern. With some half-inch lines secured to the port and starboard cleats and looped around the head of the rudder, we could pull it up tight against the stern and still have it free to swing. It would be more than good enough for sailing to windward, but going downwind, it might be too stiff for good control. We'd have to wait and see. With the sails hoisted again and set for the course, it was just one more thing to worry about. There seemed so many it just got added to the list. I'm sure it wasn't going to stay at the top of the list for long. There was already a slight nagging at my nervous system about something else.

W e had noticed it before, but it wasn't until we were down around fifteen degrees south that we thought we should look into it. The routing charts that we were using for marking our course and plotting our celestial fixes were very short on details. Only the main outline of any land or large island was shown. These are only weather charts, one for each month, so you can choose the best winds and avoid the worst storms. It actually states on them "Not to be used for navigation," but beggars can't be choosers, and it was all we had.

We were using the page for the month of March, which was when we had left Cochin. On this page, there was a small black dot on our present course, and we were going to run into it. I was sure it was a printer's error, but a check on all the other pages showed that if it was, it was the only one. There were no other unaccounted for small ink spots that might have dripped from a wayward pen. A check through the atlas showed no island to be there, but when it comes to large bodies of open water, the atlas wasn't very detailed either. The Indian Ocean is my favorite sea, and I've studied it like no other. I could have sworn there was no island there, but all the same, there it was on the chart. In this huge mass of water, in this endless empty space, this little dot of black was sitting like a taunt directly in our path. What if that spot of ink really was a rock sitting atop a volcano?

When I say it was directly in our path, that's probably overstating it. It could be ten miles either side. With only a noon fix and dead reckoning to navigate by, though, that's as good as a hit. For the last few days I had had very good noon sights and each red mark on that chart joined together in a straight line that, if continued, would run right over the spot. Our latest noon sight put it about sixty miles away. We were making a hundred and twenty miles a day along this course, so we would be on the mark about midnight.

If we really wanted to miss it, we would have to slack off the sails and bear off more towards Africa and sit at the tiller, to boot. Morale was low enough already, and changing course to take us away from our destination wasn't something we wanted to do. We decided to go as we were. I was almost certain there was nothing in the way to hit. Jack was maybe a little less sure, and Andy had an anxious night. The morning light showed nothing but rows and rows of shining white caps. It's difficult to know if we made the right decision. If there was nothing there, we would have looked pretty foolish making a big tour in the middle of an empty ocean to avoid a spot of ink. If there had been something solid there, though, we could have looked even more foolish. Whatever, the next sun sight put us way south of that troublesome coordinate and was a boost to slumping spirits.

If we could only catch a fish, we could really start singing. We were having no luck at all trying to put dinner on the table. We had snagged only two fish in the past two weeks. I can't say caught, really, because, although we had hooked them good and hard, we only got the heads onboard while some sharks had had an easy lunch. It could be there are no fish around anymore in the Indian Ocean, which isn't surprising if you see the size of some of these modern day fishing boats that prowl around the open seas. Poor fish don't have a chance with helicopters buzzing around spotting out the schools and directing the boats, which steam to the spot and scoop them up in nets as big as the Isle of Wight. On the other hand, it could be we were not paying attention enough. We would throw a line over the stern, and that was it. We would just check now and then to see if anything had taken a line, but we were getting hungrier by the day. We had a few eggs left, and the few potatoes were getting soft and spongy and growing shoots. The dried fish from the Maldives was long gone. Oatmeal mixed with powdered milk was our main fare. Good job I liked it. I never get tired of eating it mixed with baby formula (not the regular powdered stuff.) A good fish would be nice, though. We decided to set up an early warning device for when anything took the hook. Normally, after streaming the fishing line astern, we would take a loop of the line and clip it to the backstay with a clothespin. When a fish took the line, the line would be snapped out of the peg, and if you were on deck, you'd hear it. There could have been a hundred clothespins snapping on the deck and nobody would have heard them now. Not only was the wind and sea too noisy, but there was nobody on deck most of the time. We had to go topside for our morning rigging check and quite often for sail repairs, and of course, for our sun sights, but usually the deck was deserted. If we were to catch fish we had to be ready to pounce the minute we got the signal.

It's funny when you have to come up with ideas. You usually start out with the complicated ones and work down to the simple ones. We ended up tying the fishing line around our thumbs and to stop them from being ripped off if we got a big one, we put a bungee cord in the loop. Most of our time was spent lying down, so it was no problem, really, just keeping a thumb propped up on an elbow. Either our thumbs were not sensitive enough or the seas were too boisterous for the fish to come out and play because the only tugs we got were the tugs of hunger in our bellies.

North of the equator we used to harvest quite a lot of flying fish that landed on deck during the night. We seemed to have moved away from their flight path. The little we got from this stingy sea were a few small squid blown from the waves onto the main sail, where they stuck like soggy postage stamps ready to be scraped off and put in the frying pan.

It was Jack, again, on deck when the next thing happened. I suppose with him being the builder he was intuiting the failures to his vessel, which is fitting, really. At least he couldn't blame anyone else for the slow disintegration of his boat.

Up through the hatch this time to see what the fuss was about. I was imagining the mast falling down, the sails tearing away or maybe the rudder had finally gone. It wasn't anything as life threatening as that, but the compass and its housing box had been swept from its lodging place near the hatch and thrown into the cockpit well. The glass was smashed and the damping fluid all leaked away. Maybe not life threatening in the immediate, but our first reaction was to panic. Compasses are so much associated with boats that it's impossible to imagine going to sea without one. In a way, it's like the eye of the ship showing the way, guiding you around the dangers. Now, the boat had been blinded. The compass on our boat might not have been too clear sighted; in fact, it was positively myopic. Still, we used to refer to it often. Going up on deck from down below, the first thing to do was a quick sweep of the horizon to check for any shipping about that might be coming at us. A quicker glance to check the sail setting and then take our time to study the compass. It's always reassuring to have that little needle telling you that you're still on course. It's telling you more than just that, too. If the needle is pointing to the same spot, then you know the wind hasn't changed strength or direction because if it had, you'd be on a different course.

Compasses, like any other instrument onboard, are very useful, but they make you lazy. No, I shouldn't say they made us lazy, we were already lazy enough, but they do dull the senses. If you're going to fill your boat up with satellite navigation systems, weather faxes, and all the rest of the computerized junk, you may as well stay ashore and do it all by remote control. It's like driving down a summer lane cocooned in an air conditioned car, cut off from the smells and sounds and heat of the outside world. Without instruments onboard, you're forced to look at and focus on what's really happening out there. You have to look at nature holistically. Get into the rhythm. Let all your senses come into play. There are a lot of signs. It's like Bob Dylan sings, "You don't need a weatherman to show you which way the wind is blowing." You also don't need a compass to tell you the sun sets in the west.

The Polynesians used to navigate with incredible accuracy over vast distances in the Pacific Ocean, from one small island to another, and they had no compass. All we had to do was find Australia. It shouldn't be too difficult to bump into that big chunk of rock and sand with or without a compass. It's true that Polynesia had some rather sophisticated aids to navigation. One was a coconut with a hole drilled in it used to measure the declination of stars. They even had a pretty accurate star chart with all the principle stars woven onto a mat made of coconut fiber, but they definitely did not have a compass. They must have been so tuned into their environment that they could probably feel the backwash off a distant coral reef as the ocean waves pounded into it and set off a rebounding backward pressure wave. They certainly watched the flight paths of all the sea birds. They could tell by how all the clouds moved if they were lingering over an island or flying free over an empty ocean. There was no way we could hope to be as tuned in as those guys were.

Most of their basic intuition was cultivated by a profound knowledge of the sky—all the stars, their declinations, their relation to each other—and the seasons. Like migrating birds, they would have known instinctively where their place on the planet was in relation to all the signs in the heavens. Modern man has lost all this. Now we have to rely on electronic blips beaming down from space to tell us where we are when sailing on the trackless sea. I don't think Polynesians thought the sea was trackless on their great journeys around the whole Pacific.

If the Pacific Islanders could have sailed so unerringly from New Zealand to Tahiti to Hawaii to all the other islands in that vast sea, why did it take so long for Europeans to cross that piddly little stretch of water to find America? I have read more than a few times that Columbus had to wait for the invention of the compass before he could set off westward, but that argument doesn't hold any water at all. First of all, he had a compass. Compasses had been around for a hundred years or so by that time, although pretty useless things they were. The needle was not attached to a card and not set in any damping fluid, so they would have spun around wildly. They weren't even gimballed. That came in 1537. Not having permanent magnets, the needle would have had to been re-magnetized quite often by stroking it with a piece of magnetite rock. Not only that. Compass needles align themselves with the earths magnetic lines of force, but these magnetic lines of force aren't constant in strength or direction. They wiggle about all over the place so a compass reading has to be corrected to take account of these variations in the magnetic lines of force. You either have a positive variation or a negative variation. If you don't compute the variation into your course, you'll end up on the rocks. That is, if you're putting all your faith into a compass rather than following all the other signs around. It's true that Columbus on his second trip to the Americas figured out a little about the magnetic variation so that shows he must have had some kind of compass. In any case, the first good and really useful compass wasn't made until 1826.

Another thing about Columbus is that he had already been to the Azores, which I think is a far more complicated trip than crossing the Atlantic from the Canary Islands. From his starting point in Barcelona to the Canary Islands, where he stopped to refit before setting off on the real journey, he had already gone through the worst part. That would have been getting through the Straits of Gibraltar and getting enough off-ing from the Moroccan Coast. There are some nasty little southwesterly squalls that crop up there, and keeping clear of a lee shore would have been something to think about, but people had been sailing to the Canaries since before the start of the Christian era. You could hardly miss the islands. They have one of the highest volcanoes in the world as a leading mark. Even Pliny and Herodotus had something to say about them. In fact, wasn't it Pliny who let the cat out of the bag by telling the world that the islands were named after packs of wild dogs and not after those adorable little singing birds? He didn't say how the dogs got there, but obviously it was by boat, and back in those far off days, there were definitely no compasses. Come to think of it, even farther back than that, the Phoenicians were sailing all the way to Britain to get tin from Cornwall. Imagine that, crossing the Bay of Biscayne in a Force 10 with the clouds sitting on your head and with no compass. Although riding out a Force 10 three hundred years ago, I would be more worried about the sails and rigging than lack of a compass. Actually, nothing changes for a sailor. I'd have the same worries today.

So, people had been getting to the Canary Islands without compasses for at least 1500 years before Columbus. To navigate from there to the Americas, you wouldn't need a compass anyway. A clear view of the North Star and a hand on the end of an arm would be enough. To use a hand as a navigation aid, stand up on deck, extend an arm from your body, stretch wide your thumb and forefinger, put the tip of the thumb on the horizon. From there to the tip of the forefinger is fifteen degrees of arc. Leaving the Canary Islands in September when the northeast trades are well set in, as Columbus did, you're pretty much guaranteed a clear sky every night. In that month, with the sun's declination still slightly north, the sun sets a little north of due west. You'd want to sail a bit south of the setting sun, bringing the north star further down every night so it's sitting on top of your finger. When you have it there, turn the wheel to bring the boat on course at right angle to Polaris. Keep the star balanced on the end of your finger for a week or so, and you should sail right through the passage between the islands of Dominic and Martinique. If you want to go somewhere else, you can always interpolate. Probably easier said than done, and not a method taken seriously by cruise ship captains, but it would have been good enough for Columbus who didn't know where he was going anyway, even after going there and back four times.

After five hundred years of maritime research, it's still not clear where he made landfall that first time. If only he'd stuck his thumb out and stabbed the North Star with his finger instead of all those hapless natives with his sword, he might have realized that he couldn't be in China, whose latitude lies outside the span of a hand. If he'd been making for Hong Kong at twenty degrees north, he might have been on track, but reportedly he was reading Marco Polo's description of Japan that peaked his interest in going that way around to get there. When he mistook Cuba for those islands, he should have realized he was too far south, but you have to let him off, I suppose. If he'd known the real distance to China, I doubt he ever would have set out. He thought the East was only three thousand miles away so when he hit land after going just that far, I guess it was natural to assume that he had brought up somewhere on the old silk road. Final word—he didn't need a compass. Come to think of it, he didn't even need a boat. You could sit on the kitchen table and push off from the Canaries and end up somewhere in the new world. The winds and current wouldn't let you go anywhere else.

I don't like to go on about Columbus. He's a lot of people's hero. But, let's face it. Compared with the really great navigators like Magellan, Bartholomeu Dias, Vasco de Gama, oh, and let's not forget the greatest of them all—Drake, come on! Columbus is a little mediocre. In all his sailing life, he never even went south of the equator. He always had the North Star to guide him. If the lands he had stumbled onto had proved to be barren and worthless, he'd be just a footnote in a sailor's trivia book. But, lucky for him, and by extension, Spain and Europe, he'd come across a gold mine, literally. So, now he's the hero of the Americas, at least for the white guys, but it's a bit like getting a medal for winning the jackpot in a lottery.

Anyway, we didn't have a compass anymore, but we had something Columbus and the rest of them would have given their right arm for, and maybe their left leg, too. We had a five-dollar digital watch set at Greenwich mean time. So, at least once a day at local noontime, we could know not only our latitude, but our longitude as well. The difference in the time between where you are and the time at Greenwich, computed into degrees of arc will equal your longitude. In practice, we didn't use it much, though, because that meant sitting up on a sea soaked deck taking multiple sextant sightings of the sun until it reached its zenith, which is local noontime. It's not so easy to know just when the sun is at maximum height. It often seems to pause at apogee, and you can't tell if it's still going up or already on its way down. If you happen to get a bit of cloud blocking it at just that moment, then you wouldn't know what reading to use.

We used to take a sight in the morning about nine or ten o'clock, and using that sight and sextant angle, in conjunction with the almanac and another book of tables of declinations, we could compute a line of position. At that time of day, this line, when drawn on a chart, would be almost vertical, running north and south, and you are somewhere on this line. Another quick sight taken somewhere around noon would give you another line running west to east, and you're also somewhere on this line. So by advancing the first line on the course you had been steering by the time taken between sights, where the lines meet is where you're at. From very early on, sailors could work out their latitude with pretty good accuracy. Their astrolabes and backstaffs might have been more difficult to use than a modern sextant, but the results wouldn't have been that much different.

Thinking about that, they might even have got better results than those given by Jack's sextant. The sextant he was using at the time was a beautiful old brass antique he had picked up in a London junk shop. It must have sat for years on somebody's side board, lovingly polished so much that all the graduations on the arc had been almost rubbed away. You needed a magnifying glass to read off the degrees and minutes. That's the only bit of brass on a boat which should never be polished. I used a German Leica, small and light and all aluminum. It's beautiful to look at and beautiful to hold. It's the only thing I want put in my coffin. You can even leave me out, but that's got to be there.

For the next week or so, the compass wouldn't be missed at all. We were locked on this course, with the sails and tiller set, keeping the boat to a hard beat to windward. We didn't have to do any steering. We couldn't go any more into the wind, and we couldn't go any more off the wind. Well, maybe a little off the wind, but that would have meant sitting at the tiller day and night. Our tiller was lashed down, and the course was determined by the wind, which day after day, just kept piling it on. It never went down to less than thirty knots, which you might think is nothing. It isn't bad if it's up your back, but barging into it day after day was very wearing. If only we had bought more supplies in the Maldives--if only there had been more supplies to buy-- things might have been a little more pleasant. Not that life at sea is ever boring, but a day on the water is a lot longer than a day on the land, and snacks and meal times are anticipated much more than when you're living ashore.

During the day, it wasn't too bad. There was always something to do. Dashing up on deck for a quick sewing session or to take a sight, but this we didn't do every day anymore now. Our course was set and constant. We could guess within a few miles where we were. We scoured the hidden corners of the boat for cans of food that might have been forgotten and sorted out clothes to match the growing cold. The nights were the worst. Going into winter, the sun was setting earlier and the nights getting longer. Without any electricity for lights to read by, they seemed endless. If we hadn't been heeled over so far, and if the waves would have stopped spraying the decks with cold seawater, we could have sat on deck and watched the heavens revolve. As it was, we were stuck below with cabin fever.

One night, when I just had to read or go out of my mind with boredom, I thought I'd light an oil lamp. This was not a gimbled, made-for-a-boat type of lamp, but the kind you'd put on a camping table with a wire handle at the top that you could tie to a deck head. It would swing around violently and was too dangerous to use on a boat underway. I suppose Jack was going to get it together in the future when he got the money for this lark, but for now, it was up to me to improvise or lie in the dark. That night I just couldn't do without reading for a while. I thought I had worked out a system where the lamp could swing enough to keep the wick vertical and the glass from crashing into anything, but, I hadn't worked it out well enough. I had fallen asleep, the book had fallen on the cabin sole, and I woke up with Jack beating me around the head and the pillow in flames.

Chapter 17

*W*e must have fallen over a bigger than usual wave, and the lamp smashed against the bulkhead, breaking the glass and spilling kerosene all over the place. Luckily, the lamp hadn't been too full and the fire was quickly put out. In any case, everything was too damp below for it to really get a hold, but fire on a boat is one of the dreaded dangers of sailing life. Apart from giving us something to talk about for the next few hours, it was not a big crisis. There was no danger in a steel boat of getting burned down to the water line. Now, though, there was nothing to it but to lie down in the dark at night and think about what else could go wrong.

Thundering along, listening to the moaning of the wind and the sound of the waves beating against the hull and breaking over the deck, it was easy to imagine all kinds of things still left to go wrong. Already we had lost the vane. We had the rudder tied down by a piece of rope; a broken engine; no compass; the sails threatening to come apart; and hardly any food. The mast was still standing, but the rigging was under constant strain on this beat to windward. It was easy to fantasize the wire popping out of the turnbuckles. After all, only Jack knew what kind of job he had done when he set them up. The greatest worry now, though, was losing the sextant. Normally, that wouldn't be a concern at all. They were only brought on deck for a couple of minutes a day and the rest of the time were loving encased in their boxes and stowed carefully below. But on this boat, it seemed anything could happen.

Had someone put the evil eye on us? Sailors are a superstitious lot and have all kinds of taboos about what could jinx a boat. I remember one time visiting a French boat, and in the conversation, I mentioned the word, "rabbit." On French boats, for some inexplicable reason, you can't say "lapin," and even though I had said it in English, the owner was terrified that I had doomed his boat to a fathomless grave. In some countries, blue boats are bad luck. In Australia, green is out. And of course, you should never change the name of a boat. We'll I'd never change the name of a boat. That would be pretty insensitive. If your mum had named you "John," you wouldn't want someone to come along and make you change it to "Bill." Some of the old sea dogs thought women and priests onboard were bad luck, too, but I've had them all onboard, and I haven't hit the rocks yet.

When I had the priest onboard I admit I was a bit apprehensive, but the opportunity to get into the head of a man of the cloth was too much to turn down. I'd met him on Christmas Island in the Pacific. A Frenchman, twenty years the Roman Catholic bishop of the Line Islands, which are slap bang in the middle of the wide Pacific, he was desperate to get to Fanning Island, sixty miles to the northwest, to visit his scattered flock. There was no boat on Christmas Island capable of going that distance, and I said I would drop him off there. The weather was perfect, gentle trades, for a fair run over barely rippling seas. We could leave at sunset and be there at dawn. We'd have dinner on deck, and over wine, he could tell me what he *really* believed about all that mumbo jumbo. But, trust a Frenchman. He ate too much, drank too much, and went to sleep while we were still on the small talk. At least we arrived safely, and his parishioners were so happy to have him there that they loaded me up with a fruit market full of papayas and bananas.

I'm not superstitious, and I didn't expect the hand of fate to snatch those precious sextants and throw them overboard, but still, I couldn't help feeling there was more to come. What could we have done without a sextant? In theory, we could have picked a star whose declination was the same as the latitude of our destination. We could have sailed south until the star was directly overhead at its zenith and then steer east, checking overnight that it was still overhead at its zenith. Very easy in theory, but we were no Polynesians, and heading south into the winter, we didn't expect too many cloudless nights.

The day after my head had caught fire, just to show that the malevolent spirits had a nicer side, we unearthed a five-pound container of sesame butter. It had been forgotten at the bottom of the locker ever since Jack had left Melbourne over a year ago. The top layer was a bit greenish, but scraping that off, underneath was fine, and spread on pancakes was not too bad. So, not everything was doom and gloom.

It had taken almost exactly two boxes of biscuits from the time we entered the trade winds until we sailed out of them and into the variables. This belt of wind is sometimes called the horse latitudes. I guess when the term was coined they used to transport a lot of horses for all the wars going on then. Because the fickle winds come from all points, keeping the boat tacking and jibing constantly to keep on course, it was hard on the horses to keep their footing. These variable winds which blew between the trade winds and the westerlies usually lie between twenty degrees and thirty degrees south of the equator. We were already down to thirty south, and a few days later we were catching westerlies. Now came the hard part. The last few days or so of getting wind from all over the place hadn't been too bad, although it had meant standing at the tiller and lots of sail trimming. The winds had been reasonably light, and the seas quieted down. The best thing was that we could stand and walk around upright most of the time. We were noticing the seas changing. Gradually, the westerly swells got higher and higher as the winds from that direction began to take over.

This was it: what we had been waiting for since we had left India. The final run down to Australia. Everything was serious now. We were zeroing in on destiny. Up until now, those big inner tubes of hashish sitting quietly on the cabin floor had been just sort of accessories—something to sit on or fall over in the dark. Now that it looked like we really were going to make it, they took on a more ominous significance. Depending on the mood of the day, the sight of them could bring on a warm flush of euphoria at anticipated wealth. More often, looking at them brought a dampening chill into our daydreams. We knew we weren't desperate criminals. This was just a harmless little jaunt, a bit of adventure, maybe a bit of profit to finance our boat building. It wasn't like we were transporting guns or even heroine or cocaine, which you could probably make a case against. It was just harmless old hashish, the natural oily residue from the cannabis plant. Certainly less harmful than Coca Cola. We had to face the fact that not everybody saw our point of view, and while they may not be in the majority, they were definitely more powerful. We knew it wouldn't upset their conscience to put us behind bars for quite a few years. Even so, I wasn't ready to throw the hash overboard just yet. A newspaper article and the arrival of a letter had brought me here. Fate, or whatever you want to call it, had led me here—on a boat falling to pieces on the edge of the winterly westerlies on a journey that seemed more likely to fail with every passing day. But, that article and letter had been a kind of pointer, like consulting the I-Ching. You don't have to believe in anything magical to read the hexagrams. They just make the decision for you, and it's up to you to follow it through. Obviously you don't know if it's the right path or not. If you knew that, you wouldn't have asked the book in the first place, but once you take the advice, you have to stick to it. It's no good changing canoes when you're going over the rapids. You might get wet feet. With over two thousand miles to run down, we probably had about two weeks left before we found out what fate really had in store for us. Would I get to finish my boat or would I finish up behind bars?

We better make the best of it. This could be the last holiday we'd get for quite awhile. As a vacation venue, though, it wasn't all that good. The accommodation was bad and the food terrible, but to make up for that, the scenery was magnificent. We had dropped down to forty degrees below the equator, mainly so we could say that we had really been in the Roaring Forties. We'd have to come up some time as we intended to make landfall at Cape Leeuwin, which is at thirty-five degrees south. Cape Leeuwin, like the two other great capes, Cape of Good Hope, and the mother of them all, Cape Horn, has a fabulous reputation for storms. Then, it's across the Great Australian Bight, funneling though Bass Strait. I couldn't imagine what those seas must be like after a fetch that circled the world. To be suddenly nipped between Tasmania and Australia proper and where the seabed shallows, I think you'd be at a loss to find an adjective to describe the seas there. Already out here in the deep ocean, the waves were spectacular and large.

In all oceans, there's always a ground swell running, a heaving of the ocean, the aftermath left over from exhausted storms. Down here, the swells are just on a larger scale because the seas have got such a long run to build themselves up. Even when the wind isn't blowing, they don't go down because there's always another gale not far behind to keep piling them up. Swells don't make your knees knock. They might if they were close together. Then it would be like sailing up and down the Crags of Cambria. But, from the hollow of one swell to the next could be a kilo-meter apart, like sailing over the gentle slopes of the Devon Hills. It's all together different when the wind is blowing locally and whipping up waves on top of the swells. Then you really are in awe. There's nothing like it. You want to bury your head in a pillow. In fact, some of the old sailing clippers had a barrier built behind the helmsman, not to stop him getting wet or from washing overboard, but so he couldn't see the size of the waves bearing down on him. The southern ocean must be the ancestral home for all the gales that ever blew; where the spirits of every storm ever spawned roam wild.

These winds are not like the hurricanes or cyclones of the tropics, those prima donnas of the world's weather systems, whining and shrieking in spiteful destruction like a child throwing a tantrum. Down here the winds bellow like the primeval bull, and the whole place reeks of majesty and pomp. This is where the big blue whales wander, and there are none of your mincing tropic birds down here. Only the great white albatross can complement these seas. We were way out of our class. Social inferiors gate crashing Poseidon's ball. We could only hope we were so insignificant we could pass unnoticed, like a speck of dust on the carpet.

When the wind was really up and the sea was tumbling, the crests of the waves piled up so high they couldn't support themselves, and they came crashing down the face of the waves in a foaming avalanche. Then, an hour at a time was all we could take at the helm. The trick was to keep the boat on the trailing edge of the waves, and when they broke, to go down with them surfing into the troughs of the seas that were bubbling and churning all around. It was exhilarating but really tiring when steering by hand.

When the particles in a wave are careening downhill, they're going round in a circle in a vertical movement. When you're on the slide down, they're helping you. You're riding on top of the forward going circle, but at the bottom you hit the other side of this circular movement, like a brake. The stern is still slipping through butter, but the bows have run into a patch of treacle, like jamming on the front brakes of a bicycle at speed. If you don't go head over handlebars, the rear end starts flailing around trying to shake off its forward momentum, swinging the back from side to side. It was vital to stop the stern from swinging too much.

Just turning a few degrees from side to side would have exposed enough of the hull for the waves to lever the boat around broadside onto the sea. Then, we'd have as much control as an empty beer can rolling over and over down a windy street.

If we had been using a small storm spinnaker, it would have made things easier. With only a reefed-down staysail jib, though, we were limited in our options. The main was reefed right down and boomed out to port, with the staysail on the same side. Not the best arrangement on a dead run. Sometimes the wind blowing into the jib was blanketed by the mainsail. Then, the jib would collapse slowly before snapping back into shape as the wind found it again. It's quite surreal to watch this. The wind is blowing furiously. The main is full and straining, and everything on deck that can flap around, including clothes, is beating out this manic rhythm. Then, suddenly, the jib sail is starting to lose attention and is acting like it's bewildered by what's going on. For a split second, you can be deluded into thinking the wind has suddenly stopped. Oh, euphoria! Then a quick crack on the head and it's back to work. When the winds were lighter, we boomed the jib out on the other side to the main and ran wing to wing, as they say. That kept the staysail more on the job, but it made steering more of a challenge because then we had to worry about accidentally jibing the jib as well as the main. We didn't get to sail wing-to-wing too often. The winds hardly ever died down enough. They have got the stamina of eternity down in the Forties. More worrying than going down a wave was the thought of jibing the main. Although both things would have the same results—a possible rollover, a snapped off mast, a boat flooded with water, and more than likely, a free key to Davy Jones' Locker.

The wind was coming up from astern from due west. According to the weather charts, that was the predominant direction. There was also a good percentage of winds with a northwesterly or southwesterly slant. One of these winds would have suited us better. We could have had the wind more over the quarter while keeping to our course of almost due east. That would have lessened the chance of jibing. When running with the main sail boomed out and the wind right up the derriere, it's very important to stop the wind from getting behind the sail. No prob-lem at the foot of the sail where the boom is holding it out almost right angled to the wind, but at the head of the sail, where the sail narrows at the mast, the angle of the leech is more like forty or thirty degrees, or even less, to the wind. If you have the boom out to port and you turn the boat to port, the wind very quickly can get behind the sail up there and start to twist it around. Before you know it the wind is flowing down the reverse side of the sail, pushing the boat around with it. Quicker and quicker the back of the sail is becoming the front. If the boom isn't tied down and is free to swing, you might possibly not broach, but it will go through a head scything one hundred and eighty degrees and probably take away the starboard stay as the main sweeps the boom over onto its new setting. We always kept the boom tied down to leeward. Fifteen feet of heavy gauge aluminum pipe is not a candy hammer, but if we would have accidentally jibed in these seas, we would have broached for sure. The boom being tied down and the wind filling the sail from the wrong side would have pushed the boat broadside to the wave, the main sail so confused it thinks the starboard side of the hull is now the bow. We could have brought the wind more onto our starboard quarter. That would have lessened the chance for an accidental jibe, but then we would have been heading far too south. We were pretty sure the winds were coming from due west by comparing them with our plotted track line, which we had got from some hazy sun sights. Without a compass, keeping the winds directly behind us was a good course keeper. In the daytime, we felt safe enough keeping the wind just where we wanted it. There was a long narrow strip of cloth tied to the backstay. If we kept this streaming down the centerline of the boat, everything would be fine. The trouble was on the long night watch when it was so dark you could hardly make that out. Sometimes, when you had been looking away checking a star or something, you'd come back to look for this piece of cloth, and you wouldn't be able to find it. It had blended in with the dark sky. That was always a bit of a panic. Looking at the main didn't help, either. That also was difficult to see. You couldn't know how far off course you had gone. Maybe it was too late and the main sail was already getting into jibe mode. The safest thing to do was to push the tiller away from you, bring the boat's heading more south. That was why we didn't pole out the jib on the other side of the main. We wouldn't have had this escape route because the jib would haved jibed then. When your eyes had found the streamer again you could bring the boat back on course.

Even off watch you couldn't relax. You kept thinking, "Are the others having the same problems as I had keeping on course?" "Is someone going to let their daydreaming take over or even fall asleep?" We were all exhausted. What would we have done if the boat had broached? These waves were massive and powerful, and once they knocked us down, I don't think they'd have let us up too easily. The fore hatch was not so secure, even though we had it tied down from inside, and the main hatch would have been easily broken. The first rollover would have filled the boat with cold water, and if we came up right, we would have been wallowing out of control like a boxer staggering from a knockdown punch. The punch after that would have sent even more water down below until the weight of water and steel would be more than the air inside could support, and down we'd go. We didn't have the comfort of knowing there was a safety raft onboard, because there wasn't one. The rubber Zodiac was deflated and stored below, and the aluminum dinghy tied down on deck, would have been as much use as a washing machine, although it would have held more water. In any case, it most certainly would have been ripped off the deck in the first rollover. The two guys off watch and down below would have had a nasty few minutes until they drowned, but at least they'd have a comfortable grave with their bones left intact after the fish and crabs had had their fill. But, the poor guy who had been at the tiller would have been floundering around in the water, trying to stay afloat. It would be a much longer and lonelier death for him. That's why sailors thought it better not to learn to swim. Get it over quick and hope your body reaches the bottom before it's torn to pieces by sharks. Or maybe you don't worry too much about that. I didn't particulary want to drown to death. I almost did once, and to be denied that last sweet breath before the lights go out is a cruel and undignified ending.

It had almost happened in Tabarka, a small port on the north coast of Tunisia. It is a beautiful old town with the ruins of an ancient castle guarding the entrance to the harbor. Not a bad place to die, if you could do it in the sun. My stars weren't lined up properly that day. They wanted to take the sun away as well as my air. There was a lot of work going on in the harbor, dredging and building new sea walls. Most of the work was being done by a Hungarian company, and that's a strange fact in itself. The last time Hungary had a coastline was about two billion years ago, and there they were doing some serious maritime construction. They had a huge work barge anchored in the inner harbor that was three hundred feet long by about a hundred feet wide. Tied up against this was a French sailboat, which I was visiting. Clamoring over all the equipment on the barge, I was stepping onto the sailboat when one of my shoes fell off into the water. Not stopping to thing about it too much, I grabbed a rock from a pile nearby and jumped in after it. They were almost new leather sandals, and I liked them. The rock helped me to the bottom in no time. I probably got there before the shoe did. It was only ten feet deep, but with all the dredging going on, stirring up the sand and mud, visibility was almost zero. Keeping my eyes closed, I patted around the seabed with my hands and just by luck I found it right away. Surfacing slowly so as not to hit my head on the keel of the sailboat, I came up between the barge and the boat. I had only been down half a minute and was hardly out of breath.

The friend I had come to see thought this was a great chance to get a diving flipper back that he had dropped over the side a few days ago. Flush with success, I though I'd have a go at getting it back. Maybe I'd get dinner thrown in with the aperitif I'd been invited to have. So another rock and down to the bottom again. Obviously a diving flipper didn't fall straight down and must have glided off to God knows where. Moving around the bottom, feeling in the mud, I didn't have any luck that time. I was totally out of breath, but I gave it one last try. But, with my lungs screaming for air, I had to give it up. Keeping my arms stretched up, expecting to contact the bottom of his yacht, my hands touched a mass of big sharp barnacles, not what you'd expect to find on the bottom of a sailboat. I opened my eyes, but that did nothing. It was all as dark as a cave, not a glimmer of light. Then, it hit me. I was under the barge! I had no idea which way lay the yacht, which would have been the shortest way out. Already totally and completely out of air, a panic was rising, difficult to control. I could start swimming around, looking for the way out. That would have been a real panic maker. I was thinking, "So, this is how you die. What a stupid way to go, trapped under a dredging barge." These and lots more thoughts flashed on and off altogether in a nanosecond. My mind was becoming disentangled from my brain. This would have been the time for an out of body experience, but it didn't happen. It's difficult to put into words, but the subjective mind was distancing itself from the objective reality of my body, tearing away from its biological source, and yet it knew when the brain lost its oxygen, it would go, too. For the first time in my life, I was truly aware of being aware. Funny you have to die to realize you were ever alive. What saved me was a book about whales I was reading. It was still there on the saloon table. The day or two before I had read that given the comparative lung capacity and body weight of a human versus a whale, a human should be able to stay submerged for much longer. The difference apparently is in the nervous system. When the human cannot get rid of the carbon dioxide build-up in the body, the nervous systems sets up a panic alarm that shuts everything down. Whales don't have this cutoff switch, or something like that. Holding onto this idea, I decided to crawl upside down using the barnacles as handholds and going in a straight line, even if it meant going the whole length of the barge. As it turned out, I surfaced about three quarters of the way along the long side of the barge, with my hands shredded, but a small price to pay for that first sweet lungful of air. You think sex is great? Try that one. It's AIDS-free, too.

Chapter 15

*I*n the beginning, when we first met up with the westerlies, it was a really anxious time, steering by hand, trying not to jibe or broach. If we still had the wind vane, it could have been almost enjoyable. A wind vane finely tuned to steer a boat could keep a heading better than most humans. We would have been free to relax and get into this incredible ride. Given a few days, though, when we had got into the rhythm and the swing of things, it became easier. It almost became second nature. The subconscious took over and most of the tiller corrections were done without thinking about it. Like learning to drive a car with a gear shift. Hard work in the beginning, getting the brain and limbs to work together, but it gets easier all the time until the brain gets all the data it needs to print out a new circuit board. Bingo! You're in automatic. It was never as easy as that at the tiller, though. For one thing, it was not a power driven steering wheel. We were coming off a wave with the bows wanting to go one way and the stern wanting to go another. It took a lot of muscle on the tiller to keep her heading straight, but, in the daytime, at least, we could relax enough now to take in some of the scenery.

All seas are different. They all have their personality and quirks. The tropic seas are full of light and color, dazzling like a Disney movie. They make the earth feel young with a good-to-be alive feeling. Not that Disney movies make me feel that way. In fact, most of them make me want to puke, but the brightness of the colors playing on the retina, traveling down the nerve stems, and affecting the brain, give a natural high. Sailing in the tropics, you can dream of staying young forever. Down in the southern ocean, everything is monochrome with the somber mood of an ancient Greek tragedy. There's nothing young down here. The black sea and the dark grey clouds leave no doubt about how old the earth is. It's a very serious ocean with no frivolity here. If you compare the tropics with a Disney movie, then these high latitude seas are a play by Ibsen.

I suppose a lot depends on first impressions when you first sail upon a particular sea. For me, the seas around Japan will always be bad-tempered, cold and damp. The Indian Ocean, north of the equator will always be gentle and playful, full of short bright showers; the Caribbean, full of light and island music; the Red Sea harsh and dry, full of wind, like a muezzin's call; the Mediterranean sloppy and blaise, except when the mistral is blowing, and then it's got the mood of Christmas time in summer. For Magellan, the Pacific always would be just that. Pacific. Because that's how it was when he first set keel on it. It wasn't like that now. Trying to give an idea of how big these waves are is like trying to describe an elephant to someone who has never seen anything bigger than a mouse. Quite possible, I suppose, but unless you've actually seen an elephant, it is still only a two-dimensional impression. You have to see the elephant to put the real umph into the picture.

The Eskimos have lots of different words for snow, don't they? And there are a lot of different words for rain, aren't there? So, why not different words to classify waves? You would think the English language, evolving from an island race, would have sorted this out by now, but we still have to tag on an adjective like "big," "enormous," or "gigantic." I bet the Polynesians had different words for different waves. After all, they must have seen them all in their fantastic journeys all the way from New Zealand to Japan. For a start, we could call the waves in the southern ocean "boomers." That would give some impression of the sound and size. Think of a kettledrum in a symphony orchestra. A boomer has to be a minimum of twenty foot. Anything less would be a baby boomer. Over sixty foot would be a blooming boomer. We were sailing in common, or garden, boomers, and they were fascinating to watch, tirelessly rearing and breaking, heaving and swerving.

When we got tired of this, the albatrosses would come on for the commercial break. These great white seabirds with their eight-foot wingspans make their home down here and only go to land once every two years to make baby albatrosses. The rest of the time they must find it more fun swooping over the boomers. If I ever get to be reincarnated and have a chance to choose what I want to come back as, there would be no second choice. Just give me a pair of those fabulous wings. I couldn't imagine a better way to spend this reality than endlessly gliding and soaring in total freedom. I don't think they do this all mindlessly without any consciousness. I think in their own way, they have everything all sussed out.

Why do we assume that our conscious awareness is the ultimate criteria, the final standard, that the whole universe has to be judged by? Especially if we have arrived where we are through a process of evolution, which is nothing more than a random build up of atoms falling by chance into certain patterns. It can't even be called accidentally, because that would imply the existence of a prior, perfect state, which is getting into the realm of metaphysics, and evolution has no track with that. So our body and brain are nothing more than the complex fabric woven by the random movements of atoms into a design that no person can judge good or bad. How could they with no standard to judge it by? If the brain developed by chance, then so must have the mind, which is fueled by it. Our consciousness and our views of reality are nothing more than happenchance. There's absolutely no way to know if evolution has arrived us at the ultimate truth of conscious awareness. If there is such a thing as a universal standard of consciousness valid throughout the whole cosmos and in all dimension and we meet those parameters, then it's an incredible coincidence that we arrived at that understanding after so many random steps.

I always thought I'd die regretting that I'd never know the answer to what it's all about. But, maybe that is the answer. The answer is that there is no answer. How can you make any sense out of the outcome of millions and millions of pointless, random happenings? You can't possibly say, "Ah, that's it! That's how it was supposed to turn out." If that's the case, evolution would be like the monkey sitting at the typewriter. Given enough time, it would type out the complete works of our pal, Bill. No, I can't go along with that. That would be a worse plot than *The DaVinci Code*. Let's face it. Our thoughts and philosophies about awareness cannot be any more valid than the patterns of the atoms in the dust we are made of.

Oops. Sorry about that existential burp. A bit of a downer thinking that way. But, don't worry, life's not that bad. Roll up a joint, pop a pill. If that doesn't work, and it's still bothering you, you can always try burying your head in the sand by joining one of the popular religious clubs. Islam seems to be a sand pile of choice for a lot of people, but Catholicism has more theater to it. Anyway, that's getting a bit deep. All I wanted to say was that our understanding of awareness might not be the only one. People laugh at Prince Charles for talking to his plants. Me, too. But, there's got to be a suspicion that there might be something to it. All things on earth share the same kind of molecular mechanics, and so we can probably say that awareness can be judged by the creatures in the chain that have reached a higher biological level. That's why I think searching for intelligent life on other planets is a dead end. Unless they share the same DNA structure as us earthlings and have gone through the same random mutations, I can't see how they could arrive at the same understanding of consciousness. Maybe plants on our earth, not having a recognizable brain, aren't aware as we understand it, but I can't see why seabirds couldn't be. Up until recently they were our partners in the great mutations. Even just a few hundred million years ago, give or take a day, we could have been sitting down to dinner together.

One morning, I watched a family of albatrosses. I guess it was a family. There were two adults and a year-old fledgling. The young one hadn't got its white feathers yet and was still a streaky brown. They came up from behind the boat in tight formation and landed on the sea about five boat lengths ahead. They sat there, bobbing up and down on the crest, and waited for us to pass. When we got ahead, they would make an awkward run into the wind, spread out their wings, and ride the air currents up and over the waves. When they were high enough above the peaks into the strong blast of the true wind, they'd flip over, peel off, and come screaming back downwind over the boat. They repeated this over and over until I suppose it was lunchtime and they went off to see what was on the menu. You can't tell me they were doing this on automatic mode. They were either teaching the young something or just having fun. Psychologists might say that this is just a remembered present, like the working of a dog's brain, but who knows? That's probably just human vanity getting in the way. I think they were having fun like lots of animals do.

One time I was in Trincomalee Harbor. I was with Jack then, too. We decided to take a rubber dinghy down the Malabar River through the jungle. Turning the bend, where the river shallowed, the bank on one side was nine foot high and sloped down to the water. There was a small herd of elephants grazing at the top while the youngsters, giggling and laughing, slid down the slope, sitting on their backsides, four feet up into the air, splashing into the river and then scrambling and pushing to get up to do it again, having a great time. Of course, monkeys play, as do dolphins and whales and I would think all mammals. I would even go so far as to say that maybe insects have some kind of awareness. Have you ever really watched a cockroach? Probably not. First instinct is to zap it. I had a two-week intensive seminar once on cockroach behavior. I had been tied up to a sea wall at Madras harbor and at sea again had found a boarding party had breeched the food locker. These Indian cockroaches were not quite as obnoxious as the common, dark brown Germanic species. They were a lighter chocolate color with bright orange polka dots. Quite cute, but still they had to go. Couldn't stand a cockroach scurrying across my face when I was asleep. These animals were extreme strategists. Cornered, they would faint to left or right, antennas sweeping looking for an opening. Attack forward, retreat backward, play dead, anything to get away. Bit like politicians, I suppose. No matter how many battles I won, I could not get rid of them because they laid their eggs in inaccessible places. In the end I took a couple of those lizards off the wall in a Zanzibar coffee shop—those little chitchats that clamber along the walls and ceilings of the hot countries, the ones that get so stressed when they lose their tail. They got rid of the cockroaches and ate the eggs, too. In fact, they did too good a job because a long time after, I found their dried and shriveled bodies. They had starved to death, which doesn't show too much intelligence. They could have farmed the eggs and had a constant food supply. Human beings do daft things like that all the time so it doesn't prove a total lack of awareness.

Anyway, I'm pretty sure those albatrosses knew they were onto a good thing. They must have been laughing behind their feathers at these three cold, wet, bedraggled things lumbering across their turf. One thing was for sure. They were doing a better job than we were at feeding themselves. They were as plump as festive turkeys, as healthy as farmyard children. We were down to eating flour and water pancakes. Jack called them chapattis as though naming them gave more taste. But, a flour and water pancake by any other name is still a flour and water pancake. Rubbery and almost totally tasteless except for a slight bitter after-taste from the weevils in the flour. Spread with sesame butter and the last of the jam, they weren't that bad. When the jam ran out they began to pale.

The albatrosses were probably doing a better job at navigating, too, although we weren't doing too badly there. I wonder if these Great Wandering Albatrosses know where they are all the time in relation to their breeding grounds. The young ones, after they first fly away from their crooks and crannies on their lonely little ocean islands, don't return to land at all for the first five years. If, like most other migrating animals, they return to their birthplace, how do they do this? It's not like they can fly miles high to check the sea scope. I never saw an albatross fly higher than the mast. In any case, they'd be lost in the clouds. Their playground stretches from the Antarctic Circle all the way up to thirty degrees south and circles the earth. Maybe they don't go back for the first five years because it takes them that long to find it again, but I kind of doubt that. If they lived in the northern hemisphere, it would be a little easier. There, they would always have the North Star to give directions and latitude.

Down in the antipodes, there was no such convenient star. There's the so-called Southern Cross, but it's a very poor substitute. You know how it's shaped like a kite, four stars making out a diamond in the sky? When it's coming up over the horizon, it's standing vertically with the bottom of the kite pointing south. When it rises higher in the sky towards its zenith, it starts to fall over until it's lying on it side. Then, it's not even pointing to the horizon, and you have to interpolate. If you place your eyes about ten fingers to the right and drop them down to where sky and sea meet, that should be a good enough check on where south is.

Since losing the compass, we were getting good at guessing where true south lay. When the night skies weren't cloudy it was really a spirit lifter to know we were heading in the right direction and that the wind was still blowing from the west. It was much less fun thundering away in the dark, with only the wind and wave to give direction.

We could cheat now and again. We still had the little hand held compass, but using that thing was an invitation for a broken neck. It was no use using it at deck level. There was too much iron around to give any meaningful reading. Using it meant somebody climbing halfway up the mast. That was no mean feat in rain-soaked foul weather gear with the mast lurching like a drunk while one of us hung on with one hand, trying to peer through a little hole in the side of the compass. These compasses, the shape and size of a donut have a chemical light inside which is supposed to light up the compass card at night. In calm conditions they are accurate enough, but in these conditions, it was hardly worth the effort. We only did it when we were really paranoid or when there had been too much cloud cover to take a sun sight or to see the southern cross for a few days.

Albatrosses must have evolved a better way for finding their way around. They'd have to if they wanted to return to the same rock every time they got the urge to lay an egg. Then again, maybe any old place would do for their procreation, in which case, we might be better navigators than they because we now knew where we were going.

We were getting confirmation now that Australia lay just ahead. The continent itself was talking to us. There was a small, medium wave transistor radio onboard, which for the last few weeks had given up nothing but static noise. We were picking up local radio stations from out of Perth. A doubtful blessing. True, it gave us confidence in our position and acknowledgment that we were going in the right direction, but we weren't really in doubt about that. In exchange, we had to listen to all the woes of the outside world.

We heard about the trouble in the Falklands and couldn't imagine how those guys felt fighting a war in these conditions. Though they had bigger, warmer ships and better food, the sea was just as cold when you got your ship shot away from under you, and unlike us, who had only ourselves to blame for being in these wintry seas, their last act would be a salt water toast to the generals and politicians who had sent them here.

Maybe we could relate to that little skirmish in the South Atlantic in a small way, but it didn't really affect us. It was too far out of our concern like most news, but as we got even nearer to Australia, we began to pick up a station out of Sydney, and listening to that one day, we heard a story that gave us a definite feeling a prophetic déjà vu, if you can figure that one out.

*W*e had missed the very beginning of the news report, but it seemed some person had just been sentenced to twenty-eight years in jail for conspiring to import hashish into Australia. Mind boggling! Twenty-eight years just for conspiring to bring in some dope! Not even actually bringing it in, like we were. You could rape and murder your neighbor's wife and not get half of that.

What are the authorities thinking? If they want conspirators, why don't why they go after the politicians and the bureaucrats? Tobacco companies, sugar cartels, the oil companies, pharmaceutical companies, and all the arms factories? They're all into conspiracies, either to overcharge us, control us, or kill us. The world is just one big conspiracy. In fact, some conspiracies are so big people don't even realize they're conspiracies. For instance, take that guy, Mr. Kalashnikov, the man who invented that very efficient rifle used by half the world's armies and all the world's terrorists. He might not have killed anyone personally with his wonderful gun, but surely a charge of conspiracy to kill could be brought against him. Of course you'd have to stop somewhere or everyone above three years old would be behind bars, and some of those below, too.

We didn't hear, or maybe the radio station didn't say, but we never got to know how much hash this guy was conspiring to get in. Probably not very much if you consider that sentencing for conspiracy charges seems to be disproportional to the seriousness of the alleged crime. Presidents and Prime Ministers that conspire to start wars that kill thousands get re-elected with gala parties. Leaders of world religions get promised a seat in heaven along with all the earthly rewards for conspiring to brainwash our children. Little backpackers conspiring to smuggle an ounce of heroin get strung up. If we wanted to stay out of prison, maybe we should go back for a few more tons.

It's alright being flippant, but hearing something like that didn't lighten the mood any on the boat. It made us more aware of what could happen if our little adventure went wrong. When you're a little fish like we were, you can't afford to get cocky. It's okay for the big fish of the conspirator world. They can arrive in presidential jets and Pope-mobiles, but we were going to have to be very careful how we arrived. Arrival time was very near now. In a few days, we would be off Cape Leeuwin, the jutting chin of southern Australia. Already we were feeling the effects of the winter high pressure system that lies over the land. The winds were gradually getting lighter and the seas less bruising as the high pressure forced the low pressure systems further south. It was still a long way off being a summer cruise, though, and we wondered if we could make it through Bass Strait, which still lay a thousand miles away and loomed in our minds like the Mountains of Mourn.

Given the state of the boat and the food locker, we were giving serious thoughts to an alternative plan. We could make for Albany, an old whaling port, that lay east of Cape Leeuwin, tucked away safely just around the chin. We couldn't arrive with our cargo aboard, and knowing nothing of the coast about, it didn't seem too good a prospect. We still had Plan B to fall back on, which was to make for the town of Bunbury, which had a reasonable harbor and was located about sixty miles north of Cape Leeuwin across the bay from Cape Naturalist, giving good shelter from any southerlies but a bad shore in anything else. One advantage to this plan was that Jack knew the area a little. His wife lived further up the coast in Perth. He knew there were good sandy beaches surrounding the shallow bay. Jack and Andy were giving this idea more serious thought than I was. I still preferred finding a landing on Wilson's Promontory, with its many coves and inlets and no towns, but I must admit getting there at this time of year made me uneasy. Something else at this time made me uneasy, too.

One morning I had just finished my trick at the tiller. Eight o'clock in the morning, but still dark, just like a winter morning back in Manchester, cold and dark with heavy rain showers. Andy had taken over the watch, and I thought I'd go see if Jack was awake to have a little chat. Going into his little cubbyhole of a back cabin, I found him lying on his bunk, writing in a big notebook.

I'd never seen this notebook before, and I had never seen him writing, either. Neither of us kept a log or a diary, just the scraps of paper we worked out the calculations for the sights on. That in itself is strange. Both of us were avid readers, interested in history and past explorations, but of all the places we had visited or been to, not a word, not even a photo. Good job Herodotus and all the rest were not so bloody lazy. I asked Jack what he was writing about, and he said that he had found God. He had a little smile on his face, but he seemed more embarrassed than cynical.

He could have said he was pregnant, and I wouldn't have been more surprised. He must be having me on. Ever since I had known Jack, he had been a fully paid-up, card-carrying atheist. So, I couldn't imagine what god he was talking about. Obviously not the God who comes in three pieces, and you have to make him into a whole one like a cosmic Leggo game--the one he had been encouraged to bray to when he was a boy, like a donkey with heaven on a stick in front and a switch of hell on his backside. No, it couldn't be that one. Too many bad words said about that one. Maybe he had picked something up in India. They have more gods there than fleas on a dog's back, but we hadn't been there long enough for him to get any bad habits. He wouldn't enlarge on what he said, and I couldn't draw him into his usual cynicism. He was certainly writing a lot, but at least he hadn't reached the stage that most people with a god get to when they want to bash your ear with their silly absurdities.

A few weeks ago I could have understood him getting God-fever, crawling through the tropics with his brain heated with hashish, but he hadn't been hitting the pipe for a long time now. Surely, there aren't any gods lurking around down here in the wet and cold. I thought they only like hot and dusty places, or at least warm, but I guess they can pop up anywhere where there are people to lure them out. It was worrying, though, because when people find gods, they always lose a reciprocal amount of logic and reason. I didn't want Jack turning round and saying God had told him to abort the trip. If this new-found god of Jack's was going to say anything like that, though, it would have to hurry up because we were almost about to make landfall. That was a disturbing talk. Disturbing because no matter what club you belong to, you don't like it when someone up and leaves. The more people you have in your club sharing your views, the stronger you feel you are right. I don't think I'd go so far as to burn or torture anyone for joining a new club, but it's not nice to lose someone to the opposition.

Anyway, no time for that now because we just went over the continental shelf. This was the first direct proof that we were nearing Australia. Apart from noticing that the weather had been changing, due partly to the continental high pressure system, we knew now for sure that land was only about thirty miles away. The South Indian Ocean probably averages out about three thousand feet. That's a lot of water being pushed toward the landmass by the constant westerly winds. When the seabed suddenly rises up until it's only two hundred meters deep, it's not going to take this abrupt change lying down. In fact, it's going to get itself into a right state trying to get rid of all that forward momentum. It doesn't rear up like a wall, like it would if it were hitting a beach. Then it would be a disastrous tsunami-like wash out. Instead, it heaves and breathes itself up until the seascape changes into hillocks and dales. It's positively pastoral, the water in the valley being a deep, dark grey, lightening to a lush, grassy green for the last few meters of the swelling summit. Any cows grazing on these slopes would have a hard time, though, as the slopes are continuously changing shapes, the valley becoming the peaks, and the peaks sliding down to become one of the troughs. The valley is so deep that no wind arrives down there and the sails would falter and flap until the valley floor heaved up again to let the wind re-grip the sails and give some forward momentum as we raced down the next arriving slope. This tobagganing lasted about thirty minutes until we were over the edge of the bank and the sea had found its equilibrium again. What a show! It was a great welcome to Australia.

We had caught a fish, too. The first for many weeks, although not too surprising. The edges of continental shelves are always good fishing grounds. The fast food centers for our watery kin, where all the nutrients and goodies are churned up from the chilly deep. I would have preferred a yellow fin tuna or a dorado, but a fair sized bonito was way better than nothing. These fast swimming fish are red blooded and not the best meal in the sea. Not too bad in a curry or even in a spaghetti, but we didn't have the makings for any of these dishes, so sashimi it was. An old lady told me in Japan that the best way to eat bonito raw was to cut its throat and hang it to bleed to let the blood drain for a day, then slice it fine and dip it in a garlic sauce. We didn't have the time for that nicety, and we had no garlic, but we did have a tube of Japanese wasabi mustard and some soy sauce. They might have turned their nose up at in a Tokyo restaurant, but I tell you that fish was good. We kept the head and baited it with the biggest fishhook we had, a hook that wouldn't have been out of place in a butcher shop, and a long wire trace. We would see what else we could catch before maybe we were caught ourselves.

After clearing the bank and getting in smoother water, the wind went down with the seas, and by late afternoon we were almost becalmed in a smooth grey swell, which suited us perfectly. We were going to heave to anyway and wait for nightfall, where we hoped to pick up the loom from the lighthouse on Cape Leeuwin. We didn't want to get too close in daylight in case we were spotted by any ships rounding the Cape en route to Freemantle or the other way to Melbourne or wherever. In the summer, it might not be unusual to find yachts off this cape, but in winter, it might be rare enough to make the ship's lookout question it. We knew that the Coast Guard in Australia had quite an intense anti-smuggling program with ships and small aircraft pilots being asked to report any suspicious boats. The program is more active around the north and the northwest coasts, but it was still something to think about even down here.

The moment for decision had arrived. We could continue on past Cape Leeuwin and across the Australian Bight and hope to make it through Bass Strait. I think we all would have preferred this. It was the original plan and seemed the best way to get our stuff ashore unseen, but realistically, it just didn't seem possible given the state the boat was in. The rudder, tied on by rope, had worked okay in the deep ocean, but across the Bight, and especially Bass Strait, the waves would be steeper and shorter, and the rudder would be asked to work harder. That wasn't even considering having no compass, no engine, and no food. Jack and Andy seemed to be leaning toward going north, following the coast up from Cape Leeuwin and across the wide and shallow Geographie Bay to the small harbor town of Bunbury. Jack had passed through there by car but knew nothing of the harbor except that it was a small commercial port. I could go for that, but no way I wanted to arrive with the stuff onboard. I suggested that we could throw it overboard going into the harbor entrance. We knew that the tires would sink and then we could dive for them and pick them up later. The minute I said it, I realized it was a desperate idea, and probably, at this stage, I was the one most into just getting rid of it, throwing it away and forgetting out the whole thing. Jack pointed out that we didn't have the financial freedom to do that, and we should probably think a little more. Maybe this new god of his was a pragmatist, too.

There was one other way to see this through, but it depended very much on the weather. Fifty miles north of where we were lay the rocky promontory of Geographie Point. From there, the course would be just north of east, crossing the forty miles to Bunbury. If we were to round this point, keeping close to shore, Jack reckoned there was a sandy beach just south of the point near the small hamlet of Dunsborough. That seemed a better idea than trying to get into Bunbury Harbor, where Jack was sure there was a customs office.

We'd have to be lucky with the weather. With the wind any-where north through west, it would be a dodgy place to be trapped in, with the surf running around the whole sweep of the bay. It would be a dangerous lee shore, especially with no engine. Getting close enough to launch a dinghy would be even more tricky; getting it to shore and then back out through the bay and then having to claw the yacht away from the shore, close hauled. The boat would also have to be at anchor, while the dinghy went ashore, ferrying the cargo, and that couldn't be taken for granted. It might not be good holding ground, and we could end up with everything washed up on the shore.

That wouldn't be a bad idea. Maybe we could hide the stuff before anyone came. We could play the hapless mariners. We would get tea and comfort and maybe a hero's welcome. Not a bad idea, except the profit for Jack for this trip wouldn't cover the cost of his boat and definitely not his pride. Lots of better sailors than us had ended up on the rocks, but still, it takes some living down, losing a boat.

It seemed strange to be talking about dangerous lee shores and monstrous Bass Strait waves when we were sitting almost becalmed about twenty miles off the southwest coast of Australia, waiting to see if we could pick up the light from Cape Leeuwen, but we knew this was a lull before the storm. We were near a huge land mass and obviously in a different weather pattern than the deep ocean. All the winds had been called off somewhere to regroup and talk strategy. It would probably charge down from the north when it was ready, sweeping round the Cape to end up joining forces with the westerlies to the south. But, for now, the three of us could all sit together on deck the first time in weeks and eat together. Come to think of it, it was the first time we had anything substantial to eat for weeks, together or not. That poor fish didn't stay on the plate too long. We took some time looking around the boat, retying the rudder, which was getting a bit slack, tightening up the rigging, and putting a few more stitches in the mainsail. Then, just as a grey day started to turn into a grey night, there it was, right in front of us.

The loom from the lighthouse on the point of Cape Leeuwen glowed against the dark sky in spurts. We couldn't be absolutely certain about that, not having a chart, and the atlas doesn't give such information, but it was flashing every twenty seconds, giving a soft dull glow just below the horizon. There weren't any other points or dangers around to justify such a powerful light. It just had to be Cape Leeuwen.

Really, that's a very bad no-no in navigation to assume something is what you think it is, but we didn't have much choice, not having any means to verify it. Anyway, it just couldn't be anything else, and we decided to congratulate ourselves. We were exactly where we thought we were, give or take a few miles. Not bad, considering we had had no compass for the last four weeks. Granted, our course line through the westerlies had been a bit erratic, but we probably hadn't sailed more than thirty miles of wasted time.

We still couldn't decide what to do with the cargo. The hardest bit was probably yet to come. We were all feeling nervous. Not about the prospect of Bass Strait or the storm we knew would be coming soon. We knew a blow was coming because, of all the instruments you could have on a boat, about the only one left on Jack's was a barometer, and every time we tapped the glass, the needle kept going down. No, we were feeling nervous thinking of the twenty-eight years in jail that guy got for conspiring to bypass the Australian customs. I think that at that moment, I would have given the whole hundred and twenty kilos away for a cup of hot coffee, a cigarette and safe entry into Albany.

Chapter 20

We were still talking round and round about what to do when we turned on the radio for the nightly news and the weather forecast out of Perth. As we suspected, there was a cold front up north near the Bay of Sharks, near Perth. It was Force 7, becoming Force 8, the forecaster said. It was a small system but would pick up speed as it tracked down the coast. This sounded good. Maybe we could do something with it. The idea of going to meet a Force 8 storm isn't usually something to get excited about, but if the storm was traveling as fast as they said, it would be off Geographie Bay about this time tomorrow around sundown. Then, the Bay would be swept with westerly winds, raising a short, choppy sea, and making entry into the Bay a desperate trap. As the cold front passed on south, the winds would change from westerlies to southwesterlies and then to southerlies. The Bay would be totally sheltered then, and any wind would be from off the shore. All we had to do was to get up there, heave to until the storm passed, and then creep around the point into the Bay. Oh, this sounded too good to be true! Of course, it all depended on the weather doing what the forecaster said. If the cold front decided to take a rest while it built up more steam, I doubted we could hang around. If it got up to a sustained Force 9, we would be forced to run before it. Then, there would be no choice but to round Cape Leeuwen and run across the Bight and through Bass Strait.

So, we were for the moment all agreed to trust the weatherman. It was only fifty kilometers from here up to Geographie Point, where we could turn into the Bay. I use kilometers because it doesn't seem right to count the atlas in nautical miles, but if you did, it would be only about twenty-five miles, which we could cover in five hours or so. Just then, there wasn't even a promise of any wind coming down from this storm. The minute we got a hint of a breeze, we would close haul and reach up the coast, keeping well off the shore in the daytime. We didn't want people waving at us. We spent the next few hours getting the tires ready, stacking them near the companionway. We didn't want to put them on deck just yet, not wanting them to get washed overboard in the storm to come. We found the spade, checked the outboard motor and got the Zodiac pumped up and lashed down on deck. All night we lay off the coast in a cold, dark sea with the sky like a black bucket over our heads. There didn't seem to be any current running around the coast, as the next morning the loom from the lighthouse was still where we had first sighted it. Day broke absolutely colorless, not a hint of where the sun was rising. Once the lighthouse got turned off we were without a reference point. By this time, though, probably because of having no compass for the last few weeks, we knew instinctively where north and south were. Anyway, we could feel the pull of the huge landmass to the east and sense the empty ocean waste to the west. There was never any feeling of not knowing where we were or where we had to go. We just needed a bit of wind to nudge us on our way.

Around mid morning, we got our wish--just enough wind to get us under way. We kept the mainsail reefed right down. We didn't want to have to do that when the storm broke. We left the yankee jib high up on the forestay where it caught enough wind to move us through the water at about two knots. We were close hauled, heading slightly more away from the coast, which still lay hidden below the horizon.

It was then, just as we were settling down on this new course, that we noticed we were dragging something in the water behind us. Something had taken a fish head, which we had left dangling over the stern. Whatever it was, it must have been big. It was almost stopping the boat dead in the water. We always kept a pair of welder's leather gloves handy for pulling in big fish, and although they hadn't been used much lately, they were miraculously where they should be. Jack started pulling in the thick, monofilament line. It was slow going. Whatever had taken the hook was below the boat now and trying to drag the boat down. Andy and I wrapped towels around our hands, and together, pulling in short stages, we slowly started gaining. This fishing line is only a few millimeters thick and of just one strand. How is possible for plastic to be so strong? What incredible force is binding the atoms together? You can almost feel their pain at all this stretching. I can imagine all these little atoms holding hands, not wanting to be the one to let go as their arms start popping out of their sockets. You really have to admire these little guys. They held on right to the finale until what was on the end of the hook came thrashing and snarling out of the water.

It was a shark. A tawny colored thresher shark. With long sweeping tail fins, they're really beautiful animals. They win hands down on any best-looking fish contest. Beautiful or not, it was a lot of meat on the end of that line, and we were really excited. I really like a bit of fried shark, and there was enough here to put some fat back on our bones. We managed to pull it up until its jaws were level with the gunwales. Its mouth was open wide, rows upon rows of sharp white teeth. It looked to be about eight feet long, but a third of it was tail. God must have got a good design award for that. It really is a wonderful looking back end.

We were stumped about what to do next. It's not like you could bonk it on the head to kill it. Trying to stick a knife into a shark is like trying to puncture a leather football with a pencil. Sharks don't have skin. It might look like skin, but it's not. Its outer covering is made up of millions of little tiny teeth, smooth as silk brushed one way, rough as gravel brushed the other. Imagine the gene that mutated that one. It must have got a prize, too. The shark wasn't cooperating very well, thrashing around its huge tail, thwacking the hull so hard it set the boat shivering. Somehow we managed to get a loop from the halyard around its tail intending to winch it up and over onto the deck. God knows what would have happened then. A few hundred pounds of frenzied meat with teeth snapping around our feet.

Just as we started winding up on the mast winch, the shark started popping out little baby sharks, perfectly formed six-inch replicas of the mum. Andy stopped helping right away. He didn't want anything to do with killing a pregnant female. I could sympathize with that, but the thought of letting go of such a meal was a bit hard to take. It was becoming evident we were too weakened from lack of food to see this through, anyway, so Andy's compassion was a good excuse to let it go. We cut off the wire trace as close to the mouth as prudence told us, and it fell back with a crash into the sea. I doubt the fishhook, stuck in its upper jaw would stop it from snapping up its next meal, and it would probably rust out over time. Lucky bugger. I wondered if the customs man would be so kind to us if we got caught.

Anyway, we didn't really have time for this diversion, although Jack couldn't believe we just let all that protein go. We had been struggling for over an hour with the shark, the boat going round in circles, because the tiller wasn't attended to. The wind was already ratcheting up a notch with a few low wisps of straggling scud starting to blow by. We didn't want to get too far off the coast. One worry was getting too far north and maybe sailing past the point. There was no sun to get a sextant sighting, so apart from actually seeing the headland, we didn't have any way of knowing exactly where we were. The point itself should be easy enough to make out even from a distance and at night. We took a tack in shore to verify the land was close at hand and hadn't fallen away into Geographie Bay. Later in the afternoon, just as it was getting dark, on midwinter's day, we could see the coast close by. It was just a small view of land through a window in the clouds that were now rushing past with amazing speed.

Then, the wind slammed into us. We were still carrying the high cut yankee jib and it caught the first blast and heeled us over until the scuppers and the lee deck were under water. We were now flying toward the coast, the wind screaming through the rigging and the seas piling up fast. A few seconds later, the rain came, cold and stinging, plastering our hair to our heads and running in torrents down the collars of our shirts. We should have been prepared, but we were caught without our wet weather gear on, and in no time at all, we were soaked to the skin. With two pairs of trousers, and three sweaters on, we gained ten kilos in as many seconds. If we got washed over board, we would sink faster than a brick, but we had to get the jib down. This yankee jib was not such a big sail, but in this wind it was too dangerous to leave up. It felt like any minute now it would pull the stays out of the chain plates and start the mast falling. The jib sheet was as taut and hard as an iron bar. Jack was at the tiller as Andy and I tried to free the sheet from the deck cleat to give us some slack so we could pull the luff of the sail down. It didn't want to let go, it was pulled so tight. We thought of cutting the sail loose, but then we would have had an even worse situation, a hundred square foot of frantically flapping Dacron streaming out from the forestay. It would have shaken the boat to pieces. We could control the flapping if we could turn into the wind just enough to get the leading edge to start backing and take the pressure off the leach. We had to be careful with that, though. We didn't want to suddenly fall off on the other tack before the leeward sheets were slacked off. Then, we really would be in trouble with such a sail set high. With lots of yelling and watching our timing, we got the sheet slack enough to ease off, and we could wrestle the jib down. Half of it fell over the side into the sea and took another age to pull it back on deck and get it lashed down so it didn't blow free. I couldn't guess what the sea temperature was, but it felt warm enough for a bath compared with the rain., which made me feel better about ending up in the sea. At least we wouldn't be cold on the way to the bottom.

It was dark by then, and the storm was right on top of us; the wind increasing, blowing the tops off of the waves, and the rain just smashing into the sea, hissing and boiling. You had to shout to be heard above it all. No more sailing for us just then. We hove to with the jib sheet pulled tight, the sail backed to windward, with the fully reefed main hauled amid-ship and the tiller lashed down to leeward. The bows were now pointing away from the land, and we were lying broadside on to the wind and the waves, which were still from the north. You might think that sounds strange to lie beam-on to the oncoming waves, but the seas weren't big enough for the waves to crest. As the wind pushed against the sails, pushing the boat slowly back to leeward, the seas immediately to windward are flattened so the next waves arriving to this smooth patch are damped down. The jib is trying to turn the boat off the wind, but the tiller is trying to turn the boat into the wind, so it's stalemate, and the boat just rides like that until the jib sheet is loosened and the tiller freed to let the sails tack over to the other tack. It's not uncomfortable to ride out a storm like that, and sometimes, I have lay hove to for days waiting for the weather to change. Of course, you have to have a lot of room to drift, which we did—all the way to Antarctica. It felt like we had already arrived there.

The air temperature was probably around eight degrees Celsius, but it felt a lot colder with the wind blowing over our wet clothes. Now there was no need to be on deck, and we could go down below and try to find something dry to put on. That wasn't easy, either. I hadn't brought that much stuff with me, but by routing around in the dim light

of a kerosene lamp, I managed to pilfer enough from Jack and Andy to
feel dry again, but certainly not warm. Jack and I put on wet weather
clothes and went to sit on deck again. After half an hour of just sitting
on a cold, wet deck, it seemed a bit pointless, and we went back below
and lay down on the cabin sole, still wearing our storm gear. It was so
much quieter down below, and the boat had taken on a slow, cradling
movement. It was almost pleasant lying there in the dark. We had to put
out the lamp. It probably would have been okay, but we didn't see the
need for it, and we would need our night vision if and when we got the
wind shift and started sailing again. In fact, the motion was so soothing
that after awhile, we started to drift in and out of sleep. Suddenly — why
does everything have to happen suddenly? I suppose things aren't emer-
gencies unless they do, but still why not a stage between normal and desperate? A sort of ready-set-go set up? Anyway, it was sudden with no
sort of get-ready-for-this.

We had been lying hove to for all this time, the boat doing its
thing perfectly, and it should have kept doing it until we let go the lines
that were holding it in position. We had been lying with the starboard
side to the wind and heeling over to port. When, to use that word again,
suddenly, we flopped heavily over onto the other tack. Where I had been
rolling into Jack, he was now rolling into me. It was so unnatural, so
unexpected, we were up on deck in seconds, and what did we see? It was
every sailor's dreaded moment.

Ahead was a large freighter. We could barely make out the hull
and superstructure, it all blended together in the rain, but the red and
green navigation lights were very visible and set far apart, which meant it
couldn't be far off. The two white streaming lights, set fore and aft, were
perfectly in line, which meant it was heading directly towards us.

These lights were dipping up and down, showing it was making
heavy weather of it as it forged north. Instinctively, I went to free the jib
sheet, and Jack undid the tiller. Neither of us can really remember what
we did, but I know I didn't have to release the jib sheet. The sail was no
longer backed but free and pulling. Somehow the wind had got behind
the sail, and we had jibed. Now the jib full of wind had us under way and
gathering speed. We were on a run with the wind aft, but we were sailing
by the lee. Imagine this: The freighter is going north against the wind.

We are now going south with the wind behind. Our sails are out to starboard. Our only real freedom of movement is turning to port. That would put us on a broad reach to the port tack, with the sails full of wind and no lines to unhitch and haul in. If we could have assessed the situation in the first split seconds of getting on deck, there might have been just enough time to sail across his bows, but in those first few seconds, the situation was not at all clear. We had a mind's view of where the sails were when we left them, and that had all changed. Also, the tiller was lashed down to port, which would have stopped us sailing off to port right away. By the time we had a picture of what was going on, we sensed the ship was slightly to our port, so sailing right across its bows would have been a bit rash. We could have jibed and brought the main over onto the other side, but it was too late for any maneuver like that, especially in this wind and sea and on Jack's boat. If anything had gone wrong, like lines snagging or something, we would have been sitting ducks. Jack's boat had a tall mast, and there were two running back stays. Depending on which tack you were on when you jibed, you had to release one and quickly tighten up the other one or you were in danger of losing the mast. In the dark, it was a very difficult maneuver to do.

To a freighter that size running over us would have been like hitting a milk carton. They certainly wouldn't have heard our screaming: "Turn on your radar, you silly buggers!" Their radar was most likely on anyway, but it's very difficult to pick up small boats in a blow amongst all the clutter of the waves. So, there was no choice but to sail down the very narrow corridor between his port side and the extreme limit of an accidental jibe. Crazy to think of all that vast ocean to starboard that we weren't free to escape into. That's the longest sail of my life, sailing down the length of that ship. It's not like we could even see it or hear it. It was just a block of darker black moving across an already black background. In fact, we felt it more than saw it when the wash from the stern of the ship started rocking us more violently than the waves had done. God, that was close.

I can't possibly believe in divine intervention. In any case, if God had been anything of a sailor, he should have thrown off the jib sheet to windward and pulled in the sheet to leeward. That way we could have sailed off to the west on a broad reach. The only thing is, if we had tried to do that maneuver when we first got on deck, we would not have had time to uncleat the line and winch in that line. Even if we had, the boat would have needed time to pick up speed. It's not like we would shoot away like an arrow. Maybe it was the god of suddenness in charge, and because his job description denies him the right to act until the absolutely last moment, it was the best possible way out. For the life of me, I can't think of a reasonable answer for why it happened. What was so special about the precise moment when the boat flipped over on the other tack? Why not sooner? But certainly not a second later. Then, we would have gone for sure.

After getting over that excitement, we wore the ship around until we were back sailing north again, following the stern light of the freighter fast disappearing ahead of us. Of course, we shouldn't have done that, either, because we had no idea which direction he was going. He could have been heading out to sea for all we knew, but we just felt like feeling that he was making for Freemantle or Perth, still about a hundred and fifty miles up the coast. If that was true, and we were heading north, it meant the wind had come round to the west because we couldn't have made this course before without tacking back and forth. You might think, "Ah, that's why the boat jibed by itself, because of the veering wind." But, that wouldn't be right. A boat hove to would stay just as it is. True, the bows would change direction as the boat turned around to match the new wind direction, but the sails would stay exactly as they were. So, it's a good try, but I don't think that's the answer. And, don't start thinking supernatural just yet. It was providential in another way, though, being shaken awake like that. We were now on deck and noticing the wind was beginning to change. If we had been lulled to sleep, we might have missed all this and woken up too late to take advantage of the wind shift. So, maybe the freighter was sent as an alarm clock.

We eased off the sails a little and fell off more to the east to go look for the coast again. When we did find it, a sprinkling of little lights, possibly five miles away and turned north again to follow it up, we were on a broad reach, so the wind really was turning fast. Just like the weatherman said. This little cold front was going south at a fast clip. It was eight o'clock now, and we figured we had to be off the point at midnight to leave enough time to get into the Bay and out before sunrise. If only someone could come and tell us exactly how far north the point was. When you're at sea at night when it's been blowing hard and raining, there's nothing like the glimpse of a star through an opening in the clouds. It shoots the spirits right up, and when the moon starts flashing by, you feel like dancing. You just know the weather is going to get better.

Now, there was a waxing crescent moon playing hide and seek behind the clouds. It was now an eight-day old moon, about thirty degrees high from the horizon, a fat crescent looking very bright against the black clouds. In a couple of hours it would be setting and too low down to give us any help, but just now Jack thought it might help to fix our position. That was a crazy idea. A sextant sight of a star or the moon has to be taken around twilight, just after sunset or sunrise, when it is light enough to see the horizon but dark enough to get a good image of whatever you're looking at in the sextant mirror. Sometimes the moon is bright enough to see a horizon long after sunset, but usually it's always a false horizon and shouldn't be taken seriously. Jack really wanted to do it, though. I was sure it wouldn't work, but I had been the expedition's accredited navigator. I don't know how it happened that I had just taken over doing all the navigation, but since leaving Malaysia, Jack had been happy to let me take it all on. Maybe he thought it justified me being part of the trip. So anyway, it was a matter of pride that I couldn't let him do it alone.

The clouds were breaking up fast, and the rain had almost stopped. There was a wide band of open sky underneath the moon to the west. The horizon did, in fact, look to be visible so we got out our sextants and tried a few sights. I rarely use the moon to get a fix because it moves faster through the sky than the sun or stars. There are a lot more calculations to do, a lot more looking up in the tables, and a lot more chances to make an error in working everything out. Working out numbers is not one of the best things I do. Even if we got a good sight and did all the calculations right, we'd still only have a line of position to draw in the chart. And even that would be at an acute angle to the course. Still, knowing we were about five miles off the land, if we could get a line of position, would be a reasonable fix, I suppose. Jack had his sights worked out first, and he put us about fifteen miles south of the promon-

tory headland. It took me longer to wade through all the books of declination and tables of corrections and what not, and I put us just south of
Perth, which should have been a hundred and twenty miles north of us.
A quick check over my calculations and I found a whole degree of latitude that shouldn't have been there, but even with that taken off, I was
still sixty miles off, too far north of where I hoped we were. Damn. It
looked like Jack was a lot nearer than I was.

Back in the 80's when satellite navigation systems were still
expensive and not very reliable, yachties used to pride themselves on their
sextant skills. It didn't matter if you weren't much of a sailor. You didn't
have to know how to set a spinnaker or know the difference between a
barque and a Baltic trader. If you could pick up the light on Dundra
Head after a week of foul weather, then you could join the conversation.
So, I was really disappointed I hadn't done better, especially with young
Andy looking on. He had come to think that my navigation skills were
infallible. It didn't make me feel any better when together we agreed that
the conditions for an accurate fix were just not good enough, and we
threw both our calculations out. Maybe Jack was just being polite about
that because three hours later it turned out he had been right on. Must
have been luck.

Since the near miss with the freighter, the wind had been steadi-
ly sweeping round. Sailing up the coast now one hour shy of midnight,
we were running free before a southerly wind that was losing its punch.
We had closed in more with the land and were probably just three miles
off.

It was difficult to judge the height of the cliffs. The tops were a
darker silhouette against the sky, but the base was merged into the sea.
Maybe they were thirty feet or more. Thank God for the high ground,
though. If it had been a low-lying promontory, we would have not
known where it ended. There was only one small light, not very bright,
on the point, maybe a lighthouse, but it wasn't flashing. There was no
mistaking the place where the land finished--an abrupt cut-off where the
cliff rose up out of the sea. Going in nearer, we could see a huge rock or
maybe a small islet about a quarter of a mile off the end of a point and not
quite as high as the land itself. There was a problem. We could save a
lot of time if we sailed between the rock and the land, but where there's

one rock, there are probably more. I can't believe we even considered it, not having any charts or anything, but Jack thought it might be worth a go. In the end, though, we decided to go around it, and give it a wide berth. We had been running with the sails out to starboard on the port tack, so we had to jibe as we rounded the rock, keeping well away from the waves breaking at the base. That brought the moon dead astern. It was a dull orange giving off no light, sitting on the horizon ready to go to bed. It could have been wishing us good luck before it disappeared. More than likely, it was quite indifferent. It must have seen this sort of thing a million times before. Strange to think it is the same moon that was watching Joseph Conrad as he sailed his Tremolina into those darkened Spanish bays. There's food for thought. We had our differences, but sailing into bays at night to avoid the law was something we definitely had in common. It was almost make or break time. In a few short hours, we'd know the outcome of this little carry-on. Maybe it was time to invoke the souls of all the dead mariners who had ever tried to outwit the revenue man. Get them rooting for us.

Doubling round the end of the point, now heading in a southerly direction, the wind was blanketed by the land to starboard. The water in the bay, which a few hours earlier would have been choppy and spray-filled, was now as quiet and calm as a village pond. Ahead, maybe four miles off, was a string of lights on shore climbing up and away from the shoreline. This must be Dunsborough. They were our only point of reference, and we made towards those lights, ghosting along, juggling the wind, trying to keep the sails asleep with what bit of air there was spilling over the narrow promontory from seaward.

Overhead, to the west, the last of the straggling clouds were still flying by fast. To the north, the sky was now all clear. So, here was the next problem already. How were we going to get out of the bay? This little storm had worked perfectly until now. We couldn't have choreographed it better. But, this little bullet of a cold front system was shooting on by and within a few hours all the wind from any direction would be gone with it. What were we going to use to make our getaway? We could, at a push, use our Zodiac to get us out, but we had always intended to scuttle that. Slash the rubber pontoons, and let it sink to the bottom, along with the engine. I can't remember the reasoning behind this now. I think it went something like, "It couldn't have been us who ferried that stuff ashore. We've only got a rowing dinghy and we've lost the oars, too."

The lights up ahead were going off one by one and we were picturing the people in those houses getting into a soft, warm bed, bellies full, skin bathed, cuddling up to other soft, warm bodies. In their wildest dreams, they couldn't imagine someone was envying them at that very moment. Then, dead on the stroke of midnight, all the rest of the lights went off together.

Chapter
21

T he village must have had timed streetlights. There would be no one walking the dogs at this time in winter, so why waste money? This was good. Everybody tucked up in bed, and dawn a long way off. Without the lights on, though, we couldn't tell how far we had to go before running up on the beach. We were only making a few knots through the water, but that would be enough to ground us fast and hard if the shoreline suddenly got in the way. We didn't want to get too near, but we didn't want to be too far, either. We'd keep going until we got into two fathoms of water.

An electronic echo sounder would have been useful, but Jack hadn't got round to that, either. It would have meant drilling a hole in the hull to put a transducer through, and drilling an unnecessary hole below the water line wasn't something you did before thinking about it carefully. A good old-fashioned lead line was as good as anything. From out of all the other bits of make-do equipment, here was a real one. A short cylinder of lead with a good hundred and fifty feet of line attached with the fathoms marked off with colored ribbons. The bottom of the lead was scooped out to fit a piece of wax. The wax would pick up samples from the bottom and let you know what sort of ground you were anchoring in. Using a lead line isn't quite as easy as you'd think. If the boat is stopped, you can just let the line out until you feel it bounce on the sea floor, but under way it takes a bit of practice. Holding most of the line freely in the left hand and swinging the lead around with the right, judging the boat's speed, you throw the lead out ahead. The faster you're going, the further you throw. The trick is to pull in the line so it's straight up and down as you go over the lead, which you are juggling and jiggling up and down, feeling for the bottom. Before doing this, we had to bring the anchor up from down below, flake the chains out on deck, and attach the anchor rope.

This was really it. This was what we came over three thousand miles to do. Now the time had come, it all seemed a little unreal, but there was absolutely no turning back now. The adrenaline levels were rising., with Jack at the tiller, Andy ready to let the anchor go, and me standing at the bows holding the lead, looking for two fathoms of water to stop in. The first ten throws or so found no bottom, even with all the line out. Up ahead was just a black wall, not a hint of where the beach should be, if there was a beach. Jack assured me there was, but it's not like he knew the place well or had done any scouting. Maybe up at this end of the bay, the beach gave way to rocks.

I was thinking about all the books I used to read as a boy about smugglers and blockade runners. The guys in those boats were always the goodies. It was the landlubbers who needed to learn some manners. The real nasties were the wreckers, those people who lit lamps on the cliffs and rocks, so the seamen, thinking they were heading for a safe haven, instead ended up smashing their beloved boats to pieces, scattering their cargo for these ghouls to salvage. God, that's nasty. Worse than kids pulling the arms and legs off helpless bugs and things. I hoped the people of Dunsborough were nice folks and those lights we saw really were above a sandy beach.

It took about thirty minutes of ghosting along, the sails just holding in the bit of wind, the bows hissing softly, before I found a bottom at twenty feet, a bit deep for anchoring on a short scope. We decided to risk going a little further in. The seabed was a very gentle slope. It seemed to take forever to get into ten feet of water. When we finally let the anchor go, it was one o'clock in the morning, and we figured we had five hours of dark left. We had to ferry the stuff, bury it, and be under way and at least as far out to sea as the end of the promontory. All this before the sun came up. With no way on the boat and the sails lowered, it was as quiet and dark as a crypt and we were whispering to each other. Down below we lit the oil lamp, which just added to the feeling of gloom, making the winter night outside colder and even more dark. We lit the alcohol stove to make a bit of warmth and to brew a cup of tea. We didn't really want a drink. It was more of a ceremony, like Japanese warriors doing the tea ceremony before going off into battle.

I'd always thought Jack and I would be taking the Zodiac to shore, leaving Andy to watch the boat. I was kind of looking forward to that. Some action after being cooped up for so long. Standing there down below, drinking tea and talking strategy, psyching up for the final push, though, we thought it better if Andy went with the dinghy and I stayed to get the boat ready to get under way. That way, if they did meet someone on the beach, they could probably pass off for a couple of locals doing some fishing. My English accent could make them suspicious. You can't say all Englishmen in Australia are suspicious, but there's such a lingering animosity against their former jailers that they just love to put the boot in given half the chance. Of course, if they got stopped digging a big hole and putting a bunch of tires in it, then it wouldn't matter what accent they had. I don't think they'd get away saying they had a big dog.

There was enough power left in the ship's battery to leave the radio on standby, set at a frequency which we could match with the walkie-talkie. Then, it was time to go get the Zodiac over the side and the outboard engine set up on the back. The tires were dragged up from below and placed in the dinghy. God, it looked like a lot. The final touch was a couple of old fishing rods, just in case. As a subterfuge, it was not very brilliant. Not in the same league as a Pope-mobile, but you never know, you can always fool some of the people some of the time. Of course, if you've got a Pope-mobile, you can fool lots of people all of the time. Oh, and we almost forgot the spade. Naturally, when Jack and Andy were onboard the Zodiac, and I was getting ready to cast them off, the outboard motor wouldn't start.

We'd never had a problem with this engine. It was one of those good ones that must have been made on a Wednesday. It always started on the first yank, but now it seemed like it wanted to up the angst, get the nervous system even more worked up. It took a good ten minutes checking the fuel flow and cleaning the plug before it burst into life. Then they were off, heading towards the beach.

It sounded loud enough to wake up everyone from here to Perth. I could still hear it long after they disappeared into the night. The shore must have been even further away than we thought. It was a weird feeling being left alone on the deck of the boat. It was so quiet, the only sound was the hiss of the alcohol stove from down below. The stars were out, but they weren't giving off any light, and just a few yards out from the boat, the sea disappeared into a black nothingness. This must have been how it was for Brahma, sitting in the void before he thought the world into being.

That's what is so fascinating by the sea. One minute you're being knocked around like a ball in a lottery machine and thinking the end is near and the next minute everything is so calm and peaceful, you think you've been granted eternal grace.

It's a good job no cigarettes were onboard. I would have got nicotine poisoning for sure if there had been. In a situation like this, the guy who has to wait, who has no part in controlling the outcome, he's the one who gets the ulcers. There's no way I could be the driver of the car in a bank heist, sitting there praying everything is going to be okay. I'd have to be part of the action. It's just too gut-wrenching hanging around, hoping your mates don't screw up. Not that I'd ever stick up a bank. That's what real criminals and governments do--steal other people's money. It's ironic. Here we were risking life and limb to bring a bit of pleasure into some people's lives, and, if we got caught, these same official thieves would throw the book at us. Lock us up and throw the key away with a holier-than-thou look on their faces. Those Martians circling overhead sussing us out must have a hard time figuring out who the bad guys are sometimes.

Two hours later, I was still pacing round, up on deck, down below, going round and round and imagining the worst. If they didn't come back in another hour, I'd have to think they'd been caught. Then what? Obviously, I'd have to wait until the very last minute. In fact, until it got light and I could see the shore to see if they were still there or not. Even if I did leave, where could I go? Not to any Australian port. I'd have to get north into the southwest trades and try my luck in Indonesia. That was a pipe dream. Even if I could sail this boat, which was falling to pieces, alone, there was no food onboard. Anyway, if they had Jack and Andy, it wouldn't be long before the Coast Guard was out looking for the boat that they had obviously arrived on. Then, I'd get towed back into back into port, probably Bustleton.

Just then, the radio crackled to life. A message from Jack! A whispered complaint that he couldn't find the boat. A request for the oil lamp to be put into the rigging. I wasn't going to ask him how he had gone on over the air, but I could sense the excitement in his voice and figured that so far, we were still this side of freedom.

Ten minutes later, they had found the light I put out. They were back along side. They had done it. I could tell from their excitement. They could barely control themselves. We were still all whispering and moving around quietly, although I don't know why. The outboard engine hadn't been whispering. If no one had heard that, they weren't going to hear us talking. I guess that's just a wired in reaction. A natural defensive system that kicks in when you're trying to do something secretly. Politicians must spend their lives whispering.

We had to get going and get out of there. At least as far as the tip of the promontory of Cape Geographie. Then, we could make a course for Bunbury and it would look like we had never been inside the bay. Didn't I tell you fate was always kind to people doing mischief under sail? Already, there was a murmuring of a land breeze. Not enough to fly a kite in, but enough to give us a shove and get us underway. In fact, things were looking so good, we decided to give up the idea of sinking the Zodiac. It's not like we were going to become millionaires, and it seemed a waste to trash two thousand dollars worth of dinghy. We handed up the engine and hauled the Zodiac up on deck. It would have taken too long to deflate it and pack it up, so we left it for the time being. Anyway, it was full of sand that would have to be washed out. I couldn't believe it. Had we really done it? Were we really going to get away with it? Obviously, we always thought we would or we wouldn't have even started, but the end just seemed too easy. Everything had been too perfect, but we weren't complaining, and we weren't going to hang around to see. So, we upped the anchor, which was already on a short scope, trying not to rattle the chain. I can't think of anything in life more satisfying, more thrilling, than hauling up an anchor. Somehow, it's different than casting off from a dock or a harbor wall. There's a lot more physicality involved, all the pulling and straining at the birth of a new adventure. The sails I had already got ready. I had taken out the reefs in the main and had replaced the yankee with a bigger jib sail, so all we had to do was to pull them up and loosen off the sheets. We had a fair wind and only five miles or so to run out of the bay. If we got pounced on right then, the circumstantial evidence would be pretty overwhelming. It would be hard to explain what we were doing inside the bay, but once we cleared the point, we didn't care who saw us. It would look like we had just come across the ocean and were heading to Bunbury Harbor.

We were feeling pretty elated. We had just saved ourselves twenty-eight years in jail and were all floating a few feet above the deck as we ran around getting underway. Andy took the tiller, and Jack and I ran around cleaning up, getting rid of any traces of a recent trip ashore while he told me what had happened when they got to the beach. After almost running up into the sand in the dark, they had had to motor along just a few feet off the beach, looking for a landmark so they could easily find the spot again. They had finally found a tennis court that sat back from the shoreline next to a beachfront road. That's where they went ashore, digging a big hole just to seaward of the perimeter fence. They threw in the tires and covered them up with six feet of sand—or that's what he said. A six-foot hole seemed a lot of sand to move, but as long as it was deep enough to stop any dog sniffing around, it would be okay. They hadn't seen any sign of life, no lights on anywhere and nobody about.

Thinking about it then, we agreed that it was very fortuitous that the engine had broken down just south of Ceylon. If it hadn't, we would have motored through the doldrums and got through the westerlies so much earlier and arrived off Australia three months sooner when the weather was still warm enough for midnight walks and snogging on the beach.

We were just getting ready to wash the sand out of the dinghy when Andy who was standing at the tiller, scanning the horizon like a good helmsman should, shouted out a warning and pointed back along the course to where we had come—to shoreward, to the east. There was a boat coming!

It was the Coast Guard! Its red and green running lights were already visible. You know the saying, about your stomach dropping down when you're in danger or when you see something frightening? Well not only my stomach but every organ in my body dropped down to my knees. My legs suddenly became as heavy as two sacks of wet sawdust. I could hardly move, and the space where my heart had been was pounding like a steam hammer. I know now how the fox feels when it's cornered down its hole with the dogs baying and barking at the entrance. It's still free for the moment, free to run to the back of the hole and try to claw a new way out, but all is useless and the end inevitable. So, just like that fox, we knew the end was coming, but we kept on desperately trying to wash the sand and evidence off the boat. I couldn't bear to look up. I just kept my head down as Jack handed me buckets of seawater, which I was throwing half-heartedly over the deck.

Another cry from Andy that it was getting closer forced me to look up again, and sure enough, it was coming on fast. When at first the running lights had been just above the horizon, now we could see a white masthead light well above the horizon. It was obviously set on intercepting us, coming straight for us at high speed. I wasn't thinking at that moment about all the time and effort that we had put into the trip that was now wasted. I wasn't even thinking about my almost finished boat back in Japan. I was thinking about Chantal and Radja and what would become of them and my daughter back in England. She'd be okay, she was with her mum. I doubted she'd ever forgive me, though. There's nothing like failure to start off the chain of disdain. She didn't even know what I was up to. Imagine the shock when she got the letter telling her that her dad was locked up forever in an Australian jail. Just then, life was overwhelming. Too much to bear. A few more minutes, and I had to glance up again. It was almost on us now. The speed they were going, they should be coming alongside any minute.

When I looked up this time, what I saw was not the running lights or the white masthead light but what seemed to be a search light. It was high up on what must be the bridge of a huge ship, but strange, underneath the light I couldn't make out any superstructure even though it was not that dark anymore. Dawn was not that far off. It was nowhere near as dark as before. What was going on? There couldn't be a ship that big in the shallow bay. Judging from the height of the light, it would have to be a supertanker or something that big.

Then it hit me. It wasn't the light from a boat chasing us. It was Venus. The planet, Venus, was coming up behind us, rising fast like she always does when she's a morning star. The feeling of relief at that realization was like having the firing squad stood down and winning the national lottery at the same moment. I had forgotten all about Venus. The last time we had seen the planet, she'd been an evening star. That was weeks ago. Then she disappeared. Swallowed up in the incredible light of the sun and lost to sight from the Earth as it followed its complicated journey through space. It might have been shining at dawn for the past few days, but we hadn't seen it because it had been cloudy. When we saw it this day, low down in the east, the cold air over the land where it was rising must have refracted the light, split it up like a prism. So when Andy called out that a Coast Guard boat was coming, our brains took over and saw the reds and greens as running lights. That was a nasty trick the grey matter had pulled on us, but I guess it was understandable. Our subconscious must have been half expecting it to be reality, and it was going to use any props available to up the stress rate. We had finally seen through it, and we knew now that all was going to be okay, although it was a long way from over for me yet.

I'm not sure I could take anymore excitement after that last buzz, so when a real boat did come into view about an hour later, coming up from the south and rounding the point on a course that would take them across the bay to Bunbury, I couldn't muster the strength to even stand up. The sawdust in my legs hadn't dried out yet. We'd used up so much adrenaline in the last twenty-four hours that there was none left to get us excited anymore. We just sat there while it approached and passed us not two boat lengths away. It was an ocean going tugboat. Half a dozen guys showed up on the aft deck and waved to us. We were then just level with the point and already set on a course for Bunbury, forty miles away. They probably thought we had come up the coast, too, and had just changed heading. That was a good sign, wasn't it? Them waving at us? It didn't look like they'd been told to look out for a bunch of desperados.

That passing cold front was probably still blowing wildly off Cape Leeuwen by now, but for us, it was a beautiful, clear blue sky with just enough wind to keep us going. By late afternoon, we were outside the harbor entrance to Bunbury. We thought it might be a good idea to ingratiate ourselves with the authorities by pretending we were concerned and caring people. It was almost five o'clock and maybe they wanted to close up and go home for dinner. We called them up on Channel 16, using the walkie-talkies. That's the frequency for all harbor master offices the world over. They would indeed appreciate it if we could wait until morning before entering. So, we hove to and got ready to spend the last, long, cold night aboard. All the lights of the town were sparkling in the frosty air. The thought of all that food waiting there for us kept our spirits up. Our supper that night was two tablespoons of sesame seed butter washed down with sugarless, black tea.

It's only fair to warn you, if you're reading this for a tale of the sea, that you can throw it away now. This last bit takes place on land, and it's rarely pleasant or exciting to be there.

ou probably want to hear a little more about the ending of this journey. I'm sure you want to know about the payoff. Did I get caught? Did I get the money or not? Well, I could tell you the answers right now, but as I discovered, getting to the ending, even when it appears to be in sight, is rarely as easy as it looks.

Just after eight o'clock the next morning, while waiting outside Bunbury Harbor, a small launch came out to give us a tow in. We had told them the night before that we had no engine but said there'd be no problem for us to come in under sail. I guess they wanted something to do, so out they came. We had spent the last night on the boat cleaning up on our hands and knees, looking for any speck of hashish that might have got stuck in a crack. We dried and folded the Zodiac and stuffed it down below and arranged for the Antarctic expedition board to be filled in with more superfluous information.

There was one last thing I had to do, and the only thing I did on the whole trip that I did without getting everyone's approval. Jack just couldn't get himself to throw away his little hashish pipe. I had known this days back, and when he started looking for it that last night so he could conceal it somewhere, I knew he'd never find it. I had it in my pocket. I hadn't been able to throw it away yet, but I knew that he'd never consent to that. He wasn't overly attached to it. It's not like it was a family heirloom passed down through the generations, but as I said before, he's difficult to understand sometimes. He probably thought he could find a safe place. However, these were highly trained Australian customs officers about to climb aboard, better than bloodhounds at sniffing things out. They could find things in your suitcase you, yourself, didn't know were there. And, if they did find it, that could lead to all kinds of questions and suspicions. So, when the launch pulled up alongside, I dropped it over the side. "That will teach him to get a better moon sight than I did."

We weren't really worried about these guys searching the boat. There was nothing to find. There was still the chance that someone had seen the boat when we were inside the bay off Geographie Point and had done his civic duty by reporting it to the Coast Guard, but the customs men seemed to be taken in with our story of losing the engine after leaving Malaya and drifting across to the Maldives, and even about the Antarctic bit. When, like the Indian customs men, they started telling us of their successes in nabbing drug runners, we knew we were off the hook.

Down in Aussie they do everything properly and in order. Before we could get off or anyone else could board, the doctor had to come aboard to make sure we weren't carrying smallpox or something. Apart from a slight case of dermatitis around split and bleeding fingertips, we were announced fit enough to disembark. First, though, we had to throw away any food left on the boat and even cans, if we had any. They're more afraid of contaminated food than terrorist bombs in Australia. That was one law we could follow to the letter. It took about two seconds. Then, the immigration man arrived. He was a Pom, like me, not more than half a year emigrated out of England, young and efficient and pompous as hell. Of course, he couldn't shout at Jack and Andy. They have roots here, but he demanded to know where my visa was. That bowled me over. Since when did people from the motherland need visas to get into Australia? It was a new rule come in a few months before. I wouldn't have minded if he had been an aborigine denying me access to his land, but who the hell was this guy, throwing his weight around, telling me I couldn't stay? He could hardly make us turn around and sail out again. So, after making it quite clear that this was a very special exception, he stamped me in for two weeks. He did say I could get an extension after that. That made me shake my head. If he could do it after two weeks, why not just do it now? This guy was from Blackpool, just down the road from Manchester. I used to go dancing there on a Saturday night. We were practically neighbors. It just shows that for the rest of us, blood might be thicker than water, but for the immigration man, it's the viscosity of your ink that counts.

After that little two-hour welcoming ceremony, we were left alone to do what we wanted. We wanted to go to a different berth further inside the harbor, right at the back near the main gate. It was quite a ways, and a tricky maze of jutting walls and pilings. They said they'd give us a tow, but we preferred to go under sail. Standing on the customs dock, as we pulled up the sails to get underway were three guys who said they were from the local sailboat club. These guys didn't think we would be able to do it without an engine. Whatever Jack is, though, he is also a superb tactician. He could tell to a fraction of an inch the amount to let out or pull in the sails. He set them to perfection and judged to the second when to tack and come about. It was a virtuoso performance, sailing around all the obstacles, gliding up to our final berth and stepping calmly onto the dock to tie up for the last time. Drug runners couldn't do that.

Just before leaving the boat, which for me was going to be the last time, to go and telephone Jack's wife, Jack got Andy and I on the aft deck. He wanted to show us something up the mast. He pointed at the tangs halfway up the mast--the brackets that hold the spreaders in place, those short spars that keep the masthead side stays spread out. When you're the builder, you must notice all kinds of things other people would miss. It was clear when he got us to look from just the right angle that there was a crack in the stainless steel weld, opening like a tear in a piece of paper, where the bracket was bolted to the mast. It had opened about a quarter of an inch at the start of the rip and went for half an inch. There was still an inch of weld, but obviously, that would have weakened as the tear got longer. He had noticed it a few weeks back when we were thrashing through the southeast trade winds. He didn't tell us then because he thought we might worry about it. He was right there. I would have been worried to death. If the spreaders had gone, the mast would have, too, or at the very least, the top half would have. It must have been a heavy burden keeping a secret like that to himself. No wonder he was looking for a god.

Walking out the dock gates to find a telephone, I was eighty percent sure that Chantal and Radja would not be waiting. At least not in Australia. After Jack came back from talking to his wife and didn't mention them, it climbed to ninety-five percent. I still couldn't bring myself to ask him, "Are they there or not?" Lynn was staying with relatives in Freemantle, about two hours north, and all the intrepid Antarctic explorers had been invited to go and stay there. So, while we waited for her to come by car to get us, we checked out the nearest fish and chips shop.

They just opened for lunch, and we got the first batch. I don't know if it's that good every day, but it seemed to us that they made it extra special. If all you know is English fish and chips, then you can't imagine what I'm talking about. Of all the countries in the world where they serve this up, Australia has to take the prize. You have to give them credit for something. The beer is terrible. Actually, I can't really confirm that. They serve it up so cold that you can't tell what it tastes like. The fish they fried was advertised as flake, the fancy name for shark. I wondered if it was the one we had hooked and let go off Cape Leeuwen. I hoped not. After all, our destinies were linked. I wanted it to be swimming free, with a future, just like us.

When Lynn arrived alone, in an empty car, I had to stop kidding myself that I was going to see my little boy anytime soon. Lynn handed me a letter posted two weeks back from Colombo. This was the first letter that I had received since the one from Jack that had brought me here in the first place. I didn't think there would be any surprises in this one, though. There weren't. Chantal had decided to stay in Sri Lanka because she didn't think she and Lynn could get on together, stuck for weeks in Australia, waiting for us. Lynn was a lovely person, so that was just the excuse. She wrote saying that we must have arrived by now, so please come and pick her up to take her back to Japan. It was postmarked Hikkaduwa, a town on the east coast of Sri Lanka, just outside Trincomalee, but the return address was Colombo. She had obviously given no thought to the possibility that we might have had trouble with the boat or drowned at sea or worse, been caught and thrown in jail. I guess it's better to be an optimist than not, but bloody hell! French women think they can flick their fingers, and you'll come running. Well, any woman for that matter.

I wasn't so sure I was going to jump to it this time. It wasn't that I was too disappointed, but I was annoyed. I had only been ashore for an hour or so, and the problems were starting already. That's the biggest grump I've got about being on the land. Problems just seem to pile up, one after the other. There doesn't seem an end to them. Climbing up on each other's backs until they're so heavy you can hardly lift your head. At sea if you have a problem, you sort it out right away. If you can't, well, it's just not a problem anymore. I should have been enjoying the ride up to Freemantle, riding on the high of a successful end to our trip. Instead, I had to worry about what to do now. We stopped at a wayside store to get some beer. Maybe we could kick start the celebration. It didn't help much. I definitely wasn't feeling too happy.

This was the first time I had been to western Australia, and the bit I was seeing wasn't very impressive. It had a feeling about it like the people couldn't decide whether to stay or not, so they hadn't gone to too much trouble with the buildings, throwing a few planks of wood together. The overall effect wasn't that bad, but there was the impression that they could be pulled down and relocated at a moment's notice. There was some lingering image of an American cowboy town about the place, but more temporary.

There were three choices as to what I could do now. Stay in Aussie until the stuff had been dug up and transported to Sydney; go back to Japan and get on with my boat; or fly off to Sri Lanka to find Chantal. Staying in Aussie is what I had intended to do until payday, but it was doubtful if everything could be arranged within my two week visa. We weren't going to dig up our loot until we were sure it wasn't being surveilled. Then, we had to find a place where it could be stored until we could arrange some transport to get it across the country. I could have tried for an extension to stay, but that would have meant more questions and might have brought the boat back into the authority's gaze. Anyway, my job was finished. I had been hired to help get it into the country, and that had been accomplished. I was eager to get back to Japan, of course, but it was still the rainy season up there, the most miserable part of the Japanese year. It must be the only country in the world with five seasons: the usual four with a rainy season slotted in between spring and summer, and sometimes, lodged so deep it can't get out until autumn. Or, I could do as commanded and go off to Sri Lanka. I had just enough money to fly there, but it would mean waiting there until Jack had got paid off and he could send me some money to get out again.

What would you do? Right! I thought you'd go for that one. So, I know who to blame now if it turns out to be the wrong decision. But, it's true. A holiday in the sun, relaxing on the beach didn't sound too bad. I would have been happier if it had been in another direction, though. Backtracking over the same way we'd just come, looking down at the same watery waste we had just struggled so hard to get across, wasn't too appealing. I didn't come to that decision as quickly as you did, though. In fact, it took almost a week, moping around on early morning walks, crunching over the frost on the banks of the Swan Rivers.

Jack and Lynn had driven by the tennis courts a number of times since we had arrived, checking that all was okay. One day, we all went. It was on the way to Cape Leeuwen where we went to see the lighthouse. That part of western Australia, right on the Cape, must get a lot more rain than further up the coast. It really changed my opinion of this half of the continent. It was massively forested with huge ironwood trees. It looks like Europe must have looked a few thousand years ago. It's only a very tiny fraction of this huge and barren land. What a shame they can't shove it a bit further south, put more of it in those westerly winds.

If I were honest, I'd have to say I knew all along that I'd have to go to Sri Lanka. I could have left Chantal there to fend for herself but not my little boy. All that hemming and hawing was just to make it seem like I wasn't being bullied. I bought a ticket via Singapore to Colombo. When I left, the hashish was still buried, but plans had been made and all looked to be going well. I wasn't at all worried that Jack would let me down. I had telephoned my friend in Japan, and my boat was still waiting patiently and unharmed.

Two airplane journeys in less than half a year, possibly a third very soon when I flew back to Japan. This was getting to be a terrible habit. Not that I mind flying if it's not too long and the plane's not crowded, sitting back, being pampered, reading free magazines. There's a feeling of calm resignation, like being in a dentist's couch, which I don't mind at all. You have surrendered your fate absolutely to someone else's care, although I always try to get a glimpse of the captain before takeoff. If he's going grey around the temples, I usually feel better. I don't care for young dentists, either.

We had an eight-hour layover in Singapore, so I walked out of the airport to the beach for a swim. I still wasn't impressed with the seaside, but it did seem a little cleaner. Maybe they'd just finished doing a photo shoot for yet another tourist hotel. Then, we were off and flying over the exact same piece of ocean we had crossed months before. It was dark outside, and we could look down and watch the lightening spitting in the clouds below, heating them up until they glowed orange. The southwest monsoons were in full spate, and Colombo on the west coast where we were going would be wet and stormy. The east coast, though, would be dry and fine, and I hoped that was where Chantal would be. Landing in Colombo was a bit of a let down. It was dark and rainy. I knew there wouldn't be anyone to meet me, but still it would have been nice to arrive in the sunshine. I caught a bus and found a small hotel not too far from the clock tower in the center of town, somewhere behind the post office. I entered through a narrow door, down a short passageway, and up some stairs. It was a seedy place, the Globe Hotel. I hoped I wouldn't have to stay more than one night. As soon it was light, I'd go and check out poste restante for the letter, which would tell me where to go.

The hotel looked like it had started out life as a large, canteen-style restaurant and had rooms tacked up around the edges. Its walls were made from half-inch plywood, with a two-foot gap between the wall and the top of the ceiling, like all Asian hotels before air conditioning. The gap was filled in with iron mesh to make the guests feel safe. Inside these boxes, there was room for an iron frame bed and a rough wooden bedside cabinet. No ceiling fan, but a small reading lamp. There was no one else around except the guy who checked me in, wearing a longi and scratching the mosquito bites through his t-shirt. The rooms opened onto the restaurant, and the smells from years of bad cooking filled the air.

It takes a lot of nerve for a Manchurian to complain about other people's food, but I find Sri Lankan food terrible. Some people might disagree, and it's true they have great fruit there—the best mangos in the world—but the curries are just awful. Once before when I was here, I was invited to a house for dinner. In a situation like that, when the food is just not edible, I can usually muster the manners to get it down. That time, though, it was so bad, it was a case of life or death. On the floor behind my chair, there was a large ceramic pot with a broad-leafed plant growing in it. I waited for the host to leave the room, and I scraped the lot into it. I hoped it might rot away before it was discovered, but there was so much salt in that curry that it probably killed the plant first. He was a nice guy, and I was sorry I had to treat his cuisine so shabbily, but there is a limit to good manners. I know there shouldn't be. If everyone in the world had impeccable manners, there wouldn't be any trouble and strife, would there? I guess that's what Jesus was on about when he told all you guys to mind your manners and do to the others what you'd like them to do to you. But, here's a dilemma. We can't teach our kids good manners and at the same time teach them the facts of evolution. They are two contradictory concepts. I have been told to my face by a Darwinist that my cooking is terrible. I had to agree. How can you refute anything told by an evolutionist? I think I would have preferred if he had surreptitiously dumped his meal and lied about how good it tasted.

Even without the bad smells from the kitchen, it looked like it was a bad idea to book into this hotel, but I couldn't leave now. It would have been rude to turn around and walk back out. I only had to stay one night. As soon as I got the letter from the post office, I'd be off somewhere else. I didn't sleep much that night. The mosquitoes were having the time of their lives in the rainy season. It's not that I begrudged them a bit of blood, and there's no malaria here yet, but the sound of them zeroing in for the attack drives me off the wall.

In the morning, I couldn't put the hotel staff through the trouble of making breakfast, so I went outside to find a coffee house and waited for the post office to open, which it did about ten o'clock. Post offices and perhaps the railways, too, are the only places that seem to work smoothly in India and Sri Lanka, and just to show their heritage and the reason for this smooth bureaucracy, many of them still have hanging outside the Coats of Arms of the last British monarchs before independence. Inside, you get the feeling that they don't want to let go of that imperial past. Getting a little shabby now, but you have to say they're efficient, and the postal service really does work. When I was told that there was no letter for me from anywhere, it had to be because no one had written me one.

I was so sure there would be at least a message telling me where they were that I couldn't grasp the situation. I'd never considered that possibility, and there was no Plan B. Now, what? Maybe she hadn't got around to writing yet. After all, it was Sri Lanka, where the clocks only go at half speed. I would go back in the afternoon, but first I had to get my bag and change hotels. Back at the Globe, before I checked out, I decided to write a quick letter and send it to the post office in Hikkaduwa, just in case she got it, telling her to send a reply to poste restante in Colombo. One of the few frills provided by the hotel was some stationary, so I used this.

The next hotel, not too far away, was a little better. It was full of Sri Lankan businessmen—not the high powered ones, but salesman types. The best thing about it was that there was no restaurant. I was going to give it as long as possible for the rest of the day for a letter to arrive, so just before closing time, I went back to the post office. Is there anything more disappointing than not getting the letter you're expecting? Probably a whole host of things, but I couldn't think of any at that moment. I'd have to give it a little more time, but I was beginning to think it was a big mistake coming to Sri Lanka. And, what to do while you're hanging around? It's not like you could enjoy yourself when you're feeling let down and betrayed. Whereas in Perth, I'd been moping along the banks of the Swan River, now I found myself, a few days later, moping around the seafront of Gaul Face.

There was no letter the next day, or the one after that. Maybe she'd sent another letter to Australia, which I had missed. I went to the telecommunications office and placed a call to Australia and got through to Lynn. No, there was no letter and nothing was happening with the hashish either. Not a very satisfactory phone call. Maybe Chantal had contacted our friends in Japan. That would be a common point of contact. I booked another call through to Japan, and after waiting thirty minutes to get connected, was told there was no answer. I think if I had bumped into Chantal going out the phone office door, I would have strangled her.

Walking round in circles, waiting for the post office to open again, I noticed two guys sitting in an open fronted coffee shop. They looked like they knew what was up. Not your out and out freaks but not your package tourist either. I went and sat down with them. Germans, been here two months, and getting ready to dash off to India before their visa ran out. They had a bit of disturbing news. They told me that people who overstay their visas were shipped off and locked up on an offshore island somewhere. Wow, that sounded a little Draconian, but I could believe it. Immigration offices everywhere won't be happy until the whole world is one big gulag. So, as soon as I had my coffee, I took myself to the immigration office, which isn't too far from the post office. Actually, nothing is too far from the post office in Colombo, except the letter you're waiting for. I wasn't expecting them to be friendly, and I wasn't disappointed. But, being Sri Lankan, they weren't that good at being unfriendly. They'd have to work on that to get in the same league as that guy in Aussie. They did tell me that it was true about visa violators being imprisoned on an island, but they wouldn't check any names for me. That left me feeling even more desperate. If they had only got a one month visa, then they were well over that, but I was sure they would have got a two-month visa, like I did, so they still had about a week.

The next two days, in between popping back to the post office every ten minutes, I called in all the likely looking hotels where she might have stayed. If she had, she might have left a forwarding address. I felt a right fool doing that. Deserted husband looking for runaway wife. I could have kicked myself for coming here. I don't know why you thought it was such a good idea. Now here I was, trapped in Sri Lanka, very little money, no ticket out, and totally dependent on what happened three thousand miles away in Australia.

One day, when I'd been here about a week, I thought to give another call to Japan. I'd just been to catch the morning post, and nothing, as usual. In fact, I had become part of the morning ritual at the post office, and I wouldn't even have to ask. When they saw me approaching the counter, they would just wag their heads slowly and shrug their shoulders apologetically. The telephone office was about a twenty-minute walk from the post office, across a large plaza, where long distance buses left from. You had to book your call at a long counter, crowded with other international dialers, then sit on a bench and wait until your name was called. When it was, you were given a booth number. You paid later. It was lunchtime in Japan, and I knew my friend should be there. After that long preamble, I bet you think I got some good news. Well, you're wrong. He hadn't heard from her, either. I never could figure out that saying, "No news is good news." This no news was eating me up. I'd hit the bottom.

I left the phone office really dispirited, not knowing where I was going. I must have crossed the square and started going up a small side street. I was not aware that I had ever been up this street before, and I wasn't paying attention to anything except my own miserable state, when all at once, my belly started filling up with soft, warm, candy floss. That's exactly what it felt like. If I had to give a color, I'd have said pink. It was filling up from just below my navel, rising up my chest, puffing out my shoulders, straightening my back and lifting my head. At the same time, and rising with it, was a feeling of wild euphoria. I felt I must be shining like a light, so intense was this feeling. I knew without a doubt, with incredible certainty, that all was going to be okay and I would soon be seeing Chantal and little Radja again. I continued walking up the road, or more like floating up, wondering what it was all about. Where had this feeling come from? It took about ten or fifteen minutes to walk up to almost the end of the road where I noticed a man standing outside a doorway, beckoning me over, and then holding up his hand in a gesture to wait a minute.

Instinctively I knew this had something to do with this wonderful feeling I had. He had gone back through the door he had been standing outside. Then, I noticed it was the entrance of the Globe Hotel, the hotel I had stayed that first night. A couple of minutes later, he came back with a scrap of paper and a telephone number scribbled on it. He told me some woman had telephoned quite a few days back asking for me and had left this number I was to ring. The number was for a restaurant up in Hikkaduwa. "Well, thank you very much. But, how did you know I was going to be coming up the street just then?" I asked. He hadn't. He had been standing outside having a smoke, and when he saw me, he suddenly remembered the note. Okay, that part is easy enough to understand. I doubt he had many foreigners stay there, so matching my face to the woman caller is straightforward enough, but how did he get the message to me and turn on the candy floss ten minutes before he even knew I was coming. That was a good trick, but I think I know how it was done. Some people like this sort of stuff. They start trotting out all kinds of theories about clairvoyancy and what not. It's not that simple minded. It's far more interesting and complicated than plain magic. As I started walking up that street, and it wouldn't have worked if I had gone up any other, my subconscious, as usual, was constantly monitoring and filing away all the information it got through the retina, and it would have noticed and recognized the hotel man at the end of the street, and maybe the hotel, too. No small feat. It still took me ten or fifteen minutes to walk that far. There was a small rise to the road, so it would have been possible to see that distance by looking very carefully with some good glasses. But the road was quite crowded and I didn't recognize the man, even when he stopped me. My subconscious put everything together, though, and realized the missing link in the missing lady saga was the letter I had written on the hotel writing paper. Maybe I had noticed the Globe's address on the letterhead as I was writing that day, but I never saw or considered a telephone number. After all, she was supposed to reply to poste restante, and I had no intention of staying more than one night. Well, that's my theory. Of course, the subconscious had no way of knowing whether she'd telephoned, but it worked out the probability and decided that the odds were good enough to give me a treat. I love my subconscious and have a great respect for it. Certainly more than I have for the conscious me. I almost relate to it like a third person, which in a way it is. I'm no more aware of how it works or what it's thinking than I am of your thoughts, but it's up and running and has got me out of a lot of tight corners. Before Freud came along and put us straight, people obviously mistook the subconscious for some kind of personal guardian angel. That term is much more fitting.

I had thought of going to Hikkaduwa when I first got to Sri Lanka. In the southwest monsoon season, it's the only place to be. But, I didn't know for sure that's where she was, and anticipating people's actions is a dumb thing to do. She should have written to poste restante Colombo, like she said she would. I wasn't going to argue just then, though, and went back to get my bag to catch the night train to Trincomalee. I like that train, shunting across the country, especially at night, with the jungle almost inside the carriage, stopping at every station with names that gum up the mouth like Treacle, Viawadenapura, Kurenagalua, Anaradhapura. After arriving the next morning in bright sunshine, I caught a bus to Hikkaduwa. I don't know what it's like now, but then it was just a cluster of makeshift shacks selling tie-dye t-shirts and batik wraparounds, and a few scattered restaurants run by local entrepreneurs. Behind these, on one side, were tall coconut trees and on the other a beach as long as you wanted it to be. I found the restaurant she had telephoned from. They hadn't seen her for a day or two, but they thought she was staying somewhere up the road, about a half a mile away, just off the beach. Walking back down the road, I took the first opening through some trees down a narrow, sandy path that opened up onto the beach, and there she was, running towards me with little Radja struggling to keep up. I was so happy I forgot all about strangling her.

They were staying in a small house rented from a Ceylanese woman. There was a low white wall around it, separating it from the beach, and a papaya tree growing in the garden. It was the bougainvillea spreading over everything that really set it off. The paradise promised by the Prophet to his Muslim martyrs couldn't have topped my stay at that little beach house. Well, maybe, but just in one way. Their paradise was to last forever. Mine had to be interrupted after a few days. Chantal's visa to stay was about to run out. We could take care of that in a day or two-three at the most. There's a train from Trincomalee up the Jaffna

Peninsula to the port of Talaimannar, or there used to be. Now it's Tamil Tiger country, and people don't travel anymore. No doubt about it. Those guys have fenced off a fascinating part of the world. All because the Brits like their tea. Bringing in hundreds of Tamils to work the tea plantations probably looked like a good idea a hundred years back, but now they want to keep the tea and the land it grows on, too. You must admit that the name those guys chose to call themselves has such a ferocious ring, it must be hard not to heed the call.

We could catch the train to the end of that long sand spit that tries to join up with the southern tip of India. Where it doesn't quite make it, there was a ferry boat to complete the journey--a beautiful old ship, a relic from the Raj. It was steam-driven because the water is so shallow that any cooling system for a diesel would soon clog up with sand. It had a saloon, where we could sit and drink our tea from cups with saucers. Arriving at Danuskodi a few hours later, we told the crew we'd see them on the morrow when the boat would be returning to Sri Lanka. With our passports stamped inbound for India, we rode another train along another spit of sand, just wide enough to take the tracks. On the right was Palk Bay, on the left, the Sea of Mannar, both like lakes of liquid turquoise. Soon we were in Rameswaran. Do you know India? You must do. Everybody's been to India, but you might not have been down to this end, which might be your good fortune.

The next morning, back at the ferry, we passed Indian immigration, which had let us out the previous day. Right at the next desk was Sri Lankan immigration who should have let us in, but they weren't doing that. Not with the foreign travelers anyway. There were four or five of us westerners, and they demanded that we show them quite a bit of money or an onward ticket before we would be allowed to embark. We couldn't do that, obviously. A lot of patient explaining that our money was arriving at a Sri Lankan bank didn't impress them. We went back to Rameswaran. We'd try again the next day. Maybe there would be a more reasonable person at the desk. You guessed it. Reasonable and immigration don't go together. Now what? We couldn't stay here. There wasn't even a bank to get money sent to. The only building of note here was a Hindu temple. A huge wedge of cake sitting end up with an alabaster cow reclining on the top, and climbing all over the sides, dusky houris and more cows, looking like an erotic nightmare. Hey, but if you like thearter with your religion, this is the place to be. Down in the dark bowels of this temple there was an elephant chained to the floor by its hind legs, tarted up with pastel chalks and silver bells. If you placed a coin on top of your head it would bless you by plucking it off as gently as a mother plucking lint from a baby's ear.

I'm not going to bore you with how we got stuck in India for two months, which we did. Getting money sent to an Indian bank takes as long as waiting for a heart transplant. Eventually we did get a bit of money sent through and some prepaid air tickets to Hong Kong. I don't know why Jack arranged tickets to Hong Kong instead of Japan, but with the tickets was a message to ring him as soon as I arrived. So, I'd find out soon enough.

Flying into Hong Kong, looking a little out of place in our Indian rags, we taxied to the YMCA in Kowloon. We could have afforded a better hotel, although certainly not the Peninsula next door, but the Y has the best rooftop garden in town, with a great view over the harbor to Hong Kong Island, with the peak rising above all those impossible skyscrapers, and it's just a stone's throw from Star Ferry. After buying some new togs and arranging for a Chinese woman to babysit little Radja, we went out on the town, up Natham Road, down all those little alleys, lit up like Christmas trees and throbbing with excitement. What to eat first? Well, we were in China. So, we settled for an Italian restaurant. We ordered Chianti before we realized we should be having champagne, so we got that, too. Then, I remembered that I had to ring Jack. I asked the maitre'd to bring a telephone. Jack was out, but Lynn gave me an address of an office building on Hong Kong Island and said I was to go there and ask for a Mr. Li who was waiting for me. A Mr. Li, now that was intriguing! Especially given that half the people in town probably had the same name. But, it was interesting enough to keep the evening bubbling.

Little Radja hadn't had such a good time, though. We heard this from the guy in the room next to ours, back at the YMCA. The man complained he couldn't sleep because our child had cried all night. It was only just past midnight when we got back. Anyone going to sleep that early in Hong Kong deserves to be woken up. The next morning was a Friday and my birthday. The sun was shining, and the water of the harbor was shimmering with promise. I left Chantal sleeping and took the ferry across to Hong Kong Island. I found the office building thirty minutes from the harbor landing, up the hill somewhere behind the Hilton Hotel. Mr. Li's office was up too many stairs to walk, and I took the elevator. I was wondering what he'd be like and why I was going to see him.

There was a plush waiting room and a secretary who took my name, got on the intercom, told Mr. Li that I was here. I was escorted like royalty into the inner sanctum. Mr. Li was a very pleasant middle-aged Chinese man and a snappy dresser. He couldn't ask me to sit down because there was only one chair, and he was sitting in it, except when he stood up to reach across his desk to shake my hand. He said something in Cantonese to his secretary and she disappeared, coming back a minute later with a young man, dressed like all Chinese office workers with a short sleeved white shirt and dunn colored tie. He opened his desk drawer, took out a bankbook, and giving it to the young man, told him to escort me to the bank. Well that was what Mr. Li told me he said to the young man. He could have been telling him to take me away and shoot me, but I didn't think so. He also told me how much money I was going to get from the bank, but I'm not going to tell you that. The tax man might be reading this. You can let your imagination run wild, though. As a birthday present, even the Aga Khan wouldn't have been disappointed. I don't know where Mr. Li fit in within this scam of Jack's, but it looked like his friends in Sydney had more clout than I thought.

When we got to the bank a few streets away and on the second floor of another office building, the teller asked if I wanted the money in thousand dollar U.S. bills because, if I did, they would have to charge a twenty percent surcharge on every bill. God, talk about criminals. This was bank robbing in reverse. The woman behind the counter probably thought it would be easier to conceal at the airport than having it all in twenty-dollar bills. It would have been, but I didn't go through all the hassle of the last few months to give it away to a bank. So, I gave her the bag I had just bought at the shop downstairs and got her to fill it up with twenties. Outside again on the sidewalk, I shook the young man's hand and thought I better give him a tip, just in case he thought of tipping off his mates about this gweilo with a bag of money. I gave him five twenties, which he seemed pleased with, and so he should have been.

Walking down the road to catch the ferry back over to Kowloon, life didn't seem too bad. In fact, it felt bloody good. What a fitting place to get the payoff, after all! There wasn't a city in the world more suitable. Not one person in this town could condemn me or moralize at me. Hong Kong was built on drug money. It was the raison d'être for its existence. Some of the big trading companies still doing business here were built on the back of drugs, when back in the 1800's the Brits forced the Chinese to exchange tea for opium. Before I caught the ferry back, there was one last thing I had to do. I had to go to another bank, a proper one this time, with Doric columns and marble halls. I was taken down into the vaults where I could sign for and pay for a pouch full of shiny, one-ounce, krugerrands. Not that it made any financial sense, but it just seemed that a successful contrabandisto should have some gold jangling in his pocket.

Well, that's about it, but every journey has to end with the immigration man, so here he is. I wasn't expecting any trouble at Narita airport. I had been coming in and out of Japan for years, but I sensed something was going wrong this time when he took us out of the line and into a small annex room. He pointed out something in my passport that I had never considered at all. The visa I had got one year back allowing me to teach in Japan had expired just a few days prior. As I had been out of Japan for the past seven months, I obviously had not fulfilled my contract, the man informed me, and because of this, he wasn't going to let us in. I had never had a contract to break, so I couldn't quite follow his reasoning, but he was deadly serious about us getting back on the plane to Hong Kong. In a panic, I tried explaining about my boat, not too far away, waiting to be finished off. He was finding that difficult to take in. Our friend, who we had called when we were in Hong Kong, was picking us up from the airport. He must be waiting at arrival, we told the immigration man. We begged him to page our friend and get him to verify it all. He was good enough to do that, but it still didn't look too good, even after our friend vouched for us.

After sucking his teeth and pondering it all for an hour or so, the immigration man finally said that if we could guarantee financial independence, he'd let us in. "Well, that is no problem!" I shouted, opening my carry-on bag and spilling bank notes and gold coins all over his desk.

He looked suspiciously at me, then back to Chantal and Radja, cocked his head slightly, and for some reason, perhaps because he had had enough of my story by this time, too, waved us through.

I'm guessing that you might still have a couple of questions you'd like me to answer before I sign off.

Did I get to finish my boat, you wonder?

You bet! She's a beauty.

And, did I get any more letters from Jack?

Ah, well...that is another story.

ABOUT THE AUTHOR

In the 1960's and just out of his teens, John Lomas set out to see if the rest of the world was as boring as his home town of Manchester, England. It wasn't, or at least most of it wasn't.

After many years of travelling with his thumb, he made his way to Singapore. From there, he caught the French steamship, MV Cambodge, that ran routes from Marseilles trading by the Red Sea, stopping at Jabuti, Bangkok, Singapore, Saigon, Manila, Hong Kong, and Kobe, Japan. Bound for a quick trip to Saigon to see what that was like before going to work in Australia, Lomas jumped aboard. He never made it to Saigon, though. The captain refused to stop because of recent violence. Lomas didn't mind continuing on, though. In those days the journey was everything, and traveling didn't mean getting to the destination as quickly as possible. The ship carried Lomas to the end of the line at Kobe, Japan. At that time, there were so few foreigners in Japan that he soon had more work than he wanted, mostly as a movie extra and TV commercial actor. He eventually returned to Manchester, but finding the weather hadn't changed, he took a slow train skirting China back to Japan. It's been his base ever since. Is it a better base than Manchester? Well, if you're not too keen on baked beans and pig's blood sausages, it is.

Nautical Glossary

A

Aft— at, near or towards the stern; to move aft is to move back
Anchor—a heavy metal object, fastened to a chain or line, to hold a vessel in position, partly because of its weight, but chiefly because the designed shape digs into the bottom.
Anemometer—an instrument for measuring wind speed
Astrolabe—a precursor to the sextant. An old navigational device for checking the altitude of the sun or stars
Autometer—an instrument for measuring a boat's speed through the water.

B

Back—the wind shifts in a counterclockwise direction in the northern hemisphere and clockwise in the southern hemisphere; the wind is said to back when it changes contrary to its normal pattern
Backstaffs—a navigation instrument used to measure the apparent height of a landmark whose actual height is known, such as the top of a lighthouse. From this information, the ship's distance from that landmark can be calculated.
Backstay—standing or running (adjustable) wire rigging that supports the mast from the stern; a wire mast support leading aft to the deck or another mast
Beacon—a lighted or unlighted fixed (non-floating) aid to navigation that serves as a signal or indication for guidance or warning.
Beam—the transverse measurement of a boat at its widest point. Also called breadth. (2) One of the transverse members of a ship's frames on which the decks are laid
Bearing—a compass direction, in compass points or degrees, from one point to another. Relative bearing is the direction relative to the heading of the boat with the bow 0 degrees and the stern 180 degrees. True bearing is the direction from the ship relating to true north with north being 0 degrees and south 180 degrees.
Beating—to sail towards the direction from which the wind blows by making a series of tacks. A point of sail also known as sailing close hauled.
Beaufort Scale—an empirical measure for the intensity of the wind based mainly on sea-state or wave conditions.

Bent—to install the sails on the boom or the forestay

Bilges—the parts of the floors of a ship on either side of the keel which approaches closer to a horizontal rather than vertical direction. The very lowest part of a boats interior where water is likely to collect

Block—a wooden, metal or plastic case in which one or more sheaves (pulleys) are placed, through which turns of line (falls) are threaded for the purpose of gaining mechanical advantage or changing the direction of motion. Lines used with a block are known as tackle.

Blooper—light-weight foresail similar to a spinnaker but set without a pole.

Boat hook—a long sturdy pole fitted with a blunt hook at one end designed to catch a line when coming alongside a pier or mooring, to facilitate putting a line over a piling, recovering an object dropped overboard, or in pushing or fending off.

Boom—a horizontal pole or spar attached to the mast to which the foot (lower edge) of the sail is fastened

Broach—to spin out of control and capsize or nearly capsize; The turning of a boat broadside to the wind or waves, subjecting it to possible capsizing; a turning or swinging of the boat that puts the beam of the boat against the waves, creating a danger of swamping or capsizing; loss of steering. A knockdown.

Bulkhead—a name given to any vertical partition or wall which separates different compartments or spaces from one another, also adding strength. Sometimes bulkheads are also watertight, adding to the vessel's safety.

Bunk—a sleeping berth or bed.

Buoy—a floating object employed as an aid to mariners to mark the navigable limits of channels, their fairways, sunken dangers, isolated rocks, etc. (2) an anchored float marking a position or for use as a mooring (3) an anchored float to use in yacht races

Buoyancy—the capacity for floating.

Cabin—a room or living compartment for passengers or crew.

Cabin sole—tThe floor or bottom surface of the enclosed space under the deck of a boat

Celestial navigation—to calculate your position using time, the position of celestial bodies, and mathematical tables. Position is determined by measuring the apparent altitude of one of these objects above the horizon using a sextant and recording the times of these sightings with an accurate clock. That information is then used with tables in the Nautical

Almanac to determine one's position.

Chart—arepresentation on a plane surface of the spherical surface of the earth. The equivalent of a map for use by navigators.

Cleat—a fitting of wood or metal, secured to the deck, mast, or spar, with two horns around which ropes are made fast. The classic cleat to which lines are belayed is approximately anvil-shaped; verb - to belay.

Clew—the lower aft corner of a fore and aft sail, both lower corners of a spinnaker, and the lower corners of a square sail

Close hauled—a point of sail where the boat is sailing as close to the wind (as directly into the wind) as possible; sails are pulled in tight, enabling the boat to point as high as possible to the direction the wind is coming from; Also, "beating" and "on-the-wind".

Cockpit—the location from which the boat is steered, usually in the middle or at the stern of the boat.

Cockpit sole—floor of the cockpit

Companion way—the area leading down from the deck to the cabin, usually with steps (ladder)

Compass—navigation instrument, either magnetic, containing a magnetized card indicating the direction to magnetic north (showing magnetic north) or gyro (showing true north).

Compass card—A card labeling the 360° of the circle and the named directions such as north, south, east and west. Part of a compass, the circular card is graduated in degrees. It is attached to the compass needles and conforms with the magnet meridian-referenced direction system inscribed with direction. The vessel turns, not the card.

D

Dacron—a synthetic polyester material.

Davit—a small crane that projects over the side of the boat to raise or lower objects (such as smaller boats) from or to the water.

Davy Jones' Locker—nautical slang for the spirit of the sea, usually in the form of a sea devil. Davy Jones's Locker is the bottom of the sea, the final resting place of sunken ships, articles lost or thrown overboard, and of men buried at sea.

Dead reckoning—the process of plotting a theoretical position or future position based on advancing from a known position using speed, time, and course, without aid of objects on land, of sights, etc. Term comes from deduced reckoning, abbreviated first to "ded reckoning".

Deck—a permanent covering over a compartment, hull or any part of a ship serving as a floor.

Declination—the angular distance North or South of the equator, measured from the center of the earth. It thus corresponds to latitude on the earths surface.

Dhow—a traditional Arab sailing vessel with one or more triangular sails, called lateens

Dinghy—a small open boat often used as tender and lifeboat for a larger craft; a small open boat, usually carried aboard a yacht for going ashore

Doldrums—The area of calm which lies inside the trade winds near the equator

Donk—the engine

Draft—the depth of the boat below the waterline; the amount of vertical distance from a boats water line to the bottom of it's keel. (2) The depth of water necessary to float a vessel (3) The belly or chord depth of the sail, its fullness

Draw—a sail is said to be drawing when it is full of wind. (2) Said of a vessel to indicate her draft. e.g., she draws 10 feet.

E

Echo sounder—an electrical depth sounder or fish finder that uses sound echoes to locate the depth of objects in water. It does so by timing the sound pulses.

F

Fathom - a unit of measurement relating to the depth of water or to the length of line or cable; one fathom is 6 feet or 1.83 meters

Fix—A vessel's position determined by observation and navigational data.

Forehatch—The hatch towards the front of the vessel.

Forestay—A support wire running from the upper part of the mast to the bow of the boat designed to pull the mast forward. A forestay that attaches slightly below the top of the mast can be used to help control the bend of the mast. The most forward stay on the boat is also called the headstay.

G

GPS—a navigation system using satellite signals to fix a position with great accuracy.

Gaff-rigged—any sailboat with a four-sided mainsail, defined by two booms, one located on the bottom, perpendicular to the mast, and another, located on top, at an angle from the mast.

Galley — the kitchen area of a boat.

Genoa — a large foresail or jib that overlaps the mainsail. Also known as a genny. Can be expressed in percentages of overlap, e.g. 150 Genoa is 50% overlap of the mainsail.

Gimbal — a system by which an object such as a compass is suspended so that it remains horizontal as the boat heels

Greenwich Mean Time — GMT for short. Greenwich Meridian Time, also known as Universal Time or Zulu time. A time standard that is not affected by time zones or seasons. It is the time used by navigators in celestial navigation.

Gudgeons — a ring-shaped fitting into which the rudder pintle is inserted which allows the rudder to pivot.

Gunwales — the upper edge of a boat's side; the part of a vessel where hull and deck meet. (Pronounced "gunnel")

H

Halyard — a line used to hoist or lower a sail, flag or spar. The tightness of the halyard can affect sail shape.

Hanked — attaching the sail using rings or piston that are usually spring-loaded, metal hooks used to secure a sail to a stay

Hatch — a sliding or hinged opening in the deck, providing people with access to the cabin or space below; an opening in a boat's deck fitted with a watertight cover.

Head — a marine toilet or the compartment containing a toilet.

Headsail — a sail set forward of the foremast on the headstay; a foresail

Heave to — to stop a boat and maintain position (with some leeway) by balancing rudder and sail to prevent forward movement, a boat stopped this way is "hove to"; such as when in heavy seas. The idea is to bring the wind onto the weather bow and hold the ship in that position, where she can safely and easily ride out a storm.

Hoist — to lift or raise the sail

Horse latitudes — the region of variable winds at about 30° to 35° North.

Hove to — lying nearly head to wind and stopped, and maintaining this position by trimming sail or working engines

Hull — the main structural body or shell of the boat, not including the deck, keel, mast, or cabin.

I

Iron donkey — the engine

J

Jetty—a man made structure projecting from the shore. May protect a harbor entrance or aid in preventing beach erosion.

Jib—the foremost sail; a triangular shaped foresail forward of the foremast

Jibe—turning the boat so that the stern crosses the wind, changing direction. To change direction before the wind onto another tack with the boom coming over by the force of the wind. Caution is needed in this maneuver, especially in heavy wind.

K

Keel—the backbone of a vessel, running fore and aft along the center line of the bottom of the hull; the timber at the very bottom of the hull to which frames are attached. (2) A flat surface built into the bottom of the boat to prevent or reduce the leeway caused by the wind pushing against the side of the boat. A keel also usually has some ballast to help keep the boat upright and prevent it from heeling too much. There are several types of keels, such as fin keels and full keels

Ketch—a sailboat with two masts. Generally, the shorter mizzen mast is aft of the main mast, but forward of the rudder post, while a similar vessel, the yawl, has the mizzen mast aft of the rudder post. The mizzen mast of a ketch is larger than that of a yawl.

Knot—a speed of one nautical mile (6,076 feet or or 1,852 meters) per hour. It is incorrect to say knots per hour.

L

Landlubbers—a person who is inexperienced with or uncomfortable around boats.

Latitude-the distance north or south of the equator measured and expressed in degrees. The equator is 0° and the north and south poles are 90°.

Lee— the side of a ship, or a shore location, sheltered from the wind; also used in context to refer to a sheltered place out of the wind, as in the lee of the island; The area to the leeward.

Leech—after or trailing edge of a sail; the after edge of a fore-and-aft sail and the outer edges of a square sail.

Leeward—direction away from the wind. In the Rules of the Road, the leeward boat is the one farthest from where the wind is coming from.

Opposite of windward.

Locker— a closet or chest-like storage space

Longitude— imaginary lines drawn through the north and south poles on the globe used to measure distance east and west of the prime meridian at Greenwich, England (designated as 0°).

Lookout— a person designated to watch for other vessels and hazards.

M

Made fast— attached a line to something so that it could not move.

Manila Rope—before the introduction of man-made fibers, much of the rope used at sea was made from manila. Made from the fibers of banana plants in the Philippines, manila did not rot when it was exposed to seawater

Marina—a place where boats can find fuel, water and other services. Marinas also contain slips where boats can stay for a period of time.

Mast— the vertical pole or spar that supports the boom and sails.

Mast Head - the top of the mast

Meridian - a semi great circle joining the north and south poles. Known as lines of longitude, they cross the equator and all parallels of latitude at right angles.

N

North Star - polaris, the North Star, is visible in the northern hemisphere and indicates the direction of north. In the southern hemisphere the Southern Cross is used to find the direction of south

P

Pintle— a tapered metal pin which fastens the rudder to the stern by dropping into gudgeons.

Polaris— the North Star; is visible in the northern hemisphere and indicates the direction of north. In the southern hemisphere the Southern Cross is used to find the direction of south

Port—the left side of the boat when facing forward; originally called larboard. The opposite of starboard.

Port hole— a window in the side of a boat, usually round or with rounded corners.

Purchase— any sort of mechanical device to increase power employed in raising or moving heavy objects. Where two or more blocks are involved in a purchase, it is generally known as a tackle (pronounced "taykle").

Q

Quarter— that portion of the vessel forward of the stern and abaft of the beam. "On the quarter" applies to a bearing 45° abaft the beam. Every boat has a starboard and a port quarter.

R

Rag—the sail
Reach—a point of sail between close-hauled and a run, with the wind coming from abeam.
reinforced trades—
Reef - (1) the rolled up part of a sail, tied with the reef lines, that is used to reduce sail area for heavy winds; To reduce the sail area. (2) A group of rocks or coral generally at a depth shallow enough to present a hazard to navigation
Roaring Forties— the latitudes between 40° and 50°, so called because of the boisterous and prevailing westerly winds.
Routing charts—charts that show the entire ocean system's weather in one-month increments
Rudder - a board-shaped swinging vane, controlled by a tiller or wheel, and attached to the rudderpost or stern for steering and maneuvering a vessel
Run - (1)aailing away from the wind with the sails let out all the way; going with the wind, downwind sailing

S

Sail - a large piece of fabric designed to be hoisted on the spars of a sailboat in such a manner as to catch the wind and propel the boat.
Saloon— the main social cabin of a boat
Scud— low, black clouds
Scupper— an opening in a deck, cockpit, toe-rail or gunwale to allow water to run off the deck and drain back into the sea.
Sextant— a navigational instrument used to measure the altitude of celestial bodies
Sight—getting a fix on the boat's position by using a sextant
Sloop— A single masted vessel with fore and aft rigged sails
Sole— Cabin or salon deck or floor; the inside deck of the ship
Southeasterlies—wind coming from the southeast
Spinnaker— A large balloon shaped lightweight sail used when running or reaching. Spinnakers are made of cloth similar to parachutes

Squall— a sudden and violent gust of wind often accompanied by rain.

Starboard— The right side of the boat when facing forward.

Stay— a line or wire from the mast to the bow or stern of a ship, for support of the mast; rigging used to support the mast from forward or aft.

Staysail— a triangular fore-and-aft sail carried on a stay. A sail that is set on a stay, and not on a yard or a mast. On a cutter this is the sail located between the jib and the main sail

Stern— the back (aftermost) part of a boat.

Storm jib— a very strong sail used in stormy weather that helps prevent boarding waves from damaging the sail or the rigging.

Sump— oil pan

T

Tack— he direction that a boat is sailing with respect to the wind. A sailboat cannot sail directly into the wind, and must therefore sail a zig zag course to windward, at about a 45 degree angle to the wind. (3) To change a boat's direction, bringing the bow through the eye of the wind.

Tiller— a bar or handle for turning a boat's rudder or an outboard motor, thereby steering the boat.

Trade winds— steady regular winds in a belt approximately 30° North and 30° South of the equator.

Transom— the athwartship portion of a hull at the stern. The flat, vertical aft end of a ship.

V

Variables—light winds around the equator.

Variation— magnetic variation. The difference, east or west, between magnetic north and true north, measured as an angle. Magnetic variation varies in different geographic locations.

W

Westerlies—wind coming from the west.

Winch— a metal drum shaped device used to increase hauling power when raising or trimming sails, loading and discharging cargo, or for hauling in lines. A machine that has a drum on which to coil a rope, cable or chain for hauling, pulling or hoisting.

Windlass— a special form of winch used to hoist the anchors. It has two drums designed to grab the links of the anchor chains and is fitted with ratchet and braking device suitable for "paying out" chain. - A windlass revolves around a horizontal axis, as opposed to a capstan, which rotates around a vertical axis.

Windward— towards the wind. Windward is an adjective meaning the direction from which the wind is blowing. The windward side of a boat is the one which the wind hits first. "Sailing to windward" means sailing towards the wind. Opposite of leeward.

Y

Yankee jib— a foresail used on yachts similar to a genoa, but cut narrower, with its leech not overlapping the mainsail, and a higher clew.

Printed in the United States
50038LVS00004B/289-309